Aphrodite and The Mixed Grill

GREEK CAFÉS IN TWENTIETH-CENTURY AUSTRALIA

TONI RISSON

This project is supported by the Queensland Government, through Arts Queensland and Ipswich City Council, by funding through the Ipswich Regional Arts Development Fund.

Support for this project was also received from The Coffee Club.

Publisher:

Kytherian Association of Australia.
Kytherian World Heritage Fund.
Kytherian Publishing and Media.

Rockdale Post Shop
PO Box 183
Rockdale NSW 2216
Australia

Enquiries: George C Poulos.
Editor, Kytherian Publishing and Media
transoz@bigpond.net.au

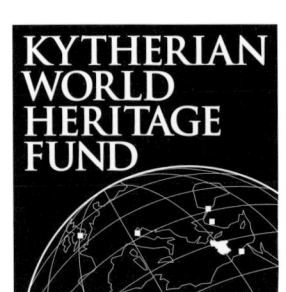

DISCLAIMER

Some information and stories contained in this book are drawn from Denis Conomos' research, from the work of historians like Leonard Janiszewski, Effie Alexakis, and Hugh Gilchrist, and from official documents such as Fire Department Block Plans and Post Office Directories. The main body of the work, however, comes from the recollections of Ipswich people who worked or ate in Greek cafés. Although every attempt has been made to verify information, the strength of oral history lies not in its power to record fact, but in its capacity to paint a detailed picture of life as it was for particular individuals. These anecdotes should, therefore, be viewed not so much as 'truth' but as memories of events that took place in the lives of particular individuals. Any representation, statement, or opinion expressed in this publication is made in good faith based on the recollections of those individuals, and on the understanding that the author is not liable for any damage or loss incurred as a result of action taken on the basis of those representations. Unless otherwise stated, most of the photographs reproduced in this book belong to the families whose stories are told here. Others are available in collections held in public libraries. Permission to use these images has been obtained wherever possible, but I apologise in advance if any have been overlooked, and this will be rectified in subsequent editions.

© Copyright 2007 Toni Risson
No part of this book may be reproduced in any form without written permission from the publisher.

Reprint January 2012
Published by Kytherian World Heritage Fund

Printed in Australia: Ligare Book Printers [02 9584 7645]
Graphic Design: Michelle Poole [0409 639 152]

ISBN: 978-0-646-47456-4

Risson, Toni, 1955 - .
  Aphrodite and the mixed grill : Greek cafes in twentieth-century Australia.
Bibliography.
ISBN 9780646474564 (pbk.).

1. Restaurants - Australia - History. 2. Greeks - Australia - History - 20th century. 3. Food - History - 20th century. 4. Immigrants - Australia - History - 20th century. 5. Greeks - Social life and customs. I. Title.

994.004893

Dedicated to Maureen Sheppard, who was the inspiration for this book, to the wonderful people who subsequently told me their stories, and to their God, who has brought us all this far by His grace.

COVER PHOTO

Marina Londy (left) from Londy's Café in Ipswich visits the nearby Regal Café after school in 1952. George Kentrotis stands proudly behind the Regal's confectionery counter with two of his brothers, two other male relatives, and two Anglo-Australian female staff. Milkshake machines, a metal straw dispenser, and scales for weighing loose lollies sit on the counter, and stylish pilasters emblazoned with the café's name and a neon sign featuring a crown frame a mirror on the wall behind them.

Acknowledgements

Andrew Antonelli Sandy Barrie Clive Beale Eleanor Beale Athena Bellas Jim Bellas Tony Bellas Blue Mountains City Council Eileen Black John Black Frank Bromley Lily Burke Marie Canfell Con Castan Alf Colless Heather Colless Len Colless Tom Colless Emanuel Cominos Peter Cominos Stamatoula Cominos Denis Conomos Paul Coward Effie Detsimas Arnold Dull Myrtle Fellows Alan Freeman Narelle Freeman Marina Girdis Jim Green Pearl Green Yvonne Hawkins Merrilyn Hicks Inscape Photography Ipswich City Council Leonard Janiszewski Manuel Kallinicos Peter Kallos Dot Kennedy Helen Kentos Bill Kentrotes Bill Kentrotis Helen Kentrotis Maria Kentrotis Vasiliki Kentrotes Jason King Ross Laurie John Lazarou Charles Londy George Londy Mary Londy Peter Londy Diana Love John Low Hugh Lunn Dani Mathewson Helene Marendy Trevor Marsden Joy McCann Jim McKee National Library of Australia Jim Pavlakis Lumbrini Pavlakis Jim Penglis Charlie Pisasale Michelle Poole Peter Poulos Effie Prineas James Prineas Manuel Prineas Regional Arts Development Fund Maureen Reinke Abbey Risson Casey Risson Don Risson Glenn Risson Portia Risson John Rossiter Michael Samios Yiota Samios Ivan Schostakowski Maureen Sheppard Maya Simonidis State Library of Queensland Jack Stathis Jim Stathis Zeta Stathis Joanne Stewart Mick Stewart Andrew Tanos Harry Tanos Maroula Tanos Sula Tanos Ruth Thompson UQ Arts Ipswich Jason Vaughan Leisa Vaughan Doris Veneris Theo Veneris Anne Wagner Vicki Willmot and the people of Ipswich.

AND SPECIAL THANKS to Michelle Poole for her wonderful graphic design, Heather Colless and Alf Colless for their work as proof readers, and Glenn Risson for his daily encouragement and support. Many of the people included in this book are in their 70s and 80s. I am both grateful for the faith these people placed in me to tell their stories and amazed at their generosity in loaning precious family photographs to someone who was, at least at that time, a total stranger. I trust that they will find this account worthy of that faith and generosity.

Contents

page 1	Introduction
page 9	The Greek Café: An Australian Icon
page 25	"A Shop Full of Dreams": The Café Phenomenon
page 37	Greek Cafés in Ipswich, Queensland: A Case Study
page 69	Mixed Grills and Milkshakes: Food in Greek Cafes
page 99	Daughters of Aphrodite: Café Brides
page 113	Serving Time Behind Bars: Café Kids
page 125	Fun and Games: Good Times in Greek Cafés
page 139	Hard Luck and Health Hazards: The Tough Times
page 149	'Oversexed, Overpaid, and Over Here': Wartime
page 163	One of the Family: Waitressing for Greek Proprietors
page 173	'Bloody Dagoes': Greek and Anglo-Australian Relations
page 187	The Other Side of the Coin: Return to Kythera
page 197	End of an Era: The Demise of the Greek Café
page 209	Café Heritage: Tracking the Signs
page 219	Conclusion
page 225	Bibliography
page 227	Interviewees
page 229	Notes

The Introduction

"I REMEMBER [...] MY DAD WHO LEFT GREECE WHEN HE WAS FIFTEEN WITH HIS HOPE HIS AMBITIONS AND A BAG FULL OF DREAMS BUT SPENT THE REST OF HIS LIFE AS A SLAVE TO A STOVE TILL HIS DREAMS WERE ALL GREASY AND HIS HOPE HAD ALL GONE."

KOMNINOS[1]

When the Australian family went touring in the 60s, Dad checked the radiator, hung a canvas water bag from the front bumper with a bit of fencing wire, and packed the boot – the roof racks too if the family car happened to be a sedan. Mum bundled the kids into the back, tossed their pillows in after them, and settled the baby into a clothes basket on the floor at her feet. There was a mad dash back into the house to check that the stove was off, or to grab a forgotten toy, and then, finally, amid cheers and well wishes from Harry and Joan leaning against the railing of the verandah next door, they were off, with everyone waving and laughing and Dad parping the horn all the way to the corner. Spirits were high. The adventure had begun.

Before long, the morning sun began to stream in the side window and the kids, weary of counting white milestones at the side of the road, were whining and snarling in the back seat:

> "Muuuuum, Clayton's touching me."
> "Make her give me back my stamp."
> "He's got one of mine."
> "Muuum."
> "Muuuuuuuuuuuuuuuum."

Until Dad swung a slap over the back of the bench seat, narrowly missing the offenders and collecting an innocent bystander:

> "Whatcha hit me for? I didn't do anything."
> "That'll make up for the time you missed out then."

So Mum tucked the edge of a nappy into the narrow gap between the glass and the top of the window. "I spy with my little eye…" she began as she wound the chrome handle up.

The nappy's shade blocked the heat that was boring through the glass and the game of eye spy bought them half an hour's peace. Dust curled behind them, coating the brave vehicle in red powder as the kids, who had no Gameboys or Walkmans, air-conditioning, mobile phones, or Poppers, muesli bars, sunglasses, sunscreen, or seatbelts, made increasingly-regular, ear-piercing inquiries regarding the estimated hour of their arrival. At last, the sun climbed to the top of a cornflower blue sky and it was time for lunch, which the 60s family called 'dinner', the evening meal being known as 'tea'.

If Dad pulled up beside a river or in a rest area, Mum broke out the Vegemite sandwiches and fruit cake, while one of the kids retrieved a Thermos from the front seat and Dad persuaded a metal contraption to pop out of a suitcase and form a picnic table and four chairs. Or perhaps a salad of cold meat, shredded iceberg, grated carrot, home-made beetroot, and thick slices of tomato and cucumber materialised from a little round caravan that had been bouncing along behind. But more often than not, whether they pulled into Maryborough, Muttaburra, Mullumbimby, Goondiwindi, Charleville, Cunnamulla, Wagga Wagga, Uralla, Babinda,

Gunnedah, Biloela, or almost any other rural town in Queensland or New South Wales, Dad would head for the Greek café, popularly known as 'the Dago's'.

With its ritzy Art Deco façade, the café was easily located in the main street. Gleaming gold letters on a mirrored sign behind the counter boasted Icy-Cold Lemon and Orange Drinks, and chrome soda fountains, eager to effervesce any of a long list of soda flavours, perched on the milk bar like robotic birds. Rumpled and weary, Mum and Dad dragged hungry kids past a dazzling confectionery counter and shelves stacked to the ceiling with Fantales, Minties, and Bex to jam into one of the polished wooden cubicles along the side wall. While they surveyed an extensive menu of grills, cutlets, eggs, poultry, joints, fish, meat pies, and toasted sandwiches, the toddler, trapped closest to the wall to prevent its escape, slapped sticky hands on a long mirror that ran the length of the café. Finally, huge plates of good, cheap food arrived and before long the travellers were on the road again, their appetites appeased and their spirits restored.

* * *

For much of the 20th century, the ubiquitous Greek café routinely opened for business before seven o'clock in the morning and closed around midnight seven days a week, except for Christmas Day and Good Friday. In addition to meals for travellers, proprietors served up hot breakfasts for workers and morning and afternoon teas for tired shoppers. For 'country people' on their weekly trip to town, lunch meant a mixed grill and a milkshake at the Greek café, and proprietors chatted with regular customers as they dispensed ice-creams for families on evening walks and milk coffee and toasted sandwiches for couples after the evening session at the pictures or a night on the dance floor.

Greek immigrants began opening food outlets in Sydney in the latter part of the 19th century.

But for many Australians, Greek cafés were more than food outlets. Bustling to the clatter of silver cutlery, the hiss of sizzling steaks, and the swoosh of soda fountains, popular cafés like the Paragon in Katoomba, the Niagara in Gundagai, and Londy's in Ipswich were public gathering places that forged an important place at the heart of Australian communities. Just talk to older Australians about them and watch their eyes light up.

Greek immigrants began opening food outlets in Sydney in the latter part of the 19th century. Their oyster saloons, cafés, fish shops, fruit shops, milk bars, snack bars, and confectioneries soon dotted the Australian landscape, and before long, the Greek café had become an Australian icon. In *Here's Luck* of 1930, humorous Australian columnist and writer, Lennie Lower, establishes a generous plate of steak and eggs at the local Greek café as an unfailing Aussie remedy for world-weariness, alongside cheering at a punch-up and a win at the races.[2] Australian painter, Russell Drysdale, also articulates the Greek café's status as a national icon, particularly of rural Australia, in his portraits of Greek outback proprietors, *Maria* and *Joe*, both painted in 1950.[3] Bob Hudson places the local Greek milk bar firmly at the centre of Aussie life in his hit song of 1975: "And they pulled up outside the Parthenon Milk Bar, and standing outside the Parthenon was this beautiful-looking sheila."[4] And in 1988, Mark Mitchell drew upon the iconic status of the Greek shopkeeping family in his 'bewdiful' characterisation of Greek fruiterer, Con Dikaletis, and his wife, Marika.[5] That the Greek café recurs in such a wide range of texts throughout most of the 20th century is evidence of the extent to which it pervaded Australian life.

Perhaps this under-representation occurs because the Greek café was simply part of the way everyday Australians lived their everyday lives

But the Greek café is not just an Australian icon; Greek shopkeeping is a quintessentially Australian phenomenon.[6] Nowhere else did Greek migrants dominate the food industry to the extent that they did in Australia. Many Greeks emigrated to the United States in the late 19th and early 20th centuries, but while American popular culture provides evidence that Greeks certainly had food-catering businesses – 'the Greek' in *The Postman Always Rings Twice* being a notable example – they do not operate the food outlets in most popular texts. Italians run the 'diners' in *The Blob* and in *It's a Wonderful Life*, and in Norman Rothwell's images of classic America, in television series like *Happy Days*, and in most Hollywood films where food outlets feature, premises rarely have Greek proprietors. Anecdotal evidence suggests that Greeks were more likely to run barber shops in America.

Despite this iconic and singular status, Australia's Greek café is under-represented in historical research – information on Queensland cafés is particularly hard to find. Food historian, Michael Symons, for example, in his landmark treatise on Australia's food history, allocates only two lines to the topic, even though he attributes the 'Mixed Grill' to Greek café proprietors. He fails to note the disproportionate number of Greek food shops, despite the fact that he refers to Australia as "a nation of shopkeepers," and, while he draws attention to the huge number of oyster saloons in Sydney's early days, he fails to mention that 70% of the 400 Kytherian immigrants living in NSW in 1911 owned or worked them, and that these oyster saloons were the direct precursor of the Greek café.[7]

Perhaps this under-representation occurs because the Greek café was simply part of the way everyday Australians lived their everyday lives. While historians traditionally target momentous subjects like monarchs, politicians, and inventors – people who change the course of history – everyday cultural practices and ephemera have, for a long time, escaped attention. As a result, few historians documented the rise of the humble Greek café. Or its demise. Neither did the general public take family photographs in Greek cafés. While families frequented them and teenagers routinely 'hung out' in them, they were not used for special celebrations. People protest the loss of human rights, the destruction of rainforests, and even the demolition of Victorian pubs, but few chain themselves to the doors of Greek cafés, or even mourn their passing, and these once popular and prolific venues have now all but disappeared from Australian streets.

But Greek cafés did change the course of Australia's cultural history and this book seizes a brief window of opportunity to capture their story. It is a story which will otherwise die with the people in whose memories it now resides. Chapter One celebrates two famous Greek cafés that are still in operation, the Paragon Café, which opened in Katoomba in 1916, and the Niagara Café, which has served travellers and locals in Gundagai for more than a century. Situating 19th and early 20th century oyster saloons and cafés within the context of Greek immigration, Chapter Two elaborates the circumstances that gave rise to the Greek shopkeeping phenomenon. To appreciate the impact Greek shopkeepers had on Australian communities, the regional centre of Ipswich in South-East Queensland is used here as a case study; in the course of the 20th century, over a dozen Greek cafés operated in Ipswich's central business district, helping to

The spread of Greek cafés throughout New South Wales and Queensland accelerated during the second decade of the 20th century. This photograph of the Busy Bee Café in Kingaroy, Queensland, was taken on the 2nd of January, 1929. Four female staff members, wearing dark uniforms with white caps and aprons, serve a multitude of customers crowded into centre tables and an early version of side cubicles. A mirror runs the length of one side of the café. From his position behind the confectionery counter, the proprietor watches over the café and shares a joke with a waitress. George Trifilis left Kythera for Australia in 1908 aged fourteen. About six years later, he bought the Royal Café in Kingaroy from his employer. In the 1920s, George opened the Busy Bee in Kingaroy, where he stayed for the rest of his working life. The Busy Bee was still trading in the 1980s.[8]

State Library of Queensland Image No. 105119

nurture a sense of community in a city built on railway and coalmining industries. After the history of Ipswich cafés is unearthed in Chapter Three, the food Greek cafés served and the technological innovations they brought to the food service industry in Australia is investigated in Chapter Four. The women's and children's stories, the escapades of drunks and SP bookies, devastating floods, murder, and wartime anecdotes, as well as more everyday aspects of café life then emerge as hitherto untold or underrepresented aspects of Australian culture in Chapters Five to Nine.

Chapter Ten gathers the stories of local women who worked for Greek proprietors. Because Greek cafés flourished at the interface between an anglophile Australia and a new wave of 'foreigners', they are used in Chapter Eleven as a means of understanding the relationship between Greek and Anglo-Celtic Australians. The focus then shifts from the cultural importance of cafés in Australia to reveal the devastating impact Greek migration had on Greek villages. The tiny Kytherian village of Fratsia, which was home to many of Ipswich's café proprietors, is now almost a ghost town, although one proprietor at least has remigrated to spend his later years amongst the homes of his ancestors. Having investigated the role the Greek café played in Australia's cultural history from its origin in the late 19th century and through its heyday in the 1940s, 50s, and 60s, the book concludes with the reasons for its gradual demise in the closing decades of the 20th century.

While families frequented them and teenagers routinely 'hung out' in them, they were not used for special celebrations.

So pull up a chair, order a drink, and enjoy – the wonderful story of the Greek café in 20th century Australia.

CHAPTER ONE

The Greek Café: An Australian Icon

Harry Londy's brother, Charles, settled in Bundaberg, where he opened the Blue Bird Café. This photograph was taken in 1929 before the café was renovated.

"Very little is known about the country, and scarcely anything is worth mentioning"

A reference to Australia in a Greek geography book from 1832.[9]

I love nasturtiums. Most people don't cut these humble blossoms for display in a vase, but for a brief time they sprawl across the garden in a riot of vivid colour, and if you suck the tip of a flower a droplet of sweetness spreads across your tongue. But then they die back, leaving almost no trace that they were ever there at all. Greek cafés are like that; their colour and sweetness spread rampantly across the Australian landscape for one brief episode of the nation's history, and then they were gone.

An early Greek food outlet typically consisted of a front counter that sold bottled oysters and cigarettes, a small, plain dining room with several sets of tables and chairs, and a rear kitchen that served light meals. The second decade of the 20th century, however, saw significant changes. The title 'Café' replaced 'Oyster Saloon'. Female waitresses replaced male staff. Rear kitchens served a greater range of food. And cafés adopted the 'classic form', a style and layout that endured for two generations. This 'classic form' was

In this photograph of the Paris Café in Clermont in the 1940s, proprietors, John and Marouli Faros, stand behind a glass-fronted confectionery counter, while dining room tables fill the back area. Lights and fans hang from the ceiling, and a refrigerated cabinet, front left, advertises ice confectionery, probably Peters Ice Cream.

State Library of Queensland Image No. 41530.[13]

marked by a milk bar equipped with soda fountains and modern electrical machines, an elaborate front confectionery counter with a glass showcase, boxed chocolates, and jars of sweets, and a dining room that could include counter seating, centre tables and chairs, and booths – commonly known as cubicles – along mirrored side walls.[10] Art Deco, the international architectural and decorative style that developed as a celebration of the machine age in the 1920s, is characteristic of the 'classic form' and is typically associated with Greek cafés as they existed during their lengthy 'golden age' from the mid 30s to the late 60s.[11]

The Art Deco aesthetic permeated nearly every design aspect – fashion, architecture, industrial design, furniture – and never really went out of style. It is particularly evident in carefully preserved café buildings like the Paragon Café in Katoomba and the Niagara in Gundagai.[14] Before looking at these, however readers should note that Greek cafés assumed a multitude of forms. They ranged from those like the Paragon, which was the epitome of elegance, to others like the Crown Café in George Street, Brisbane (near the Treasury Building), which 'café kid', Julie Nichles, says, "didn't aspire to anything ritzy; we just sold very simple stuff – tea and sandwiches was the go most of the time." [15]

A photograph of the Logos (Logothetis) brothers' café at Blackall, taken in 1920, illustrates the layout typical of early rural cafés. A row of tables runs down each wall on either side of a row of centre tables. Jars of lollies line the shelves behind a glass confectionery cabinet, where a set of scales sits ready to weigh purchases. Three soda fountains are mounted on the milk bar, with a glass straw dispenser with a metal top nearby.

State Library of Queensland Image No. 102468 [12]

This shop in Murwillumbah, NSW, demonstrates the restrained elegance of the Art Deco style that was popular in cafés of the 20s and 30s. Chrome outlines, black tiles, curved glass corners and milky green glass are typical of the style.

The Garden of Roses in Edward Street, Brisbane, featured angel statues, each bearing five lights, which were positioned along the walls. A fountain held pride of place in the foyer. Possessed of a distinctive ambience, the café served French and German pastries, cakes, and bread cooked by French and German chefs. Food was more expensive than it was in most Greek cafés, but waitress, Ruby Cassimatis, recalls, "It was worth it to have the surroundings." Catering for professional people, or what Ruby calls "a better class of people", the Garden of Roses not only had silver cutlery and even

When Charles Tsiros opened the 'elite' Garden of Roses around 1917, he set a new standard of elegance in Queensland cafés based on cafés he had experienced as a young boy in America.

State Library of Queensland Image No. 49929

silver tableware, but also employed French terminology. The menu listed meat pies, for example, as pate de fois gras. The Garden of Roses was part of a three-café complex that also encompassed the Continental and the Ellisos. These were more basic cafés; with cheaper meals and less elaborate décor, they appealed to a different demographic. As a marketing concept, Tsiros' complex was ahead of its time.[16]

Another magnificent café, this time in far north Queensland, was Cominos' Café in Cairns. Emmanuel and Peter Cominos recall that their father used to describe his shop as a 'departmentalised café'. Each of the departments – cakes, confectionery, milk bar, sandwiches, etcetera – had its own register and separate accounting system. Emmanuel recalls that his father didn't know how to boil water, but he certainly knew how to run a café. Complete with dumb waiter, the three storey café could cater simultaneously for two weddings on the two upper levels, while still operating the ground floor dining room, which, with tables in the centre and cubicles along mirrored walls, seated up to 100 customers. Peter remembers that when the café was renovated before the Second World War, it employed 75 staff, including three generations of Cominos, and boasted a kitchen – complete with the latest electric dish washers and potato peelers – that was so modern and well-designed that the Brisbane General Hospital consulted Peter's father for advice on food preparation. The female staff looked "absolutely spiffing." They wore white pinafores and if they got so much as a spot on their 'pini', they had to change.[17]

Cominos' Café had a confectionery counter from which customers could purchase cake decorations and which sold more confectionery than Coles in Queen Street, Brisbane. It also had a bakery with delivery vans that supplied bakery items to most of the district. Like many Greek cafés, it served home-made ice-cream. The milk bar, however, was an outstanding feature – it opened onto the street so customers could be served without entering the shop. The café used water-driven fans and hired out crockery. Even before the Second World War, it had takeaway, although not deep fried food, and catered for office meetings. Many Cairns workers had standing lunch orders. With an upstairs piano lounge, toilets and free showers complete with fresh towels for travellers, and a three-storey atrium in the front part of the dining room that was hung with baskets of ferns and caged canaries, Cominos' Café was a much-loved and very elegant destination for travellers and locals alike.[18] Like the Garden of Roses, however, Cominos' Café, has long since disappeared.

While some cafés were elegant venues with lace tablecloths, silver service, bentwood chairs, carpeted floors, and unique Art Deco features, others were more basic, especially those in country towns. Elements of classic café form and of Art Deco style are evident in Greek cafés in Ipswich, as are varying levels of sophistication, although none is as magnificent as the Garden of Roses or Cominos' Café. Of the many Greek cafés in Ipswich in the 40s, Londy's Café is the one most people remember. It was a large, 'double' café with two entrances and three curved display windows that featured an opaque, milky green glass typical of the Art Deco style.[19] Water trickled down the inside of one window to cool the fish and stop flies settling on the glass. Londy's had separate areas for fish, cigarettes and confectionery, the milk bar, and toasted sandwiches. There were booths along the mirrored walls and tables in the central space. The Regal Café, on the other hand, only a few doors away, was so narrow that it seems likely the café was built in a laneway between two existing buildings.

> Cominos' Café was a much-loved and very elegant destination for travellers and locals alike.

Arguably the finest example of the iconic Greek café is to be found in Katoomba in the Blue Mountains. Katoomba was Australia's first holiday resort. It was an early retreat for

Despite its long, narrow shape and simple design, the Regal Café's Italian wall tapestries, dark interior, and memorable ambience feature prominently in the community's recollections. Two soda fountains are mounted on the bar on the left-hand side of the café, and one of the tapestries can be seen above the narrow cubicles opposite the counter.[20]

colonials seeking relief from Sydney's summer heat and its unique rock formations and waterfalls, bushwalks and panoramas have enjoyed enduring appeal as tourist attractions since explorers first crossed the Great Divide in 1813. Wild, rambling gardens and quaint cottages perched on the edge of the picturesque and often mist-shrouded Megalong Valley enhanced Katoomba's appeal for city-dwellers Bus trips from Katoomba to the Jenolan Caves were also popular. By the 1920s, Katoomba had 270 hotels and guesthouses. Of these, the Clarendon and the Palais are among those still standing, as is the most magnificent of them all, the Carrington Guesthouse at the top of Katoomba Street. These guesthouses were popular honeymoon destinations and couples who celebrated their golden wedding anniversaries at the turn of the 21st century are likely to have spent their first days of married life in one of them.

After honeymooners had visited the Bridal Falls, climbed the Golden Staircase, and surveyed Megalong Valley from lookouts overhanging sheer cliff faces, or when drizzle kept them from outdoor pursuits, numerous Greek cafés were ready, at almost any hour of the day or night, to serve steaming milk coffee

Don and Lorna Risson, who married in Gilgandra in May 1948, spent a week's honeymoon in Katoomba. They stayed at the Redlands Guesthouse and visited attractions like the Three Sisters and the Jenolan Caves.[21]

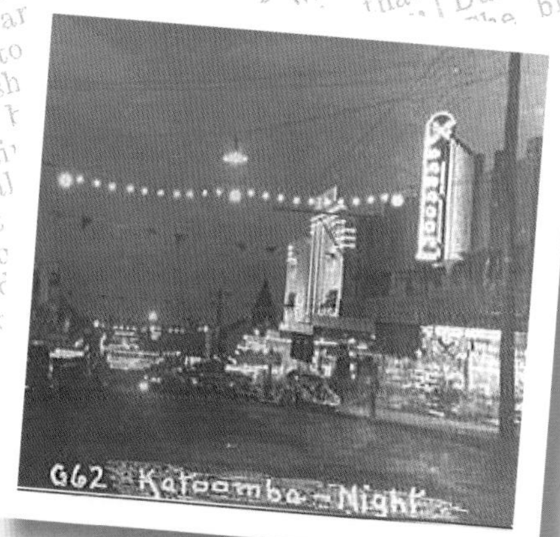

with golden toasted sandwiches, freshly-made waffles with maple syrup, mouth-watering sundaes, sodas that came in a surprising array of flavours, and a wide range of confectionery. During the 1950s, at least ten Greek cafés operated in Katoomba: the AB (All-British), Aroney's, the Savoy Café (beside the Savoy Theatre), the Niagara, Astor, Victory, Florida, and Waratah cafés, as well as the Plaza Café at Echo Point.[22] Five were within a stone's throw of the Carrington Guesthouse.

And the most splendid of them all was the Paragon Café.

The Paragon Café

The Paragon is a very fine example of an Art Deco café, but, more importantly, it was included on the National Trust Register in 1975 and is one of the few cafés to have survived the enormous changes of the 20th century. It now ranks with the Three Sisters, the Scenic Railway and the Skyway as one of Katoomba's must-see tourist attractions. Zacharias Theodore Simos (Jack) was born in Kythera in 1897. He had little money and almost no English when he migrated to Australia with several other boys in 1912, but he found work in Greek cafés until he had saved enough to establish a confectionery shop in an existing Devonshire tea-room at 65 Katoomba Street in 1916. In 1924, he bought the premises and used Katoomba's Orphan Rock as a trademark to characterise the Paragon Café's commitment to 'stand-alone' excellence.

After a trip to Kythera and Europe in 1929-30, during which he made careful observations of European café culture and confectionery manufacture, Jack returned with 17 year-old bride, Mary Panaretos, and a renewed vision for the Paragon. Plans were soon afoot to extend the premises with two dining rooms at the rear. The Banquet Hall, finished with Pre-Columbian décor, was completed in 1934, and the Blue Room, in the style of an ocean liner with mirrored walls and a sprung dance floor, was finished in 1936.[23] Fresh flowers from the family garden welcomed patrons, chocolates were slipped into the hands of small children, and the Paragon's grand Art Deco style, hand-made ice creams, and freshly-made cakes, pastries and crisp waffles were soon popular with locals and tourists.

Like many Greek proprietors, Jack supported his community. The Katoomba Rotary Club, for example, of which Jack was a foundation member, met at the Paragon on Monday nights for 55 years from 1937-92. After Jack died in 1976, Mary managed the café for a further ten years. The Simos family finally sold the Paragon in 2000 and Mary died the following year. But the Paragon Café has presided at the heart of Katoomba's main street for almost a century and is still going strong. The beautiful exterior with its blue tiles, gold lettering, raised and recessed entry, unique leadlight

The year after Jack Simos bought the premises in Katoomba Street, he refitted the tea-room with soda fountains, a marble milk bar, and booths of Queensland maple. Alabaster-coloured, low-relief sculptures of classical Greek figures adorning the dark timber-panelled walls exemplified the Paragon Café's classical elegance.

design, patterned overhang, and display windows framed with embossed copper frieze and copper corners is still intact, and the original interiors have altered little since 1936. Although the new owners are not Greek, they are committed to carrying Zacharias and Mary Simos' dream of a paragon among cafés into the new millennium.

Many Australians will remember standing spellbound before the Paragon Café's front display cases, gazing at elegant chocolate boxes resplendent with curlicues and gold lettering and silver dishes brimming with jewel-like, sugar-encrusted marzipans. And stepping over the threshold into the café's dim, almost ecclesiastical interior to inhale the rich aroma of dark chocolate and agonise over exquisitely presented confectionery, which is always lined up in neat rows in the glass cabinets, is a moment not easily forgotten.

The cocktail bar in the Paragon Café is one of the finest examples of Art Deco in Australia.

While overseas, Jack arranged to import several special ingredients and gleaned new ideas for packaging confectionery. As a result, the Paragon Café won particular renown for its confectionery and hand-dipped chocolates, which were manufactured above the shop and sold in elegant boxes featuring Katoomba's Orphan Rock.

Silver dishes, resplendent with streamlined female figures characteristic of the Art Deco period once displayed confectionery in the Paragon's shopfront windows. Although the silver dishes have gone, confectionery is still manufactured above the shop and sold in boxes reproduced in the original style, and these are proudly displayed in the front windows amid flowers, old china, original furniture, and swathes of mist-like tulle.

The Niagara Café

Another Greek café still to be found in operation presides over the main street of Gundagai in western New South Wales. Established by the Castrission family in 1902, the Niagara Café, although much less grand than the Paragon, is a fine example of a country Greek café. For more than a century, the Niagara has served the needs of local families and refreshed generations of weary Australians travelling the Hume Highway between Queensland and Victoria. Of even greater significance is the café's classic décor, which, like the Paragon's, remains much as it was in the 1930s.

The Niagara Café was originally divided into separate women's and men's dining areas, as was common at the time, until remodelling in 1928 brought mixed dining and new silver tableware. The café was refurbished again in 1933, this time in the popular Art Deco style. With a triple-curved glass shopfront and monogrammed glass doors, the Niagara is a priceless example of cafés built during the Art Deco period.

Art Deco features are also typical of the American milk bars and drugstores that had a significant impact on cafés in Australia. American servicemen stopping in Gundagai during the war were so impressed with the Niagara's modern style that they are reported to have exclaimed, "Ahhhh! Home, Sweet Home." The American influence is further evident in the café's name. An image of Niagara Falls is painted over the front entrance and repeated on the china and serviettes. At one time, the café had a deep blue ceiling covered with tiny stars, which, until it was destroyed by fire, amazed all who saw it.[24]

The Niagara's other claim to fame concerns the unexpected visit of a small party which arrived under cover of darkness at the height of the Second World War. No one recounts this story

Cubicles or booths are typical of the Greek café style. The Niagara Café's cubicles, while less elegant than those of Katoomba's Paragon Café, have distinctive fluting along the top of the partitions. The simple but stylish wall mirrors above each cubicle are classic Art Deco. Greek and Australian flags, symbolising the attitude of many Greek café proprietors, obscure beautiful Art Deco lights. A museum-like space along the side and rear walls proudly displays the café's story, the town's history, and the owners' particular interests.

A simple chrome, yellow, and black geometric design on the facade of the long curved milk bar, and a gleaming metal sign behind the counter are among the classic Art Deco features retained in the Niagara Café in Gundagai.

Not only will travellers who visit the Niagara Café experience a slice of living Australian history, but they will also be rewarded with the knowledge that they have played their part in ensuring that the Niagara will still be there when the next generation calls.

better than Brisbane writer, Hugh Lunn, who is also fast becoming an Aussie icon, so I'll let him tell it:

> One night in 1942, during World War 11, the owner, Jack Castrission, was locking up his café at midnight when he was disturbed by a loud banging on the closed door. He went to the glass to tell the intruders to bugger off, but changed his mind when he saw who was knocking. It was the wartime Prime Minister, John Curtin. With him were Artie Fadden, the previous prime minister, and Ben Chifley, who was to become the next prime minister. They'd been on a fundraising mission for the war effort and were on their way back to Canberra. So Jack opened up the Niagara Café and put on a slap-up meal of steak and eggs.[25]

Badly in need of hot food and a brief respite from the cold, the visitors were so impressed with the generous meal, and the equally generous measure of country Greek café hospitality, that they returned regularly and increased the Niagara's tea ration into the bargain. Jack Castrission celebrated the occasion with new café china that was emblazoned with a monogram commemorating the visit, and this is still on display in one of the front windows.

The café passed to another Greek family in 1983, but it seems that the Niagara is still in good hands; Nick Loukissas, who emigrated from Greece in the mid-50s, has made few changes to this rare and wonderful example of Australia's history.[26] Travellers who pass by the roadhouses on the Hume Highway to make the short detour into Gundagai will enjoy traditional Greek café fare that can include cups of tea served in silver teapots aged by the hands of thousands of Aussie travellers who have gone before.

Their years of continuous operation and classic décor set the Paragon Café in Katoomba and the Niagara Café in Gundagai apart. For every Greek café that remains as a window to a bygone era, hundreds of others have disappeared. Redevelopment in inner-city areas has wiped away every trace of the significant numbers of Greek cafés in cities like Brisbane and Ipswich.

Even if cafés remain in operation, they have often been stripped of their classic charm in an effort to 'keep up with the times' and remain viable in a contemporary marketplace. Shops like the Central Milk Bar in Ipswich, for instance, have been converted to takeaway outlets, their front walls opened up to maximise street front potential, in order to survive. In country towns, however, where change has been slower and developers are less likely to have obliterated entire blocks, evidence remains of the Greek immigrants whose determination and hard work left their mark on rural Australia. Here the exteriors of café buildings often remain intact even if the premises are used for another purpose. The newsagency in Miles for example, was once the Majestic Café. Art Deco lettering and design elements, curved or stepped display windows, leadlight panels above the door, and recessed entries are clues to the possibility that a building was once a Greek café.

In a highly competitive marketplace, it is difficult for small businesses to survive, and when an old café building changes hands its future is always in doubt, especially if councils place little value on a city or town's shopping heritage. What lies in store for another of Katoomba's famous landmarks, the beautiful Café Niagara?

Travellers who pass by the roadhouses on the Hume Highway to make the short detour into Gundagai will enjoy traditional Greek café fare.

● The skeleton of the North Star hotel stood out starkly in the night. Picture: **Lyle Radford**.

BLOCK FALLS

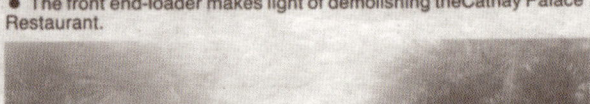

● The front end-loader makes light of demolishing the Cathay Palace Restaurant.

THE face of Ipswich's central city area changed in a few hours yesterday with the demolition of four Brisbane St stores.

By staff reporter
KERRYN RAMSEY

Corvettes, Second Hand Records, Ian Crighton Chemist and the Cathay Palace Restaurant bit the dust within about three hours of each other yesterday morning.

The shops were on the block proposed for Stage 1 of the $120 million Kern Corporation redevelopment.

Kern managing director Barry Paul said yesterday that after demolition was completed and building applicatins were approved, foundations would be laid for stage one, involving 13,000 sq m of retail space.

Yesterday, one lane of Brisbane St was blocked off to prevent falling debris from the buildings endangering cars or people.

The North Star Hotel, the subject of much controversy concerning its demolition, was still standing last night, but not totally intact.

Most of its awnings were pulled down, and the inside was bare.

Spectators lined up on the opposite footpath during the day to catch a last glimpse of the stores.

Kern Construction has advertised more partial closures of Brisbane St this weekend and next weekend between 6am and 6pm to allow for more demolition work.

On April 24, Kern Corporation submitted a building application to Ipswich City Council for the $30 million stage one redevelopment which includes a major department store and about 10 specialty shops.

The council is expected to announce its decision concerning the application within the next few weeks.

Mr Paul of Kern Corporation said stage one would include a 12,018 square metre major department store which will be the major tennant of the entire project.

"It will be equal to any in Australia in presentation and quality of merchandise," he said.

Mr Paul said the name of the department store would be announced next week.

● This is no tropical island downpour — it's the dust from the demolition work engulfing spectators. The photo was taken from St Paul's church.

● Brisbane St looked like a bomb was dropped in the middle after the demolition work yesterday.

Above: Katoomba has retained some of its old café buildings, but fate was not so kind to Ipswich's Greek cafés. A Queensland Times article from 1986 reports the demolition of a block of shops in the heart of the Ipswich CBD. Lyle Radford's photographs capture the moments after the building that once housed the Regal Café was razed, but before the North Star, where Londy's Café traded, was demolished. The white bi-fold doors of Londy's Café, at that time owned by the Samios family, are visible in the top photograph.

Right: The Café Niagara in Main Street, Katoomba, with its superb façade and classic lettering, is a prime example of Art Deco architecture. Once a thriving business run by the Poulos family, later a chemist shop, and more recently a restaurant, the Niagara was closed for business when I visited in November, 2006.

CHAPTER TWO

"A Shop Full of Dreams": The Café Phenomenon

The Greek shopkeeper was a familiar face in the Australia of the 1940s, 50s, and 60s. George Kallinicos settled in Ipswich after several years of café experience in Toowoomba and Mitchell. In the Ritz Café in Bell Street, he is surrounded by piles of confectionery, a sign advertising pure lemon drinks, soda fountains, milkshakes machines, and a malt dispenser, all of which were typical of Greek cafés during this period.

"If there is a single word which summarises the lives of most Greeks in Australia early in the 20th century it is shop-keeping."

HUGH GILCHRIST 1:190 27

The first Greeks to arrive in Australia landed involuntarily – as convicts – like many of their Anglo-Celtic counterparts. Seven Greek sailors, who were convicted of piracy in the Mediterranean, were aboard the British transport vessel, Norfolk, when it docked at Port Jackson on the 27th of August, 1829.

Although three of them had been sentenced 'for the term of their natural life', all seven were pardoned in 1836, after the newly-independent Greek government lobbied for their release on the grounds that the sailors' actions "were in pursuance of assisting the liberation of Greece from Turkish domination." The two who chose to remain in Australia, Andonis Manolis and Ghikas Boulgaris, are Australia's earliest confirmed Greek settlers. Another three Greeks arrived as free settlers in the 1830s. One of these was Katherine Crummer, nee Aikaterini Plessos, the wife of an army officer, who arrived in 1835.[28] While it appears, however, that Australia generally held little appeal for the Greeks of 1832, thousands would make their home here over the course of the next century.

> *The men who sailed for Australia or America sent what money they could and dreamed of the time when they would return home as wealthy men*

Many Greeks are passionate about their rich and ancient heritage and even third and fourth generation immigrants experience a strong connection with the native land of their ancestors. But the Greeks have always been a migratory people. Sailing for distant horizons, they ventured into foreign lands and established colonies in the wake of Alexander the Great's conquests, but, of particular relevance to the story of Australia's humble Greek café, they were also repeatedly forced to flee political instability and the poverty of an arid landscape.[29]

The land in many parts of Greece, particularly on some of the islands, is barren and rocky. Families commonly lived a hand-to-mouth existence in these areas and menfolk were forced to leave their homes in search of work. If they moved to the cities or to the mainland, they could visit their homes and families occasionally, but for those who travelled further afield to pursue their dream of a better life this was impossible. The men who sailed for Australia or America sent what money they could and dreamed of the time when they would return home as wealthy men or bring their families to join them in their new lands.

Migration to Australia

The 1850s saw a stream of Greeks leave their impoverished homeland for Australia's gold fields and by 1871 three hundred Greeks lived in Australia. Because no administrative barriers prevented Greek immigration prior to WWI, the number of Greeks living in Australia by 1900 swelled to one thousand, and that figure doubled over the following decade. By 1910, there were more Greeks in Sydney than there were Chinese or Germans, the other main non-British people groups.[31]

The Asia Minor catastrophe of 1922 brought thousands more. When the Turks drove the Greeks out of Asia Minor, razing and burning the city of Smyrna, capturing hinterland towns, and committing terrible atrocities, more than a million refugees flooded into Athens and Piraeus as Greek inhabitants fled to the ports, most with no possessions at all.[32]

Conomos gives a chilling account of the Kokonis family's plight in the days after the Turks entered Smyrna:

> *One night, shortly afterward, they heard a loud noise, and, looking out, they saw Smyrna ablaze. As the fire got closer to the house they decided to flee. Taking what they could with them, they went out into the street, where thousands of Greeks were jostling with one another, making desperate efforts to escape. [. . . .] There was no boat available, but*

On barren, rocky islands like Kythera, families lived a hand to mouth existence searching for sustenance and employment. To make matters worse, fathers and sons were often absent, forced to search for work in Athens or Piraeus. Women struggled to feed their families, some working fields or digging graves to put food on the table. Even young children had to work hard when they were not at school.[30]

they met a friend who had a house on the esplanade overlooking the wharf. [. . . .] From the balcony they looked down on a scene of indescribable chaos and panic. Hordes of people were massing on the water's edge, desperate to catch a boat and flee. [. . .] In the sea were many floating bodies – bodies of people who had drowned themselves to escape the Turks, or been pushed into the water by the Turks.[33]

Populations swelled overnight in areas already struggling to support inhabitants, and finding a better life in far-off lands was suddenly a necessity rather than a dream. For many refugees, Australia, like America, was imagined as a land of golden opportunity.

When the United States imposed limits on immigration in 1924, the rate of Greek migration to Australia escalated, although those wishing to enter Australia at that time required forty pounds or a sponsor's written guarantee. By 1928, a quota restricted entry to those Greeks who could supply a landing fee of between 50 and 200 pounds, while the figure was three pounds for British immigrants. In 1930, entry was closed to all Europeans, except those with relatives in Australia or 500 pounds in the bank. Temporarily halted by the Second World War, the flow of Greek immigrants continued with the influx of European people to Australia in the 1950s and 1960s.[34]

Thousands of Greeks made their way to Australia and Conomos gives some engaging accounts of migrant journeys. He describes incidences of older men acting as guardians for boys travelling on ships alone and finding them employment in cafés when they arrived. Immigrants often disembarked at Sydney, travelling by train to their final destination at places like Castrission's café in Gundagai or Cominos' café in Cairns. Sometimes signs were hung around their necks or they were given into the care of Australian passengers. Language was only one of many problems migrants had to overcome, but one of Conomos' most telling accounts concerns a young man, Theo P. Comino, who arrived in Sydney in 1922 on his way to Brisbane. A friend took him to Central Station where he boarded a train bound for Brisbane:

[Referring to railway canteens along the way, the friend] instructed Theo to tell the person serving him 'Ti skoni', which are Greek words meaning 'What dust'. He would then be served with tea and scones. At the first stop, the Australian took a hungry Theo to the canteen where he said the words 'Ti skoni' and was given tea and scones. The Australian ordered a pie, and Theo, whose hunger was not satisfied by the tea and scones, wished that he too could have ordered one. At the next stop the same thing happened. Theo said the words 'ti skoni' and was given tea and scones while

the Australian ordered a pie. This continued at every stop until the train reached Brisbane, by which time Theo felt that he had had enough scones to last him for the rest of his life.

To boys and young men used to small islands where tiny villages were a few kilometres apart, travelling through the vast, wild country of western NSW or northern Queensland must also have been a daunting experience.

Like older travelling companions, Greek coffeehouses played important roles as unofficial reception centres and employment agencies. Many immigrants arrived in Australia with the address of a kafeneion, often situated above a café, where they would find Greeks sipping strong, black coffee, playing cards, gambling, and discussing affairs. Usually, one of those present originated from the same area as the newcomer and would find him work and accommodation, often with someone else who was enjoying the companionship of the kafeneion. At other times, it was a Greek café proprietor like Jim Bellas who provided the assistance.[35]

Jim Bellas came to Australia as a 16-year-old in 1936. After the war, he owned the Star Café in the Hibernian Building in Albert Street, Brisbane, directly in front of City Hall. The Brisbane City Council eventually demolished the block to redevelop King George Square, but because the shop was in the centre of Brisbane Jim estimates that about 40% of the Greek immigrants coming into Brisbane during that time passed through his hands. Jim was well-established in his new homeland prior to the post-war migrant influx, so he was able to find new immigrants work and accommodation. But making room for fellow countrymen as they arrived in Australia was just part of life for most Greek migrants. Jim's wife, Athena, who grew up in West End, remembers that the verandah of her grandmother's house was always crowded with

Frank Hurley. King George V Square & Town Hall (nla.pic-an23208124).
Photograph courtesy of the National Library of Australia.

Jim and Athena Bellas in their Brisbane home with a photograph of their second café, also the Star Milk Bar, which was demolished during extensions to the Carlton Crest Hotel in the lead-up to Expo 88. Jim's service to the community was officially acknowledged when the State Government awarded him the Queensland Migrant Service Award (inset) in recognition of Outstanding Voluntary Service in Migrant Settlement.

migrants waiting to find somewhere to live. "It was that little bit of help that got them on their feet," she says. Travelling companions, kafeneia, and café proprietors helped immigrants to settle in the strange new land, but it was the dream of returning to Greece with their hands filled with rewards of their labours in the land of plenty that would sustain men through the hardships that lay ahead.

Chain Migration

Kinship is a central feature in the evolution of Australia's Greek café. For destitute and dispossessed Greeks, the journey to the other side of the world was made possible only by the assistance of relatives and associates. When early immigrants settled in Australia, they worked long, hard hours in order to save enough money to bring others from Greece. This process of sponsoring relatives and countrymen, known as chain migration, was so successful that by 1947 twelve thousand Greeks lived in Australia.[36] Not only did chain migration enable generations of poverty-stricken Greeks to emigrate, but it also helped the newcomers adapt to a sometimes hostile environment and become established in their newly-adopted country.

Some cafés were responsible for establishing dozens of families in this way. After Theo Comino opened the first Greek café in Charleville in 1908, for instance, the Greek community of about 60 people who were living in the area during the 50s and 60s gives us a glimpse of the impact a single café could have on Greek migration to an area. The Niagara Café in Newcastle is another example; it resulted in some 113 members of the Karanges family being established in Australia, many in other food service businesses.[37]

Chain migration was a mutually beneficial arrangement, assisting sponsor and newcomer alike. Imported 'cheap labour' helped early businesses to survive, as did the unpaid labour of women and children in later years. Some newcomers lived like slaves, working 20 hour days, seven days a week, for scant pay and a bed of sugar bags on a restaurant table. Despite this, many served unofficial apprenticeships in these establishments and were soon able to open their own shops, often with money loaned by their sponsor/guardians. They, in turn, brought others from Greece. This 'ripple effect' resulted in a kind of arterial flow that avoided ghettos forming in capital cities and created strong Greek communities throughout Australia.[38]

The Regal Café in Ipswich is a prime example of the role cafés played in the chain migration process. George Kentrotis (left) was the first of his brothers to emigrate. He worked in a relative's café in Ipswich until he saved enough money to buy his own. Then, one after another, George brought his three brothers to Australia. Jim (right) remained in partnership with George, married, brought his brother-in-law to Australia, and provided work for him in the café until he was able to buy a business of his own. All three of George's brothers eventually bought into their own businesses.

Chain migration also explains the close relationship between Greek café proprietors. Most of the Greek shopkeepers in Ipswich came from the island of Kythera – in fact most came from a single village, the village of Fratsia, which perhaps supported only about 40 people at the beginning of the 20th century, and most of these would have been related. Many island villages were emptied of men during the early decades of the 20th century, making ghost towns of places like Fratsia. The devastating effect chain migration had on the villages that emigrants left behind is a forgotten aspect of the story of Australia's Greek café and this is explored in Chapters Five and Twelve.[39]

Arthur Comino and the Shopkeeping Phenomenon

If chain migration is a central feature of Greek migration to Australia, the entry of Greek immigrants into food catering is a singular phenomenon. Early Greek immigrants were mostly illiterate, itinerant bachelors, who intended to work hard, save as much as possible, and return home wealthy men. Arriving in Sydney, they spread throughout rural New South Wales and up into Queensland, working as labourers, maritime workers, fishermen, market gardeners and canecutters. By the 1890s, however, a surprising number had gravitated to food service industries. In 1911, 70% of the four hundred Kytherians living in NSW owned or worked in fish shops, oyster bars, and restaurants and a 1916 survey similarly reveals that most Greeks were employed in cafés, restaurants, and fruit, fish and confectionery outlets. As the first Greeks with whom Anglo-Celtic Australians had contact, Greek shopkeepers pioneered Australia's post-war multicultural society and even in 1981, when they represented less than 2% of the total population, Greek immigrants still owned 1/3 of all takeaway food shops in Australia.[40]

The man credited with founding Australia's Greek café industry is Athanasios Dimitrios (Arthur) Comino, who arrived in Sydney in 1873. Like many who were to follow, he left Kythera to seek a better life. The story of how a Greek immigrant came to open a fish shop at 36 Oxford Street, Sydney, in 1878 is veiled by the mists of time, and his story, like the adventures of his mythological ancestors, comes in several versions, but none is better than that recorded by Conomos:

> *Athanasios, having left [a colliery in Balmain] because of illness, was out of work when he went into a fish shop to have a meal. While there, he watched the proprietor drop the fish into boiling fat and then take it out a few minutes later, put it on a plate and serve it to a customer. Athanasios was struck by the simplicity of the process. It occurred to him that such an occupation would require little experience or hard labour. He suggested to his friend John Theodore that they open a fish shop. His friend agreed, and so it was, according to this account, that in 1878, the two of them opened the first Greek fish shop in Sydney.*[41]

There is an even more delicious facet of the legend. Comino and Theodore were familiar with fish, having been born to the island lifestyle of Kythera, but they knew nothing of oysters. Upon receiving their first order for battered oysters, the pair battered, cooked, and served them still in their shells.[42]

It's a great yarn, and one that is worthy of a place in Greek mythology, but by whatever means Comino came to open his fish shop, a Greek had certainly gained a foot-hold in Sydney's food-service industry, and it was, as Conomos explains, "an event that was to have far-reaching consequences for Greek migration to New South Wales and Queensland."[43] Comino's shop was the foundation of the Kytherian community in Australia. He soon brought his brothers out to Australia, they brought their friends, and by 1911, 400 Kytherians had immigrated to NSW because of this initial shop. When you consider that only 3,000 people now live on Kythera, while some 60,000 Australians were born there, Comino's 'foot-hold' in Sydney's food-service industry is a very significant event.[44]

While the story of Athanasios Comino varies, one thing is clear; non-Greek fish shops were trading in Sydney prior to 1878, but Comino's business was a roaring success. Although he began with little knowledge about cooking fish, no money, and even less English, Comino possessed other qualities that caused his food-catering venture to flourish. First, he was quick to see the popularity of oysters in Sydney and 'cashed in' on the oyster trade, soon becoming widely known as 'The Oyster King'.[45] In addition, hard work, determination, and the kinship structure of Greek families caused the business to prosper and Comino soon opened other fish shops.

As his employees learned the food-catering business and gained the experience and capital necessary to establish their own shops, generations of young Greeks were soon following in Comino's footsteps. The 'ripple effect' of chain migration in the first two decades of the 20th century saw hundreds become established in oyster saloons throughout NSW and Queensland. Oysters were packed in ice and shipped by train even to remote western towns. A remarkable feature of this period, however, is the age of the men. Although many were boys when they left Greece, they demonstrate an unusual capacity to save, send money home to meet family obligations, and invest in further enterprises. Some were managing cafés in their teens and many were proprietors in their early 20s.[46]

Most of the Greek shopkeepers in Ipswich came from the island of Kythera – in fact most came from a single village

Oyster Saloons were not restricted to coastal towns and cities. This photograph of wool wagon teams moving along Eagle Street in Longreach was taken around 1910. Athens Oyster Saloon can be seen on a sign on the front of the shop in the centre of the image. This is likely to have been run by a Greek proprietor, one of many who established oyster saloons in towns throughout rural Queensland and New South Wales.

State Library of Queensland Image No. 145136 (See also image No. 141526, No. 10635, & No. 169189)

Comino proved that starting a fish shop required no education and little initial capital, and the necessary skills were easily acquired. It may also have seemed a logical enterprise for the Greeks who had sea-faring or farming backgrounds. The food industry at that time was also relatively free from the 'interference' of health inspectors and independent of the union restrictions on foreign labour that affected heavy industry prior to the 1940s.[47] More importantly, Greek immigrants were willing to endure the long hours, hard work, and harsh conditions necessary to succeed because they knew their families still endured the poverty and war-torn existence they had left behind. They also accommodated Australians by anglicising their long Greek names and adhering to a British-Australian menu. And they supported their local communities. Many also appear to have been astute businessmen. In the late 19th and early 20th centuries, the oyster was the equivalent of the quiche in the 1980s and the sun-dried tomato in the 1990s. Greeks 'cashed in' on this popularity and their Oyster Saloons or Palaces, as these fish shops were often called, thrived. And these were the precursors of the Greek café.

Although he began with little knowledge about cooking fish, no money, and even less English, Comino possessed other qualities that caused his food-catering venture to flourish

While the stories recorded here concern immigrants who stayed in the café trade all their lives, many immigrants made new lives for themselves and their families through other business. Harry Corones, for example, is well-known throughout western Queensland as the creator and life-long publican of Charleville's historic Hotel Corones. But Harry, like many Greek immigrants who prospered in other fields of endeavour, 'found his feet' in Australia through a café. The Hotel Corones is an increasingly-popular tourist destination. Objects, photographs, and other documents on display in the hotel foyer and in the upper-level smoking room chronicle Charleville's history and the Corones family's life. Tourists take guided tours of these exhibits, and $10 'yarns' over Devonshire tea further exploit the fortunes of the famous pub. While Harry's illustrious 60-year career as a publican is celebrated, little mention is made of the fact that his new life in Charleville began with a humble café.

Although Harry is a legend in western Queensland, he was a penniless Kytherian immigrant when he arrived in Australia in 1907. After a start in Freeleagus' Paris Café

The Oyster Saloon was the precursor of the Greek café. Lollies, ices, and tobacco are advertised on the shop front behind a group of men, probably the Greek café proprietor and staff and a number of local customers, as they pose in front of N. Andronicos' Olympia Café in Allora some time in the early 20th century.

State Library of Queensland Image No. 60934.

in Brisbane, Harry went to work for Theo Comino in his Alfred Street café in Charleville in 1909. He bought the café in the following year. Around 1912, he closed Theo's original shop and opened the Paris Café in Wills Street, opposite the present Hotel Corones. Undeterred when the café burned down some time after 1913, Harry built a new shop, also called the Paris Café, on the corner of Wills and Galatea Streets. It was in his capacity as proprietor of one of these cafés that Harry impressed Paddy Ryan (or Cryan), a travelling representative from Perkin's Brewery. Harry's conviviality prompted Paddy to suggest that Harry lease the Charleville Hotel. When Harry protested that he had neither money nor knowledge of the hotel business, Paddy assured him that the Brewery would finance the deal and that Harry would soon learn the trade. By 1912, Harry was a publican.

While he was in Sydney on his honeymoon, however, Harry learned that the Charleville Hotel had also caught fire. Not easily discouraged, he rebuilt and operated the hotel until the ten-year lease expired in 1924. Between 1924 and 1929, at a cost of 50,000 pounds, Harry built his dream, the Hotel Corones, which has since played host to movie stars, pop stars, politicians, royalty, and aviators, as well as thousands of everyday Australians.[48] The young, penniless Kytherian was well on his way to this life-long, prosperous career and legendary status within little more than five years of his arrival in Australia. And his career began with a humble Greek café.

Using Ipswich as a case study, the following chapters trace the extraordinary story of young Greek men who, having fled poverty-stricken islands like Kythera, found themselves building a network of shops throughout Australia. Many, of course, never returned to Greece; they stayed in their adopted homeland, eventually bringing Greek women out to work beside them. With the aid of packing cases and Minties tins, young children soon joined the army of Greek-Australians at sinks and cash registers across the country, and the Greek café and the Greek shopkeeping family became Australian icons.

Hotel Corones

CHAPTER THREE

Greek Cafés in Ipswich, Queensland: A Case Study

"Oh, Londy's was where you went. You should have seen the Easter eggs – they had a big display right up to the ceiling and people came from Brisbane just to see them."

Ipswich resident at
St Mary's Hostel, raceview

Historians claim that nearly every town in Queensland and New South Wales had a Greek café, and bigger towns had more than one.[49] Many proprietors worked their way through a string of cafés in different towns until they became firmly established. Others operated their cafés for long periods of time.[50]

What these observations fail to articulate is the sheer number of Greek cafés trading in some towns at various times throughout the twentieth century. By 1906, there were already three in Warwick, for example. Dalby had five in the 1930s, and in the 1950s, Katoomba had about ten and Tamworth at least seven.[51] No fewer than ten operated in Ipswich during the 40s and 50s, and that's just in the central business district. The aim of this chapter is to examine in more depth the incidence of Greek shops in a single town and to understand the impact they had on a local community. Ipswich makes an excellent case study because, unlike Brisbane, it is small enough to enable a complete survey and, unlike smaller rural towns, big enough to offer a range of experiences of café life.

While Comino's fish shop, which opened in Sydney in 1878, represents the genesis of the Greek shopkeeping phenomenon, Queensland towns soon acted as magnets for immigrants who had been 'apprenticed' in New South Wales. As a result, Greek cafés and oyster saloons are recorded in Brisbane as early as 1893. By 1910, there were 26.[52] One of the first really successful proprietors was Gianis K. Mavrokefalos from Ithaca, who opened a café in 1901. Known as John 'Gero' (Old Man) Black, he pioneered Brisbane's café industry and, like Comino in Sydney, performed the role of 'sheet-anchor', sponsoring relatives and countrymen to migrate to Australia, employing them until they had worked off the price of their passage, arranging accommodation, providing counsel and guardianship, and, often, loaning them money to open their first shop. As others replicated the process, chain migration brought thousands of Greeks to Queensland, and Greek cafés were soon spreading across the Queensland landscape, as they were in New South Wales.[53]

It may be that there were no Greek cafés in rural Queensland towns in 1900, but within a decade, 33 cafés were operating in 22 towns, half of them with Kytherian proprietors. Gympie, Maryborough, Bundaberg, Rockhampton, Mackay, Ayr, Townsville, Mareeba, and Cairns near the coast, Warwick, Toowoomba, Allora, Oakey, and Pittsworth across the Darling Downs, and Longreach, Chinchilla, Charters Towers, Charleville, Roma, and Goondiwindi to the west had oyster saloons or cafés by the end of the 1910s. By 1920, Greeks traded in at least 52 towns, including those in the far west and far north like Muttaburra, Hughenden, Kuridala, Innisfail and Babinda.

By 1891, several Greeks had settled in Ipswich, and from the end of the 19th century were becoming established, as they were elsewhere, in the food service industry. Conomos notes that Ipswich was one of eight provincial Queensland towns in which Greek café proprietors were laying the foundations for Greek settlement as early as 1910.[55] Records show that Greek-born Mrs Asica Matton was a widow and a shopkeeper in Ipswich when she was naturalised in 1903, and that Ioannis Mavrokefalos (John Denis Black), a 42-year-old oyster saloon proprietor, Efstathios Mavrokefalos, a shop assistant aged 28, and cooks, Gerasimos Mavroudas, aged 38, and Nikolaos Skavos, aged 31, were working in Ipswich in 1916.[56]

According to Conomos, Ipswich's first Greek oyster saloon/café opened in 1901, when John Dennis Black, a relative of John 'Gero' Black, opened the Australia Café in Brisbane

Ipswich's first Greek oyster saloon/café opened in 1901, when John Dennis Black, a relative of John 'Gero' Black, opened the Australia Café in Brisbane Street

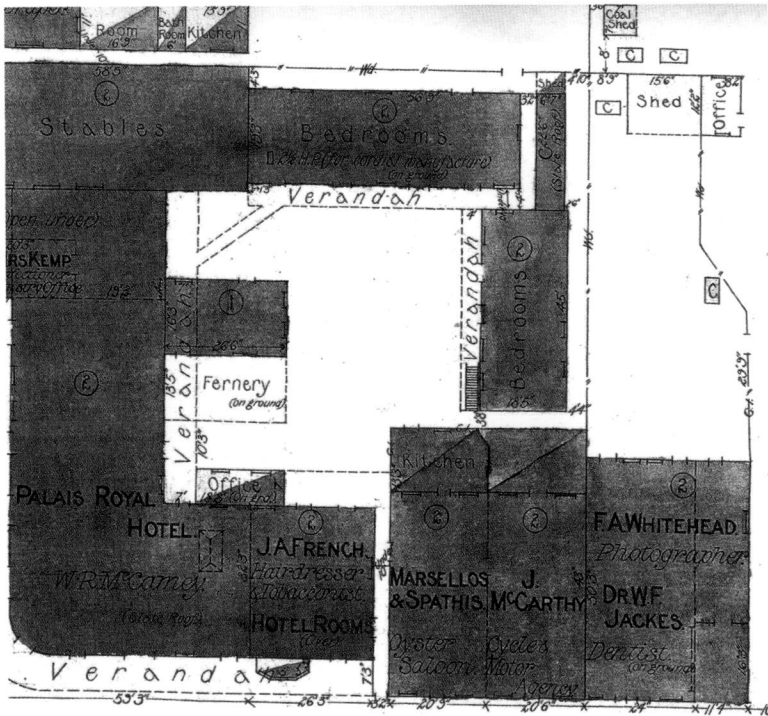

Fire Department Block Plans of 1918 show Marsellos and Spathis' Oyster Saloon (near the intersection of Brisbane and East Streets) and Whitehead Photographic Studio.

Street.[57] He was 27 years old at the time. Black opened a second oyster saloon in Nicholas Street in about 1914.[58] Peter Spathis, also a Greek immigrant, met Black during a trip to Ipswich in 1915, after which he and fellow employee, George Marsellos, helped Black run the two cafés.[59] Then, according to Elpiniki Black, her brother-in-law became ill in about 1916, and she and John went to Brisbane to run his Ithaca Café in Queen Street – the Mavrokefalos family came from Ithaca – so the Blacks sold the Australia Café and the Nicholas Street oyster saloon to Spathis and Marcellos.[60]

Since two oyster saloons under the ownership of Spathis & Marsellos appear on the Ipswich Fire Department Block Plans of 1918, one in Brisbane Street and one in Nicholas Street, the first Greek café in Ipswich, Black's Australia Café of 1901, can then be identified as a business at 80 Brisbane Street, uphill from the corner of the Brisbane and East Street intersection beside of the Palais Royal Hotel.[61] Peter Spathis later refers to one of his shops as the City Café, and later photographs show both the name, City Café, and the name of its owner, Peter Spathis, on the front of the building at 80 Brisbane Street, indicating that Black's saloon had a change of name at some point.[62] Local residents also remember this shop as the City Café in the 1940s. Of all the buildings that housed Greek cafés in Ipswich, this is one of the few that survives today.

The City Café had several subsequent Greek owners – Strategos, then Stathis (a relative of Strategos), and then Jack and Pat Cassimatis, who owned it until Jack died in the 70s. The exact date that it closed for business is unclear, but the City Café, Ipswich's first Greek café, may have been one of the longest-running Greek cafés in the country.[63] It is possible, however, that Greek food outlets may have operated in Ipswich prior to Black's oyster saloon – the earliest one that Conomos is able to identify. If Mrs Asica Matton was a widowed shopkeeper in 1903, presumably she and her husband operated some kind of shop prior to that time, perhaps even in the 19th century, and this could have been an oyster saloon.

One of the difficulties in researching the history of Greek immigrants is that oral history is sometimes the only means of gathering certain information. Because the informants used depend on contacts known to

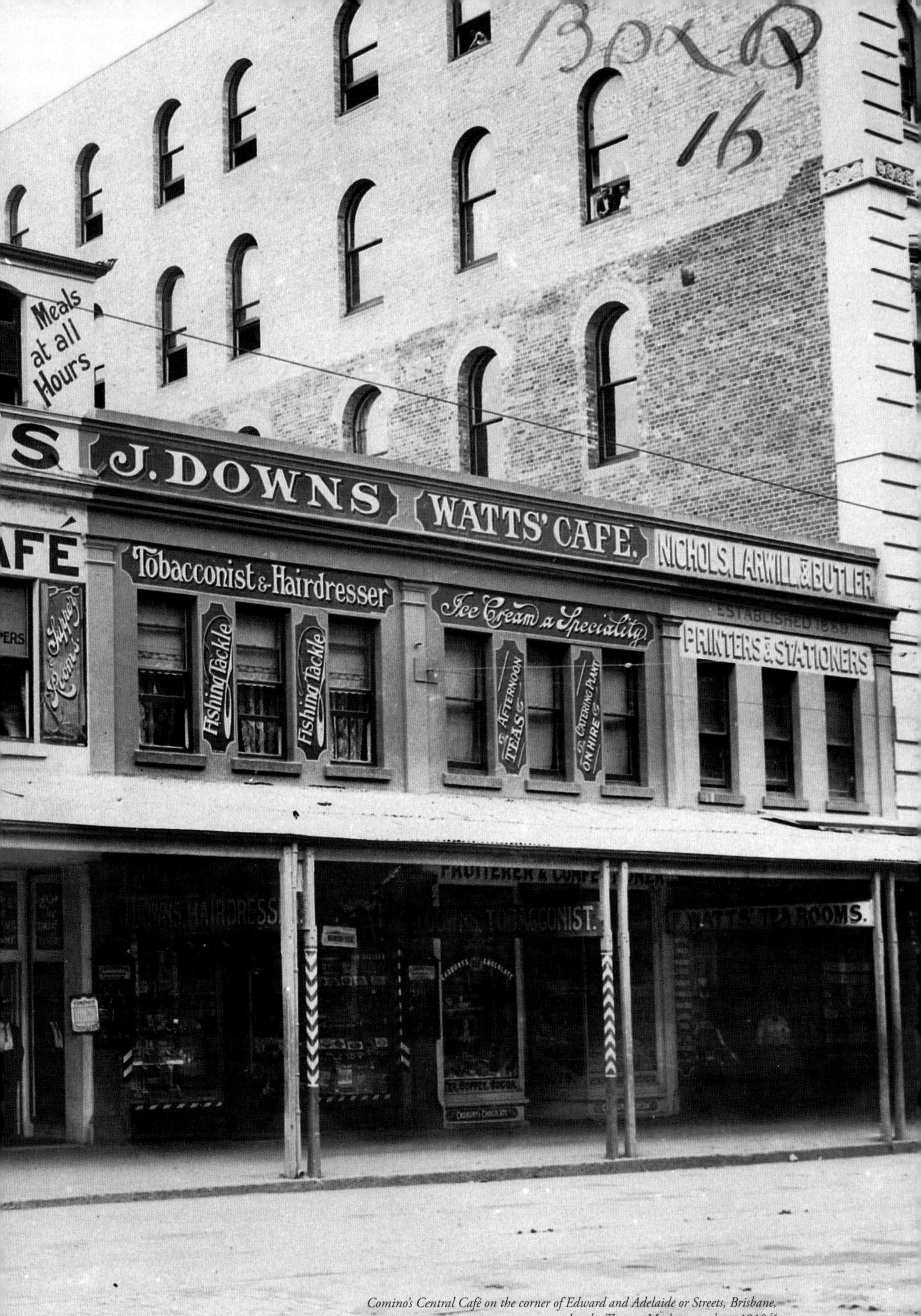

Comino's Central Café on the corner of Edward and Adelaide or Streets, Brisbane, taken by Thomas Mathewson about 1910.[54]

The City Café at 80 Brisbane Street was once the Australia Café, the first Greek café in Ipswich. A photograph taken during Spathis' ownership from 1916 to 1933 shows advertising for the café's Oyster Grill Rooms and Ladies Special Dining Rooms on the top floor windows. The photograph opposite was probably taken in the 40s.

the researcher, whole spheres of information that exist outside of the knowledge of those informants can be overlooked. While Conomos has documented an extraordinary body of information, his work may be critiqued as being weighted toward Kytherian history because he is Kytherian. Aphrodite and the Mixed Grill may be similarly critiqued, not because the author is Kytherian, but because the contacts known to the author are those people who had shops in Ipswich, and most of these are Kytherian. Since the name Matton is not listed in the Index of Names at the back of Conomos' book, it is probable that the Mattons were not Kytherian. They may have come from Ithaca, and it is not unlikely that they ran an oyster saloon prior to the one Black established. Given the kinship ties of Greek immigrants and the 'ripple effect' of chain migration, Mrs Matton may even have sold her business to Black after her husband died.

In addition to the Mattons' shop, local historian, Beryl Johnston, lists C. H. Chubb as the proprietor of an oyster saloon in Bell Street, Ipswich, in 1876, but the 1918 Block Plans give no clue as to the shop's whereabouts. The Greeks often anglicised their names, but there is no proof that Chubb was Greek.[64] Given that Chubb's shop predates Comino's shop in Sydney by two years, and given that 'Chubb' is not listed in the Index of Names at the back of Conomos' book, Chubb is unlikely to have been Kytherian. He may have come from another part of Greece, such as Ithaca, the homeland of Ipswich's alleged first Greek proprietor, Ioannis Mavrokefalos, but the name 'Chubb' does not occur in any of the sources used here to trace the evolution of

the Greek café. Oysters were very popular in Australia in the late 19th century and Greeks were not the only proprietors who had oyster saloons. Oysters had been popular in London for centuries – in Pickwick Papers of 1837, Charles Dickens wrote that there was an oyster stall to every half-dozen houses – so it is quite likely that Chubb was among the oyster saloon proprietors in Australia who were not Greek.[65]

In addition to the two Marsellos & Spathis shops, the 1918 Block Plans show that another oyster saloon, owned by Stratigos & Company, traded in Brisbane Street.[66] According to those plans, there may also have been a fourth Greek shop at that time. Marble Bar, Thomas' premises in the middle shop of the Rawlings Building in Brisbane Street, was possibly a Greek café.[67] Again, the name 'Thomas' does not settle the question of the proprietor's ethnicity. Neither is there any indication of the kind of business operated on the premises. The word 'bar', as in milk bar or public bar – was used in the context of a long counter at which customers stood to be served, but it is unlikely that Marble Bar was a hotel, since other hotels are designated by the word 'hotel' on the Block Plans. In addition, Gilchrist notes a café called the Marble Bar Café in Grafton in the same decade and Conomos lists several Greek cafés in other towns that were called Marble Café, pointing out that the name was derived from the marble imported from Italy for use in café counters.[68]

Happily, an article in the Ipswich Advertiser confirms that Marble Bar was a milk bar, although it gives no indication of Thomas' ethnicity, and Buchanan includes a photograph of the shop in her recent history of Ipswich.[69] It could have been a Greek shop. To place these three, or possibly four, oyster saloons within the context of food outlets in Ipswich in 1918, eight other food outlets are evident on the Block Plans. Greeks therefore owned over a quarter of the food outlets at that time, possibly more.[70]

Ipswich residents remember that, in addition to two fruit shops with milk bars, there were at least ten Greek cafés in the Ipswich CBD during the 1940s/50s. To assess the total number of Greek catering businesses that operated Ipswich during the twentieth century, it should be noted that those 12 businesses do not include Mrs Matton's shop, the two oyster saloons in Brisbane Street in 1918, or Black's second oyster saloon in Nicholas Street. When Marsellos left the Spathis & Marsellos partnership in about 1918, Nick Sklavos took over his share, running the Nicholas Street saloon while Spathis ran the City Café.[71] Spathis and Sklavos must have later dissolved their partnership, since Sklavos owned the Nicholas Street saloon outright with his brother, Theo. The Sklavos brothers unfortunately lost this business during the depression.[72]

These 16 businesses do include the Café Australia in Nicholas Street, which the Londy family owned briefly in the early 20th century, and which later gave way to a business called the Sydney Fruit Mart.[73] Since the Sydney Fruit Mart is indicated in the 1918 Block Plans in the approximate position in Nicholas Street where Greeks had a business called the Sydney Café in the 30s, 40s, and 50s, it seems likely that the Sydney Café and the Australia Café traded in the same premises with different owners at different times. In addition, an early photograph of Nicholas Street, now the mall, shows an oyster saloon in a position similar to that of Marsellos & Spathis, as indicated on the Block Plans. Because the photograph probably predates both the 1918 plans and Black's purchase of the Nicholas Street saloon in 1914, this could indicate a further, and even earlier, Greek business, bringing the total to a possible 18.

> "The Greeks never knocked back anything that would make a dollar."

The total number of Greek cafés in Ipswich also depends on how you define 'café'. And this can be complicated. While the Greek café evolved from the late 19th century oyster saloon/fish shop, and many maintained a strong fish section, the addition of milk bars and soda fountains and the emphasis on confectionery defines the shops of the classic era. But many shops, including Londy's Café, sold fruit and vegetables. As Bill Kentrotis of the Central Milk Bar notes, "The Greeks never knocked back anything that would make a dollar." Although they had no dining rooms, the two fruit shops in Nicholas Street had milk bars. Penglis' Fruit shop looks like a milk bar in photographs of the Ipswich streetscape because of a large Peter's Ice Cream sign. I am not listing the two fruit shops as cafés, but am including them in this survey because they had milk bars. Chapter Four further defines what is understood by the term 'Greek café'.

The ten cafés mentioned by Ipswich residents who were interviewed for this book also did not include two Greek cafés that opened after the 1950s – Tony's Café, which Jim Pavlakis ran in the 60s, and the Central Milk Bar, which the Kentrotis family took over in the 80s – or those beyond the CBD, or convenience stores, or contemporary café bars such as the one in the Hotel Metropole, redeveloped in recent years by Michael Samios, also a Kytherian. It should also be noted that Greeks owned numerous cafés in the districts surrounding Ipswich: the Andonara family had a café in Rosewood, which was sold to non-Greek Australians in the early 40s; among others, there were cafés in Boonah and Kalbar

The "Marble Bar" Hairdressing Saloon, located on the corner of Brisbane and Nicholas Streets. This interesting shop has exterior electric lights. (courtesy Margaret Bodetti)

and Laidley, the latter having been established prior to 1908; Fonda Marendy had a café in the 60s at Redbank beside the School of Arts; Bill Comino traded at Lowood; Kosmas Kallinicos had a café in Gatton.[74] In addition, Ipswich Greeks owned businesses other than cafés – Anthony's Drapery, for example – and this is still the case. The Ipswich area, then, had a large number of Greek business people and many cafés.[75]

Respondents remember the following cafés in the Ipswich CBD: Marendy's Café Australia, Londy's Café, the Regal Café – possibly on the site of Stratigos' oyster saloon of 1918 – the City Café on the site of John Black's original oyster saloon, the Metro Café, Veneris' Hamburger Bar, Tony's Café, later Tony's Snack Bar, and the Central Milk Bar and Café – all of which were in Brisbane Street – the Ritz Café in Bell Street, the Sydney Café in Nicholas Street, and the Wintergarden Milk Bar in East Street, as well as Nick Penglis' Fruit Shop, Nick Vergotis' pie stall, and George Petrohilos' Big Apple in Nicholas Street.

As was the case throughout Australia, numerous Kytherians settled in Ipswich. The Londy, Kentrotis, Marendy, Pavlakis, Stathis, Samios, Kallinicos, and Veneris families are all from Kythera. The pattern of chain migration brought many members of some families to Australia, and almost all of the Ipswich Kytherians came from one place, the tiny village of Fratsia. The impact that such an exodus had on such a small village is a remarkable story too, and this is explored in later chapters. Reputed to be the home of the goddess Aphrodite, Kythera was certainly the birthplace of many Greek families who owned cafés in Ipswich.

This photograph was taken facing south up Nicholas Street, Ipswich, about the turn of the century. The oyster saloon in the centre of the picture is possibly Black's second saloon which he operated from about 1914. Because it predates 1914, the photograph suggests that either a proprietor operated the shop at an earlier date, or else that this is a different shop. Note the Blackall Monument at the intersection of Brisbane and Nicholas Streets, which is now situated on top of Denmark Hill. [76]

Greek Cafés in the Ipswich CBD from the 1940s

1	THE CITY CAFÉ Closed in the 70s	80 Brisbane Street beside the Palais Royal Hotel on the East Street corner.	John Black (1901) then Marsellos and Spathis. Spathis (1915-33) sold to Jim Strategos, who sold it to a relative, Nick Stathis, who sold to Cassimatis in the late 40s.
2	THE METRO CAFE Lease not renewed after a kitchen fire in 1963	93 Brisbane Street, almost opposite the City Café.	George Andrews (Andreatidis) opened at the end of WWII – sold to Nick Stathis late 40s.
3	THE CAFÉ AUSTRALIA Closed 1950	Brisbane Street, three doors down from the bank on corner of Bell and Brisbane Streets (Trustee building).	Peter Spathis sold to Londy brothers some time after 1918. Sold to Harry Marendy about 1935.
4	LONDY'S CAFE Demolished late 80s in Kern development	The right-hand half of the North Star Hotel building on the corner of Brisbane and Ellenborough Streets where cinemas are now.	Originally the Paris Café. 1925 – Londy family. Sold to Coplin brothers from Sydney in 1958 and then to Samios brothers in 1963.
5	THE REGAL CAFÉ Business closed 1977	155 Brisbane Street beside Bayards several doors down from Londy's (medical centre now).	George and Jim Kentrotis – from early 1940s until George retired in 1977.
6	THE CENTRAL MILK BAR AND CAFÉ Leased March 2006	Still opposite the Ford dealership in Brisbane Street, beside where the Vogue Theatre once stood.	Maria and Bill Kentrotis bought the Central from Smith, a non-Greek Australian, in 1980.
7	VENERIS' HAMBURGER BAR	Brisbane Street opposite Bell Street junction.	Tony and Doris Veneris – closed about 1950.
8	TONY'S CAFÉ Closed about 1980	55 Brisbane Street near the Gordon Street junction.	Tony and Doris Veneris, from about 1950 until Tony was murdered in 1962 and Jim Pavlakis bought it. Closed about 1980.
9	THE SYDNEY CAFÉ Tanos family left in 1961	10 Nicholas Street, between Risson's Produce and T C Beirne's at the northern end of town.	Londys' originally, then Con Honianakis from about 1930, and Harry & Christopher Tanos from 1951.
10	THE RITZ CAFÉ Sold 1968	In Bell Street beside the Ritz Theatre approximately where the food court is now.	George Kallinicos – from 1942.
11	WINTERGARDEN MILK BAR Sold 1958	In East Street beside the Wintergarden Theatre where R.T. Edwards Electrical is now.	John (George Kentrotis' brother) and Helen Kentos from about 1950.

City Café

The City Café was a much larger shop than many later Ipswich cafés and photographs show that waitresses at one time wore dark uniforms with white caps and aprons. Peter Spathis sold the City Café in about 1933 and opened other shops in the heart of Brisbane. Jim Strategos took over the café, later selling it to Nick Stathis just before WWII. Several Ipswich residents claim that while wedding receptions were held at Whitehouse's Café and at the Capitol Café, both run by non-Greek Australians, they were not held at Greek cafés. This is not strictly true. The City Café had function rooms above the café and wedding receptions were held there. Nick Stathis' son, Jack, remembers that his father turned the upstairs area into a billiard saloon during the war and divided the café into two – a fish shop on one side and a café on the other. When Nick sold the City Café to his wife's cousin, Jack Cassimatis, some time after WWII, he bought the Metro Café across the street. A drawing of this section of Brisbane Street shows the City Café and the Peter's Ice Cream sign on the building opposite is probably the Metro Café.

Above: Nick Stathis in front of the City Café with local policeman, Roy Schultz.

The wedding of Jim Strategos' daughter in 1941 was the last function to be held in the reception area above the City Cafe because, according to Jack Stathis, food and staff were difficult to procure during the war years. Jack is the handsome young man with the wayward tie third from the left in the front row.

Metro Café

George Andrews (Andreatidis), one of the many Greeks who adopted an English name to live in his adopted country, opened the Metro Café after the war. The Metro Café was situated at 93 Brisbane Street, where Action Realty has traded for some years. The Dorothy Bell Cake Shop was beside the café and then there was the Bank on the East Street corner. In the other direction, there was a fruit shop and then an alleyway which housed McKenzie's Mining and Hardware with a flower shop at the entrance, and then another Greek café, the Café Australia, owned by the Marendy family. When Nick Stathis sold the City Café, he and his family took over the café across the road.

Individual cubicles were a feature of Greek cafés. A local resident remembers, "They had these big, wonderful booths and we could all pack in there together and talk about whatever we were doing – probably only bought a milkshake." The Metro had booths along the side wall and a confectionery counter that sold loose lollies weighed in bags and, in later years, an extensive range of pre-packaged lollies that came in packets, boxes, and tins: Throaties, Irish Moss, Arctic Mints, Life Savers, Jelly Beans, Smarties, Orchard Kisses, Marella Jubes, Nestlé Milky Bars, McRobertson's Scorched

Almonds, Cadbury's chocolates, Easter eggs, as well as Aspro, Vincents, and Bex can be seen in the background of photographs of staff behind the Metro counter. (Above)

The Stathis family lived opposite Saint Stephens Presbyterian church in Limestone Street, about where Tomato Brothers is now situated, and several local girls, who worked as waitresses in the Metro, lived in rooms underneath the house. Buses pulled up at the bus stop in front of the café and the last bus always waited until the cafés closed up around 11pm. The kitchen at the Metro Café caught fire in 1963, when a toaster was left on, and the lease on the building was not renewed.

Londy's Café

If the City Café was the first Greek café in Ipswich, Londy's Café is one most people remember. The first thing they will tell you is that Londy's was a 'double' café with two entrances and three curved display windows on the street. Water trickled down inside one window to cool the fish and stop flies settling on the glass. Sadly, the curved windows were removed when Londy's was 'modernised' after WWII. Londy's Café was situated on the right-hand side of the bottom floor of the North Star Hotel building on the corner of Brisbane and Ellenborough Streets, now the site of the cinema complex. It had separate areas for the fish department, the confectionery and cigarette counter, the milk bar, and the toasted sandwiches area. There were booths along the mirrored walls and tables in the central space, and a juke box that was popular with young people. But when Ipswich residents reminisce about the era of the Greek cafés, the feature they universally recall is Londy's Easter egg display, which was so impressive that people travelled from Brisbane to see it. Later owners, the Samios family, maintained the tradition.

Londy's also had a neon sign, which many believe was the first neon sign in town. It was green and yellow and featured a fish that flicked its tail and blew bubbles. This kind of image, along with particular traditions or features like Londy's Easter eggs, remain in people's memories long after cafés have gone and people have forgotten even where they were, much less details about menus and furniture. Many cafés were designed around a theme – Hollywood, Mexican, Australian – so that the name and décor evoked particular imagery. Brisbane writer, Effie Detsimas, remembers a near life-size wooden cut out of a winking chorus girl that greeted patrons who came to her father's High Hat Café in Fortitude Valley after the Second World War, for example. I remember the cream-coloured wall friezes of Greek gods and goddesses on the dark wood panelling at Katoomba's Paragon Café not far from my grandmother's house. Ipswich people remember Londy's Easter eggs. Like Cloudland Ballroom's crescent moon, or the Aeroplane Jelly jingle, these are icons of an era that evoke strong memories for people who lived through the heyday of the Greek café. They are as powerful in this regard as the smell of an old school port or the taste of Nana's Christmas pudding.

When Ipswich residents reminisce about the era of the Greek cafés, the feature they universally recall is Londy's Easter egg display, which was so impressive that people travelled from Brisbane to see it.

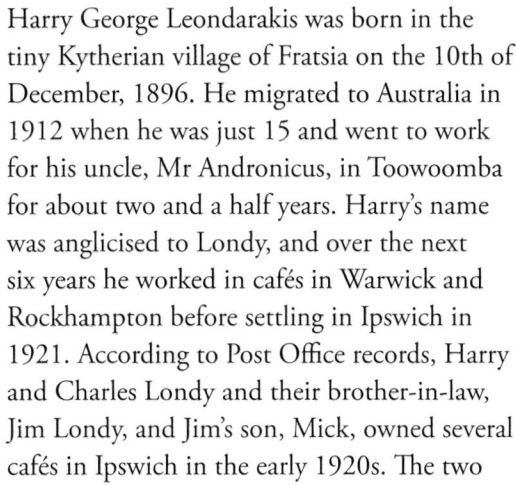

Harry Londy (standing second from left) with staff and Regal Café proprietors outside Londy's Café in the forties.

Harry George Leondarakis was born in the tiny Kytherian village of Fratsia on the 10th of December, 1896. He migrated to Australia in 1912 when he was just 15 and went to work for his uncle, Mr Andronicus, in Toowoomba for about two and a half years. Harry's name was anglicised to Londy, and over the next six years he worked in cafés in Warwick and Rockhampton before settling in Ipswich in 1921. According to Post Office records, Harry and Charles Londy and their brother-in-law, Jim Londy, and Jim's son, Mick, owned several cafés in Ipswich in the early 1920s. The two in Brisbane Street were called the Café Australia and the Paris Café.[77] They sold the Café Australia to Harry Marendy in the 30s, while the Paris Café became known simply as Londy's. Cafés were commonly known by the name of the proprietors.[78] According to his son, Peter, Harry was naturalised in 1922 and opened Londy's Café in 1925. He married Theodora Marendy in St Paul's Cathedral opposite the café in the following year, and lived in Ipswich for the rest of his life in a house near the intersection of Limestone and Thorn Streets. They had four children: George, Esther, Peter, and Marina.[79]

Some proprietors rubbed shoulders with famous people in their capacity as food caterers. The staff of the Kosciusko Milk Bar in Cooma, NSW, for instance, became firm friends with Robert Mitchum and Peter Ustinov when the café won the contract with Warner Brothers to cater for their crew, which was filming *The Sundowners* in the Snowy Mountains in 1959.[80] The staff and customers at Londy's had their brush with fame too. One Ipswich resident recalls Bert Hinkler landing his plane in Queens Park early in the 1930s. The park is close to the centre of town, and after lunch at Londy's, which was laid out like a feast, Hinkler offered to take staff members for a ride in the plane.[81]

Harry's son, Peter, recalls that the financial basis of his father's success was this: never take out a loan for something unless it's income-producing, and if it's not income-producing, wait until you can afford it. But Harry's business success was also the result of his attitude towards his customers. Harry Londy is remembered as a friendly proprietor who met new customers at the door, showed them to a table, and introduced a waitress to them.[82] When he died in 1948, aged 52 years,

> *Harry's business success was also the result of his attitude towards his customers.*

NORTH STAR HOTEL, IPSWICH

Theodora ran the café with the assistance of a female relative from Toowoomba, until she sold it to the four Coplin brothers in 1958.[83]

The Coplins were also Greek. Arnold Dull is a local resident whose family had a dairy farm near Amberley in the 50s and 60s. He delivered milk as a 15-year-old with his father. They had a three-ton truck and carried the milk into the cafés in big milk cans, which they tipped into the stainless steel canisters kept in the milk bar. The Dulls delivered to several cafés in the Ipswich area, but Londy's Café was always the last job on the run because Harry Coplin would make them a free meal and send them home with a truckload of food scraps for the pigs. This was in the days before cafés had to use pasteurised milk and farmers were forbidden to feed their pigs food scraps.

Harry would serve Arnold and his father a delicious meal of pies with peas 'n' gravy, sausages and vegetables, fish and chips, or a plate of oysters barbequed on a hot plate with cheese and Worcestershire sauce, which was Arnold's favourite.

The proprietors took every opportunity to 'pull a young bloke's leg', however, and Arnold remembers the day Harry introduced him to a 'new variety' of tomato. It had just arrived in town, Harry told Arnold, and was normally eaten green. The proprietor offered to let the young, 'green' dairy farmer try one of the strange tomatoes. Arnold bit into the shiny, green fruit only to find that the 'tomato' was an unripe persimmon. His mouth suffered discomfort for several hours. On another occasion, when Arnold's dad remarked on the flavour of Harry's chicken soup, the proprietor took them into the kitchen to let them in on his secret recipe. Harry held a raw chicken aloft over the pot of soup and poured boiling water into the cavity and out through the chicken's neck into the pot. "To this day," says Arnold, "I don't know whether he was havin' me on or not."

But Arnold's favourite memory of Londy's Café is of the day Harry Coplin gave him a lift down to the Vogue Picture Theatre at the bottom of Brisbane Street, opposite the Gordon Street intersection. Harry drove a big Mainline 500 utility, and on this occasion he didn't just drop Arnold off at the theatre, but he drove the Mainline right through the front windows of the Vogue and into the foyer. Harry said he had swerved to miss a child running across the street, but Arnold says, "I didn't see any children." Sergeant Bob Titcombe was in the foyer at the time, keeping an eye on the bodgies and widgies who frequented the inner-city streets in those days. He helped Harry push the utility back out through the window of the theatre and sent the proprietor on his way once more. There were no breathalysers in those days.

The Samios brothers purchased the café from the Coplins in 1963 and ran the business until it closed in the late 80s, when the beautiful North Star building, built in 1893, was demolished in the redevelopment of the city centre. The Samios family maintained the Londy's tradition of a huge Easter egg display.

The Regal Café

George Kentrotis emigrated from Greece in 1927, aged 20. He too came from the tiny Kytherian village of Fratsia. George worked for relatives at Londy's Café until he saved enough money to bring his brother, Jim, to Australia. In the early 40s, the brothers bought a café three doors from Londy's. No information is available about the history of the Regal Café prior to 1940, although a photograph of Brisbane street, taken in the late 20s or early 30s, shows a café in the same position to the left of Bayards, and the sign on the awning, although indistinct, appears to read Regal, or perhaps Royal, Café. The Kentrotis brothers' café was a particularly long, narrow shop, possibly built in a laneway between two buildings. Local residents remember the four large tapestries. These were in the café when George bought it and hung on the walls of the Regal Café for as long as the building was owned by the Kentrotis family; one was a Venetian scene and another depicted a bullfight.

George and Jim soon brought out their remaining two brothers, John and Peter, to join them in the café business. When he was 53, George returned to Greece to find a wife. In 1957, he married Vasiliki, also from Fratsia, and the couple and their three children, Joanne, Bill, and Marianne, lived in nearby Roderick Street. The Regal was open from 6am to 11pm seven days a week, closing at midnight on Fridays and Saturdays. Breakfast was served from 6am, when workers called in for cigarettes, coffee, or takeaway toasted sandwiches on their way to work. George and Vasiliki's daughter, Joanne, recalls that Fantales, Jaffas, and Minties made an enticing display arranged in front of

The Samios family during the 1960s: Kathy Samios, her sister-in-law, Mary Samios, and brother, George Samios

mirrored glass in the confectionery counter, along with an array of loose lollies. George is particularly remembered for giving lollies to children when their parents came to the shop.

Narrow two-seater booths lined one side of the café and longer booths for families lined the other. The wall mirrors next to these booths were daily cleansed of children's fingerprints, and this job often fell to Joanne. Typically, six staff worked a shift: Jim cooked in the kitchen at the back of the shop, with a waitress helping out during busy periods; one staff member, usually Jim's wife or an older local woman, had the job of washing up; two people, one of whom was George, handled counter sales; two waitresses took orders and served meals. The waitresses took customers' orders at the tables and returned with the bill, and customers paid at the front counter on the way out. As was the case with most Greek cafés in Ipswich during the 50s and 60s, the Regal Café staff wore casual clothes rather than uniforms, although waitresses wear blue and cream uniforms in an earlier photograph (See Chapter Ten).

George retired in 1977 at the age of 73, having operated the Regal Café for 36 years. He died in 1980. The shop was leased to others and used for various businesses until it finally closed as a second-hand record shop when the building was demolished in 1986. Joanne has kept the Regal Café's soda fountains and the milkshake machine, some order pads, a heavy stainless steel milkshake container of the type used prior to aluminium containers, and several battered silver dishes engraved with the name of the café. Thousands of Ipswich residents enjoyed ice-cream sundaes and milkshakes from these vessels. As the tuckshop convenor at Blair State School, Joanne continues to work in the food catering industry.

The Ritz Café

George Minas Kallinicos came to Australia in 1935 at the age of 16. He too came from the village of Fratsia. George was 'apprenticed' in cafés in Mitchell and Toowoomba before he and his cousin, Kosmas Kallinicos, converted a warehouse in Bell Street, Ipswich, in 1942. The new shop was situated approximately on the site of the present food court, and was called the Ritz Café. On leaving the army in 1947, George returned to the café and bought out his cousin's share. In 1951, he went to Kythera and entered an arranged marriage with Demetra and they had three sons – Minas, Manuel, and John.

The café was situated next door to a stylish new theatre. The Ritz Theatre, which opened in 1940, was the first air-conditioned picture theatre outside of Brisbane and featured Dunlopillo foam latex sets (the seats in the Wintergarden were wooden) and a 'symphony' of coloured Neon lights controlled by a dimmer switch. In keeping with the Art Deco elegance of the theatre, the Ritz Café was decked out in cream and green, with black glass, mirrors, and lots of chrome.[84] Manuel Kallinicos remembers that café staff and children would begin frantically rolling chips in newspaper five minutes before intermission, in readiness for the onslaught to come.

Manuel also recalls the rock and roll dance competitions, which were sometimes held on Friday nights at the Ritz Theatre in the 50s-60s; he particularly remembers the men with pointed shoes, slicked back hair, tight pants, and matchboxes tucked into their sleeves. Several residents commented that farmers on their weekly trips to town tended to patronise

> *Manuel also recalls the rock and roll dance competitions, which were sometimes held on Friday nights at the Ritz Theatre in the 50s-60s*

George Kallinicos as a young man behind the counter of the Mitchell Café (third from the left) and outside the café with another employee.

one café in particular. Manuel recalls that for farmers from Fernvale, Lowood, and Esk, it was the Ritz Café, and they usually came on Wednesdays and Thursdays. "People would have the same meal every week."[85]

Like many other cafés, the Ritz had an extensive confectionery counter and milk bar on one side near the entry to the shop. Until it was gutted and refurbished in the early 60s, the cafe had a raised area filled with tables at the back of the café. The cubicles were also taken out during renovations to allow greater flexibility, and Peters Ice Cream installed a new stainless steel milk bar and refrigeration unit. Like the City Café, the Ritz had an upstairs function room, where weddings were held in the 40s and 50s. George renovated the upstairs area in the 50s and operated it as a billiard parlour, where cribbage and five hundred and listening to the races were favourite pastimes. The Kallinicos family ran the café until 1968, when the building was sold to Cribb and Foote and finally consumed in the Kern redevelopment in the 80s.

The Ritz Picture Theatre being built in the late 30s.

A Queensland Times photograph of Bell Street in the early 1940s shows the Ritz Café beside the Ritz Picture Theatre.

Ritz Café before renovation.

Veneris' Hamburger Bar and Tony's Café

Tony Veneris was a Kytherian immigrant who began his time in Ipswich as an employee at the Ritz Café in Nicholas Street. He eventually leased a shop in Brisbane Street opposite the Bell Street intersection and opened a hamburger bar. Crystallie (Doris) Canaris was born in Townsville to Greek parents from the island of Castelloroso, off Rhodes. In 1946, when Doris was 22, she married Tony and came to live with him in Ipswich. Tony was 32.

When the bank later took over the building where he ran his shop, Tony bought the block of shops on the left-hand side of the Parkside Picture Theatre (later known as the Vogue Theatre) opposite the Gordon Street intersection in Brisbane Street, and opened Tony's Café. Smith's milk bar had been trading on the other side of the theatre from the early days of talking pictures, but the cinema industry was so popular in the decades before television and videos that both shops flourished. In 1956, Doris and Tony had a son, Theo.

Tony's dreams of a long and prosperous life in Australia came to a sudden end in April, 1962, when he was murdered and the café takings stolen. It was the first time a crime of this nature had ever happened in Ipswich and the story was front-page news in Ipswich

Tony in his new shop.

and Brisbane papers over the next months. Like Doris, Theo was five when he lost his father, and, ironically, when he was a teenager, Theo got his first job at Cribb and Foote's hardware. This department was on the site that had once been the Ritz Café, where his father had started work as young Kytherian immigrant many years before. Theo has now been in the hardware business for over thirty years.

Doris sold the café to Jim Pavlakis and opened a book exchange and Ipswich's first Coffee Lounge and art gallery in another shop in the same block. Both Jim's café and Doris' book exchange were flooded in 1974. At 82, Doris still opens the book exchange whenever she feels like it.

Doris is second from the left and Tony is in the corner in their first shop. Tony's father is on the right-hand side of the picture.

Tony's Snack Bar

When Tony Veneris was murdered in 1962, Jim Pavlakis took over Tony's Café, which was known thereafter as Tony's Snack Bar. Jim was a very popular proprietor, continuing to offer good food at reasonable prices long after most of the Greek cafés in Ipswich had closed down. His sister, Maria Kentrotis, who had sponsored Jim's emigration to Australia, helped her brother at Tony's Snack Bar. Maria was particularly responsible for the chips, which, according to her daughter, Effie, were renowned throughout Ipswich during the 1970s. Maria carefully selected the potatoes she used for her chips and cut them by hand, always with a special silver knife, because, says Maria, silver is softer.

Hot chips were a popular take away item for families, who sometimes bought ten dollars worth and often ate them between slices of buttered white bread. The chips were so popular that if the café ran out, customers were happy to wait for half an hour while a fresh batch was peeled, chipped and pre-cooked for deep-frying. Effie remembers that her mother's chips, wrapped in newspaper, "were 'the flavour of the day' at Tony's Café." Effie believes that people seemed to enjoy the bout of nostalgia that accompanied eating chips wrapped in newspaper. When the law was changed so that chips had to be wrapped in white butcher's paper, Effie's brother, Bill, bought end rolls of newsprint paper Queensland Times. "Chips were wrapped in white paper after that," Effie recalls, "Much to the disappointment of regulars."

The proprietors were very happy to have the young people around, although newspaper reports of this time will reveal general community alarm over the lappers and their car culture.

Tony's Snack Bar was a favourite hangout for the 'lappers' during the 70s and 80s. Bill and Effie were teenagers at the time and other young people felt comfortable being in the shop, where they would cram into the cubicles and talk about their cars, often buying only an iced coffee or a can of Coke, or just sitting on the footpath outside. Effie recalls that locally-made Jacaranda Iced Coffee was the number one drink in the 70s. The proprietors were very happy to have the young people around. Although newspaper reports of this time will reveal general community alarm over the lappers and their car culture, the proprietors report that the young people never caused any trouble. Jim married childhood sweetheart, Lumbrini, and in the late-80s returned to Greece as a result of ill-health.

Maria Kentrotis and Doris Veneris at Tony's Snack Bar.

Central Milk Bar and Café

Maria's son, Bill, 1980s.

Melissa, Lumbrini, Jim, Maria and Effie.

Bill behind the counter of the now-empty shop.

The Central Milk Bar and Café in Brisbane Street was originally built by a non-Greek proprietor, Bernie Smith, at least as early as the 1950s. It is situated near the Gordon Street intersection on the right-hand side of where the Parkside (Vogue) Picture Theatre used to be. Maria Kentrotis and her son, Bill, bought the Central Milk Bar in 1980. Five years later, they renovated the café and added cubicles. Maria carried on the tradition of hand-prepared potatoes for the Central's hot chips. After almost a quarter of a century of cutting chips in the two cafés, Maria believes that if the bags of potatoes she has prepared for chips were laid end to end they would stretch right around the Queensland coastline. She could be right.

Effie was a young adult when she started working in the Central Milk Bar with her mother. "I remember when the bra factory was up the road," says Effie. "The girls only had 25 minutes for lunch, so we were very busy at one o'clock. We hated anyone else turning up at the same time. Most would order earlier in the morning so that made it easier." Effie remembers that the girls from the factory attracted the boys. "Young boys loved to come in just to perve at the girls," she says. Recalling those years at the Central, Effie says, "I'm sure that Mum has been proxy to some marriages in Ipswich. I know I was to one couple; they had separately confided to me over the counter that they liked each other, so I took the opportunity to introduce them." The Central, Ipswich's last Greek café, was leased to non-Greeks in 2006, but has since closed down.

The Sydney Café

The Sydney Café traded at the bottom end of Nicholas Street between Risson's Produce Merchants and T. C. Beirne's Department Store. Once owned by the Londy family, and known as the Australia Café, the premises is marked as the Sydney Fruit Market on the 1918 block plans. Con Honianakis operated the café with his sister and brother-in-law from about 1930. Don Risson from the neighbouring produce business recalls that Con's sister, Mrs Madulakis, always wore a black dress and a black apron and had a small black dog that understood only Greek. He also recalls that Mrs Madulakis, or 'Sister', as she was known, made the best ice-cream he ever tasted in his life. And there was always a pot of soup on the stove out the back in winter, to which Don was welcome to help himself whenever he wanted.[86]

The café was originally two shops – a milk bar and a fish shop – with a connecting door, but because of a winning casket ticket, Con was able to renovate, removing the wall to make one big shop. A dispute that arose in relation to the ticket led to a famous court case, which was later televised in an episode of *Consider Your Verdict*. Greeks often gathered for weddings and dances at the Trades Hall across the road from the Sydney Café. On one of these occasions, Con was missed, and someone went across to road to find out why he had not arrived. Con had closed up the shop for the night, but they found the proprietor inside. He had died of a heart attack at the register counting the day's takings.[87]

In 1949, 28-year-old Harry Tanos came to Australia to join his older brother, Christopher, and in 1951 the pair leased the Sydney Café, trading under the name Dunn & Co. to avoid some of the ill-feeling directed at immigrants. Christopher had worked as a cook in Harry Corones' famous Charleville hotel prior to coming to Ipswich. Unlike the proprietors of the other Greek cafés in town, whose homes were close to the city centre, the Tanos family lived in rooms above the shop. They were also among the few Greeks in Ipswich who did not come from Kythera.

Harry on arrival in Australia.

At that time, Nicholas Street was the main route between Brisbane and Toowoomba and the Sydney was very busy. It had cubicles on both sides and could seat sixty people. On Saturday nights, when they were particularly busy, they operated with a staff of six. Harry was the cook and he kept up with the three waitresses by developing a system that enabled him to fill orders quickly without making mistakes. He used to put out the plates for the different meals in separate areas of the kitchen – steaks, fish, mixed grills, and so on – so that the orders never got mixed up. He boasts, in fact, that even with three waitresses, the orders could never get ahead of him.

The Sydney Café was particularly renowned for its fish and chips, which were sold wrapped in newspaper. Local resident, Ivan Schostakowski, has fond childhood memories of Harry's chips. After a session at the Ritz Picture Theatre in Bell Street, he would collect McMahon's soft drink bottles, which patrons rolled down the sloped floor to the front of the theatre. Ivan could carry ten bottles, one on each finger, around the corner into Union Street and around into Nicholas Street to the Sydney Café, where Harry would trade them for a bag of crisp, hot chips. McMahon's was a local manufacturer, and in those days, paid a refund on the return of soft drink bottles.

Chris and Photini Tanos at the end of a hard day's work at the Sydney Café

Patrons from the North Australian Hotel across the road often ended the night with a meal at the Sydney Café, which closed at about 11pm. While Gundagai's Niagara Café entertained prime ministers, Harry remembers one particular customer at the Sydney, whom he later discovered was Joh Bjelke-Peterson, later the Premier of Queensland. Joh often called

The milk bar of the Sydney Café in 1954/5: Christopher Tanos, his wife, Photini, Ipswich-born Georgina and her husband, Charlie Kitas, who was the son of Harry's cousin, and, on the right, Harry Tanos. Two of the four soda fountains mounted on the milk bar dispensed cold water.

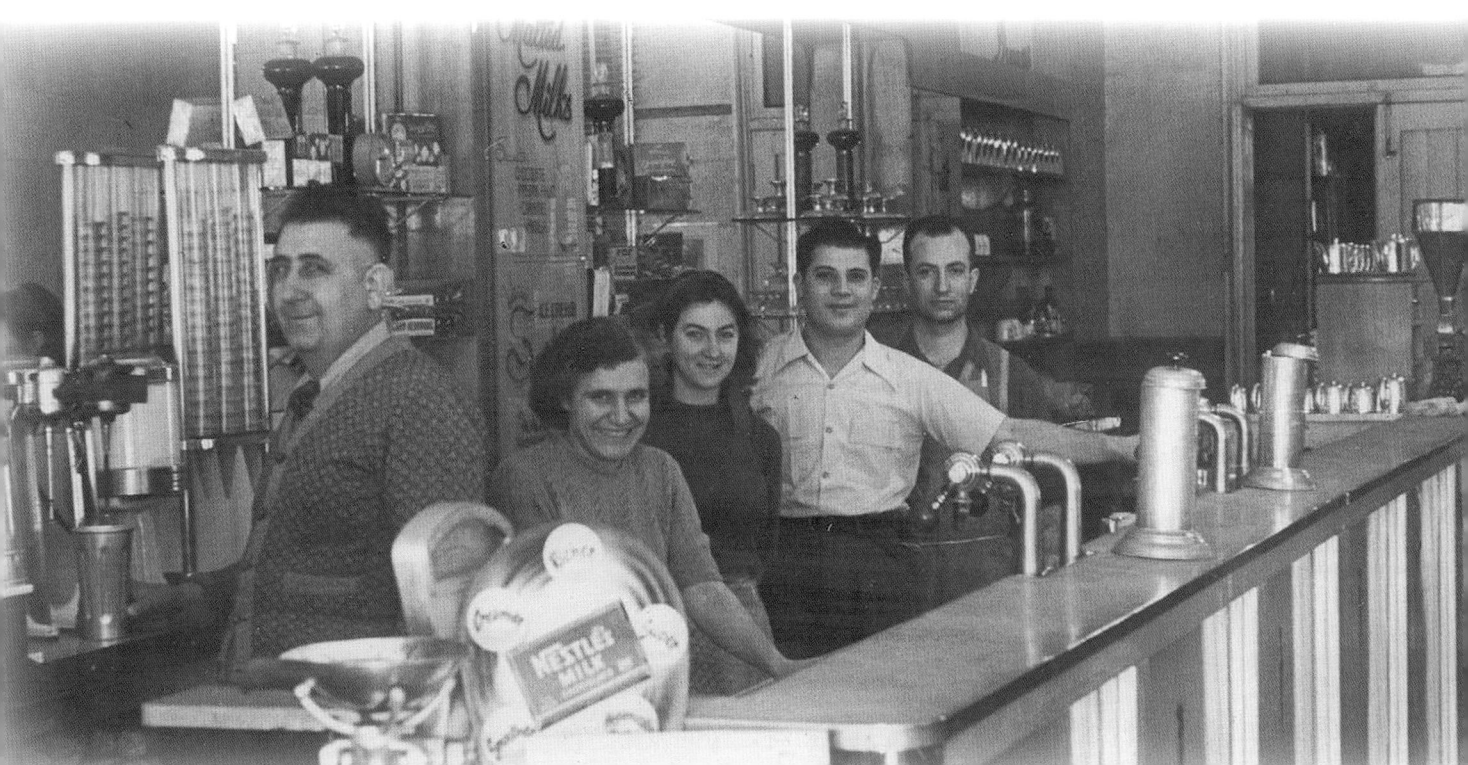

in for a meal on Friday or Saturday nights on his way home to Kingaroy after Parliament had finished. Bill Hayden, who later became Governor General, was a policeman in Ipswich at the time and was another of Harry's regular customers.

> "In the olden days, I have to have an appointment to talk to him during the day."

In the early 60s, Harry travelled around Europe before going to Cyprus to find a wife. He married Maroula in 1962, but in his absence, the Sydney Café was facing serious problems. Health inspectors insisted on renovations to the kitchen, where an old wood stove coated everything in layer of soot. The building's owners, however, refused to sell the shop to the Tanos brothers and Harry and Christopher were unwilling to outlay the significant cost involved when they could be forced out of the premises at any time. They closed the shop and the owners sold the building to T. C. Beirne for extensions to the department store.

Harry and Maroula bought a convenience store in Lutwyche Road, Brisbane, the following year. Until 2002, they survived road-widening schemes, the removal of neighbourhood homes, and even Charcoal Chicken and McDonalds. Maroula is active in the Greek community and her culinary skills are particularly renowned. Once a week, Harry enjoys playing cards and talking to the "other young men" at the Greek Club. Maroula recalls, "In the olden days, I have to have an appointment to talk to him during the day. He loves talking." For a man of 85, Harry has an astounding memory for detail. He plans to outrun his grandfather, who died at the age of 115.

Don Risson's produce business was two doors from the Sydney Café. In 2006, after nearly 50 years, Don visited Harry in his Lutwyche Road shop and caught up on old times.

Wintergarden Milk Bar

John Kentos was one of three brothers George Kentrotis brought to Australia through the Regal Café. John married Helen and bought the milk bar beside the picture theatre in East Street during the 1950s. They ran the Wintergarden Milk Bar together. John planned to make as much money as possible for a few years and then get out of the business. He and Helen installed a juke box and fitted the shop out with neon lights and long mirrors. They did a brisk trade at interval and after the pictures, and stayed open to serve late suppers for the dance crowd that returned from Brisbane late at night. Business boomed, although Helen remembers that she got really sick of the juke box. In 1958, John decided that the latest fad, Television, had come to stay and that people wouldn't want to go to the pictures anymore. The couple sold the milk bar. Their story is related in more detail in Chapter Five.

John Kentos behind the counter of the Wintergarden Milk Bar in the 1950s

Wintergarden Picture Theatre. Image published in Robyn Buchanan, Ipswich in the Twentieth Century: Celebrating 100 Years as a City 1904-2004. *Ipswich: Ipswich City Council, 2004, page 87.*

Penglis' Fruit Shop

Unlike many Ipswich proprietors, who were Kytherians, Nicholas Penglis belonged to a prosperous family from Asia Minor. When the family was expelled by the Turks in 1922, Nick came to Australia. He spoke five languages and worked at numerous jobs, including a stint in a mine at Broken Hill. Miraculously, he was the only person to escape when the mine collapsed. Nick eventually married English girl, Vera Smith, and had three children – John, Jim, and Ruth. The Penglis family established a fruit shop in Nicholas Street, Ipswich, between Berry's Smallgoods and the Commonwealth Bank, in 1942. Female staff wore white pinafores with Penglis embroidered in red on the lapel and the men wore navy aprons. Vera was deservedly proud of her fruit displays in the front window, which, according to her children, were works of art. Jim used to cook his evening meal in the shop and the smell of simmering garlic and tomato wafted out into Nicholas Street.

When the Americans set up camp at Amberley in 1942, Nick won the contract to supply the base with fruit and vegetables. He supplemented market produce with lettuce, beans, cucumbers, and eggs from the family's 10-acre farm on the corner of Cascade and Thornton Streets. Nick worked the land with a horse and plough and the assistance of two Italian internees, who were assigned to him. Vera rode the horse to a bus stop on Cemetery Road each morning, so she could open the shop while Nick went to the Brisbane markets.

When Nick was called up for service, Vera had to run the shop, order supplies, manage the farm, and deal with the Italians, who spoke very little English and could be uncooperative when they chose. Fortunately, after about three weeks, Nick failed his medical.

The job of feeding 200 hens, collecting and washing eggs, picking vegetables, and gathering wild mushrooms fell to the Penglis children when they came home from school. Ruth also remembers having to stock the shop's fridge, as well as threading brown paper bags on pieces of string to hang on nails hammered into the shop walls. Customers carried their fruit and vegetable purchases home in these bags. Jim worked fulltime in the shop after he finished scholarship.[88] Nick sold the business in 1953. At that time, he had 10 fulltime staff and three trucks. In 1954, Jim bought a milk run, supplying local cafés with bulk milk, and in 1956 he went into the fish business. He ran a fish shop near the Prince of Wales Hotel in Brisbane Street and supplied fish wholesale to Coles and Woolworth's. Jim left Ipswich in 1976, but continued to supply many Ipswich cafés with fish and groceries.

PHONE 1179   PHONE 1179

N. T. PENGLIS

NICHOLAS STREET, IPSWICH

Wholesale and Retail Fruiterer

Penglis' shop and the Big Apple further down Nicholas Street were primarily fruit shops; the lack of dining rooms sets them apart from the traditional Greek café. I am, however, including them in this survey of Greek shops because both had milk bars.[89] Ruth recalls that the milk bar in their shop had a marble top and, like other Greek cafés in town, had soda fountains and a refrigerated unit that stored McMahons soft drinks and Peters Ice Cream. Large Peters Ice Cream signs are visible in several photographs.

Unfortunately, little information is available to date for Marendy's Café Australia in Brisbane Street and Petrohilos' (Peters) Big Apple in Nicholas Street. The families in both were Kytherians and were related to the other families in Ipswich.

Non-Greek cafés also operated in Ipswich during the 40s and 50s: Brian Madden's Red and White Milk Bar in the Trades Hall building in Nicholas Street, Marsh's Majestic Café in Bell Street, and Whitehouse's Café in Nicholas Street, to mention a few. Despite the fact that there were at least ten Greek cafés as well as the non-Greek cafés in Ipswich at the time, older residents recall that it was sometimes hard to find a seat. During this period, many people went to the pictures several times a week, because television was yet to invade most homes, and there were dances with big dance bands every night, even on Sunday nights, when St Mary's Catholic church hosted a dance. Residents remember that the last bus used to leave town just as the last dance was beginning. Since the last dance was usually reserved for a special partner, it was a 'toss-up' whether to catch the last bus or walk home. Often, walking home seemed the best option.

The accounts in the following chapters detail café life as remembered by proprietors and their wives and children, waitresses, and local Ipswich residents. It is interesting to observe that women's and men's stories often exhibit different emphases; while men recall achievements and events, women focus on labour and relationships. Most female respondents said they knew 'everyone' and are still well-known from their years in cafés and many recall interactions with specific customers. Maureen said she enjoyed her time at Londy's because the employers, staff, and most of the customers were good to work

Peter and Helene Marendy worked in the Café Australia with Harry and his wife until they bought their own business at the five-ways. In this photograph, they visit the Samios family at Londy's Café.

A photograph taken in about 1920 shows café staff outside the Café Australia, which Harry Marendy owned in the 1950s, but was at the time part of a network of shops the Londy Brothers owned in Ipswich. Fruit is arranged in the window on the left, while the other side holds an elaborate display of confectionery. George Londy (Charles Londy's son) remembers that professional window dressers in the employ of the larger confectionery companies dressed the confectionery windows in cafés.

Signs at the front of the shop indicate that light lunches and soda fountain drinks were specialties of the café. The man on the right of the photograph is Jim Londy, Harry and Charles Londy's brother-in-law, who later had a shop in Bundaberg.

with. Like Maria, Maureen made many friends and was known by all who came in and is still remembered as the girl at Londy's. Helen Kentos spoke of knowing whole families of a broad cross-section of the Ipswich community. Men rarely mentioned this aspect of café life and few recalled specific customers: Peter Londy explained how his father always had fresh fish even if there was no fish in Brisbane; Jack Stathis related wartime incidents; Peter Cominos described the modern machines, techniques and designs in his father's 'departmental café'. Chapters Five and Six record the accounts of women and children who worked in Ipswich cafés, but first, the following chapter investigates café food as a means of defining 'the Greek café'.

CHAPTER FOUR

Mixed Grills and Milkshakes: Food in Greek Cafés

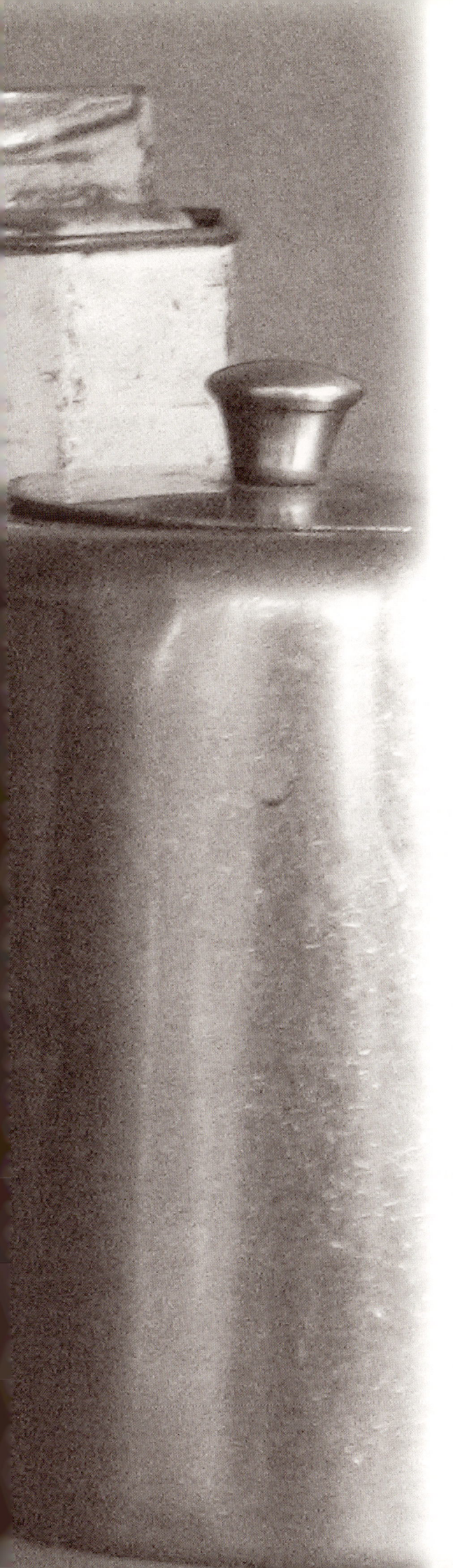

'AUSTRALIANS ARE LARGELY CARNIVOROUS AND ADDICTED TO TEA.'

DR PHILIP MUSKETT, 1893 [90]

When conversation turns to the subject of Greek cafés, it becomes apparent that many Australians – particularly younger Australians – mistakenly believe that Greek cafés served Greek food. This is not the case. Unlike Chinese proprietors, who tantalised Australian tastebuds with Special Fried Rice, Chow Mien, and Sweet and Sour Pork, Greek proprietors did not introduce the food of their homeland.

Neither was making great coffee their primary focus, as it is for the proprietors of contemporary cafés, where making coffee is both a science and an art form and coffee has a menu all its own: Cappuccino, Macchiato, Long Black, Flat White, Latté, Vienna, Edith Piaf, Affogato, Mochaccino, Skinnychino, Decaf Cappuccino, Babychino, Why Bother, Iced Coffee, Frappe . . . the list goes on. The Greek café is best defined as a particular union between a Greek social model, American food-catering ideas, and British taste, but before looking at the food that resulted from this union, it is worth clarifying some ideas about cafés and coffee in Australia, particularly in relation to the coffee sold in Greek cafés.[91]

Café Culture

Tea houses, refreshment rooms, and bakeries were popular food outlets in Australia prior to the evolution of the Greek café, and coffee shoppes, coffee lounges, and snack bars served the needs of Australian consumers during and after its demise. Department store cafeterias were also common until the shopping centre arrived with its ubiquitous food court in the 1970s. But Greek cafés and milk bars were "our original café culture."[92] After their gradual demise toward the end of the 70s, there was a lack of similar haunts and hangouts until a new café culture emerged in the 1990s and cafés again sprang up like mushrooms in inner-city blocks and suburban streets.

According to journalist, Luke Slattery, the contemporary café craze[93] dates from about 1985 and is an emblem of European style that governs a whole way of life. It is about a sense of sophistication, which Australians acquired while travelling in Europe. Although Slattery evokes images of Simone de Beauvoir conversing with Jean Paul Sartre in smoky Parisian cafés, he explains that the allure of French style and sophistication, rather than political agendas and civic events, drives Australia's café craze. Melbourne historian, Andrew Brown-May, in his fascinating investigation of Melbourne's coffee scene, also associates coffee culture with social maturity and a "presumed or longed-for European sophistication."[94] And most coffee-drinkers would agree; surely the brownish liquid alone cannot be worth $4. When it arrives with a heady aroma and an elegant design swirled effortlessly into a velvety crema, the perfect cup of coffee arouses a sense of sophisticated otherworldliness that is almost beyond price, especially if it is served 'al fresco'. One minute the coffee-drinker is wedged into a chrome chair, perched in no-man's land between pedestrians bustling along a crowded footpath and car fumes spewing from four-wheel drives streaming along the main drag, and the next she or he is draped stylishly over a chair in an imagined sidewalk café in Paris or Milan, where dappled light filters through European foliage and wistful music drips like a blessing from a cloudless, Wedgwood-blue sky.

Brown-May reveals, however, that this European sophistication adhered to cafés in Australia at least three decades before 1985. The "watershed between a drab restricted past and a modern and cosmopolitan present" came when a young Australian called Peter Bancroft was captured by Italy's emerging post-war café culture and brought the first espresso machine to Australia in 1952. Bancroft built Melbourne's first espresso café in 1954 – Il Capuccino (one p) in St Kilda – and then plunged into the business of selling Gaggia machines to others. Melbourne's 'revolution in a coffee cup', as Brown-May describes the

This photo was found attached to the side of the espresso machine in the Popular Café in Mullumbimby and is reproduced here courtesy of that café.

ensuing years, was "a slow but steady realisation of the fragrant pleasures of the espresso taste, and a delight in the bright 'steam-hissing, gilt encrusted machine'." By 1957, Australia had 400 espresso machines.[95]

Since Melbourne has a large Greek population, supposedly the third largest outside of Athens, and since Greeks were firmly established in the café business long before 1952, it is reasonable to assume that Greeks played a vital role in bringing espresso and its sophisticated, cosmopolitan café culture to Australia. But apart from Bancroft, most of the other 'pioneer players' in Brown-May's account are Italian: Cimbali, Pavoni, Monici, Crivelli, De Marchi, Varrenti, Brunelli, Pellegrini. Italians are renowned neither for growing coffee nor for being great coffee consumers. They are, however, associated with technology. In 1901, Luigi Bezzera and Desiderio Pavoni, patented the first espresso machine, an apparatus designed to extract the flavour from coffee beans under steam pressure. After the machine was exhibited at the Milan Fair in 1906, technical innovation inched its way forward to 1947, when Giovanni Achille Gaggia created a machine that better controlled the espresso process. The bar owner from Milan had discovered the secret to producing a less bitter coffee with a creamier top.[96] Coffee grinders and roasters, along with pasta makers and tomato mashers, were among the mementos of identity Italian immigrants brought with them from home, and from the beginning of the 20th century, it was their technological innovations that revolutionised coffee-making.[97]

Between 1951 and 1961, 150,000 Italian immigrants arrived in Australia. Many settled

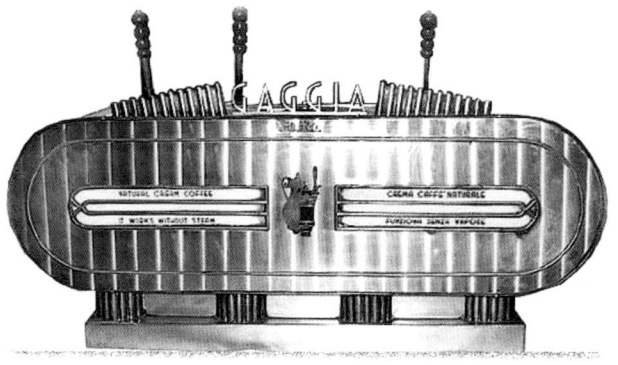

Photograph courtesy of Marvellous Melbourne, "Café Culture." http://www.museum.vic.gov.au/marvellous/postwar/café.asp.[98]

The Legend's customers "were primarily linked to a pursuit of style." The refurbished café opened at 280 Bourke Street in 1956. Having utilised the talents of sculptor, Clement Meadmore, to complete the makeover, it had a mosaic tile exterior and an Italian-style stone floor and drop lights. The Legend closed in 1970, when the building was demolished. See Marvellous Melbourne. "Café Culture." Permission pending. http://www.museum.vic.gov.au/marvellous/postwar/café.asp.[100]

in Carlton, earning the Melbourne suburb the moniker, 'Little Italy', and after Bancroft acquired the distribution rights for Gaggia in Australia, these immigrants embraced the new technology in Melbourne's espresso bars. Brown-May makes no claim that his is either a record of elementary firsts or a complete history of Melbourne's café scene, but, having identified Melbourne as Australia's 'coffee capital', he locates key people and practices involved in the early days of Melbourne's coffee culture.[99] Of the many innovative, successful, and much-loved cafés in his account, most do have new Australian proprietors, but almost all are Italian. He notes only two Greek cafés.

Just prior to the Olympics in 1956, Ion Nicolades transformed his family's café next to the Tivoli Theatre in Bourke Street into the Legend Espresso and Milk Bar.[101] Nicolades introduced croissants and open sandwiches, gelati, cassata, baklava and galaktoboureko, and Italian meals like spaghetti, minestrone, and risotto. He recalls that prior to this they served 'the old family café fare' of baked beans or eggs on toast accompanied by coffee that had stewed in an urn all day. The new menu also boasted Espresso, Long Black, Cappuccino, Vienna, Macchiato, and Mocca, all of which cost one shilling, and the staff and barista were Italians. The second Greek proprietor, Paul Theodore, emigrated from Greece in 1949 at the age of 16 to work in his uncle's Eat More Milk Bar and Confectionery in Swanston Street. Theodore recalls the coffee and chicory "dishwater" served in the early 50s, but when he took over Le Jardin in Collins Street in 1956, it became, reputedly, the most modern café of its time, serving 800 cups of espresso per day.[102]

It would appear, then, that either few Greeks in Melbourne had cafés – and most historians do record only cafés in New South Wales and Queensland – or else those who had cafés did not take part in the unstoppable "coffee juggernaut" of the 1950s.[103] Clearly, some Greeks did run cafés in Melbourne, and, given the chain migration process elaborated in chapter two, isolated shops are inconsistent with the development of Greek cafés in city areas. Perhaps, then, most continued to serve the 'stewed dishwater' recalled by Nicolades and Theodore, whose espresso machines, Italian meals, and Italian baristas reflect the surrounding Italian espresso bars, making their cafés the exception rather than the rule.[104] That being the case, what kind of coffee did most Greek cafés serve?

Coffee

Australians have been drinking coffee since the earliest days of white settlement; having been purchased en route in Rio de Janeiro, it arrived with the First Fleet in 1788. Marcus Clarke describes the brew he saw simmering over pans of charcoal in Melbourne street stalls in the 1860s as "dark and strong by means of burnt sugar" and "chicoried to a very large extent."[105] D.H. Lawrence, in his representation of Australia, *Kangaroo* (1923), claims that Australian coffee had "lots of chicory in it."[106] The standard of local coffee during the depression was decried as being "made on hot milk and some ghastly essence," and Americans posted to Australia during the Second World War detested both the 'overstewed' coffee and the coffee and chicory essence served in local cafés. Brown-May claims that the 450 businesses registered as cafés in 1939 sold a "turbid greyish liquid loosely known as white coffee, or a darker, gutless brew just a loosely known as black coffee."[107] Many of the 450 businesses were Greek cafés, and those that did not embrace the espresso revolution of the 1950s continued to sell coffee that fell far short of the rich, aromatic sensation introduced by Italian immigrants and the sophisticated, other-worldly experience that is coffee today. It is significant that few historians even mention the coffee served in Greek cafés.[108]

In the 1940s and 50s, the coffee in Ipswich's Greek cafés was a straightforward affair; it was certainly not the primary reason patrons frequented them. Maureen, a local waitress who worked at Londy's Café during this time, recalls that coffee was made on milk, kept hot in a big urn with a tap at the base, and served in silver pots. Narelle, whose mother worked in nearby Marendy's café, remembers that coffee was made with chicory essence. These accounts correspond with that of Toula Comino from Comino's famous Cairns café, where coffee was made with chicory and milk using steam from the milk bar to heat the milk. Each of these women notes, however, that this silver-potted, steaming, milky brew was immensely popular, especially as an adjunct to toasted sandwiches.

The Greeks are renowned for strong, black coffee, and Ipswich residents who knew proprietors well recall seeing them drink a concentrated brew that was taken with a glass of cold water and left a thick, black sludge

Photography courtesy of Jason King, Bells Milk Bar, Broken Hill.

at the bottom. Greek (and Turkish) coffee is made by combining a finely-ground powder with sugar and water in a briki (or ibrik). The mixture is brought to the boil until the crema rises, and then served in a small cup. Instant coffee, first mass produced in 1906, was introduced to Australia in 1940s, and popular brands, Bushells and Maxwell House, played a major role in popularising the coffee-drinking habit in post-war decades, as did Bickfords', Griffiths', and Bushells' coffee essences.[109] In addition, women recall making coffee at home in the 50s and 60s by adding hot water to a mixture of chicory essence and tinned condensed milk. Perhaps the coffee that the Greeks served in their cafés was influenced by these methods, rather than by those employed in other European countries, or by the new Italian technology.[110] At least some of the 400 espresso machines in Australia in 1957 did find their way into Greek cafés, however, and Maria, who worked with her husband, Jim Kentrotis, in Ipswich's Regal Café, recalls the arrival of the Regal's machine.

R.I.P. Time marches on and, sadly, the long-awaited espresso machine, which once dispensed coffee in various guises for the customers of the Regal Café in Ipswich, now rests in pieces beneath the Central Milk Bar.

When Maria came from Kythera, she worked in her sister and brother-in-law's café in Mareeba until she married Jim. During her time in Mareeba, a salesman, possibly a representative of Peter Bancroft, sold a machine to Maria's brother-in law, so when the salesman visited the Regal Café after Maria and Jim were married, the Kentrotis family placed an order for one of the new machines. According to Maria, the Kallinicos family of the Ritz Café, who were related to the Kentrotis family, did not want to be outdone, so it was agreed that the two cafés would take delivery on the same day. The machines arrived, on the same day, in 1958, and were the first espresso machines in Ipswich. What is interesting in this account is that, while Melbourne enjoys a reputation as Australia's coffee capital, not only did espresso machines make their way to Ipswich within six years of their arrival in Australia, but they also found their way to Mareeba in far north Queensland some time prior to that.

Many Greek cafés acquired an espresso machine, but they did not necessarily use them to make espresso. Maria recalls that her family did not approve of the 'burnt' taste of the new coffee, so they made cappuccino by continuing to combine Turkish coffee and milk, which was then frothed up with steam from the machine. Maureen Reinke, who worked for Jim Pavlakis in Tony's Snack Bar also made coffee with Turkish coffee powder and milk frothed with a cappuccino machine. But cappuccino was eventually made by the process for which the machines were designed. In the 1970s, Maria's niece, Joanne, recalls making cappuccino with ground beans at the Regal Café and serving it in a cup, as is the contemporary practice. Other popular drinks included hot chocolate and black coffee and tea, which were served in pots. These reports cannot be used to generalise about the evolution of coffee-making in Greek cafés, but the point of these accounts, and the comparison between Greeks cafés and the espresso bars of their Italian counterparts, is that coffee with its associated sense of sophistication were not the focus of Greek cafés. Most Greek cafés were not sophisticated

This contraption is the original tea dispenser from the Regal Café. One flick of the handle dropped enough tea for a teapot and flicking the handle back again produced a stronger brew.

establishments and they did not aspire to create an exotic experience. As indicated earlier, the Greek café was a particular union between a Greek social model, British taste, and American food catering ideas.

The Kafeneion: A Greek Social Model

Greek café proprietors were familiar with the tradition of the Greek kafeneion as a social model. The kafeneion, or coffee house, is a privately-run commercial enterprise, where men can satisfy their thirst. But, more importantly, it is a place for social gathering, a communication centre, and an ideal venue for transacting business. At the kafeneion, men meet, eat, drink, gamble, and talk politics.[111] While Italian immigrants placed food high on the list of things they most disliked about Australia, Greek immigrants, partly because the kafeneion was so much a part of their lives, listed Australians' home-centredness as a social behaviour that seemed unnatural to them: "All Australians do is to go home from work, eat, watch television and go to bed. What sort of life is that? It would drive you mad."[112]

It perhaps escaped their attention that many Australian men used the local pub in a similar fashion, while women waited for hours for them to come home, or sent children to fetch them. Nevertheless, for Greek café proprietors, informal public gathering was an integral part of the ritual of serving coffee, and informal public gathering around a cup of coffee was part of the way they believed life should be lived.

Harry Tanos of the Sydney Café grew up in Cyprus, where his father had a kafeneion. Harry helped out at night waiting on tables. Little food was served, but running between

The kafeneion offers men entertainment and companionship through drinking coffee and playing card or board games, as well as the opportunity to engage in the traditional Greek pastime of kouvenda or 'lively conversation'.[113]

tables with glasses of tea, coffee and orzata, a fruit cordial, was Harry's main occupation. He explains that men would buy three coffees for a pieca, which is the equivalent of a cent, and sit all night drinking and talking. Admittedly, Harry is now in his 80s, but, even at that time, the coffee cost very little. The exact price is irrelevant, however, because according to Harry, people had no money so most of the coffee was given on credit anyway. Harry's story demonstrates the true nature of the kafeneion. His father's shop was not a money-spinner and the men did not go there for a meal or even for the coffee. The kafeneion was a gathering place.

> *"Greek owners made you feel welcome, you grew up feeling wanted," "All the country folk would flock to the café"*

Coffee has its origin in the chance discovery by an Ethiopian goatherd named Kaldi in the ninth century. Since then, it has been valued for its culinary uses and medicinal properties. It has been viewed as a mark of sophistication in the life of a city and as one of the forces at work in creating hotbeds of sedition. It has been prescribed by 16th century apothecaries as an aphrodisiac and by 21st century advertisers as a foolproof precursor to romance.[114] As Brown-May so succinctly observes, "Coffee is at once a drink, an obsession and a cultural cipher."[115] But whatever people believe about coffee, few would challenge its capacity to stimulate a convivial atmosphere. While some claim that 'the café' was born in 17th century London as a unique kind of civic space where political parties met and people found out about city events, others claim that the Greek kafeneion existed in Greece from the commencement of coffee-drinking in Europe.[116]

Ray Oldenburg dubs informal public gathering places 'third places', home being first and work second. He explains that every great culture evolves an indigenous version of 'third place': French cafés, German beer gardens, Turkish baths, English pubs, and the like.[117] For Australia, it was the Greek café. Conomos notes the role it played in Australia's social life between 1910 and 1960:

> *It became a popular gathering place for people. From 7am to midnight, seven days a week, it was a refuge, where a person could always find something to eat or drink, talk to friends, and rest his weary legs. The Greek café was where you had your morning tea when shopping, or had a meal if you were a visitor to town, or supper if you had been to the pictures at night. Whether you were on your way to work at 7am in the morning, or wandering through town at 11pm, you could be assured that the Greek café would be open, and the Greek proprietor would be there to talk to you, and serve your needs.*[118]

Interviews with residents in rural townships confirm that the Greek café was the heart of the community: "If there were cattle sales it was where you meet to discuss prices and sales," "It was where you went, where you met your friends," "Greek owners made you feel welcome, you grew up feeling wanted," "All the country folk would flock to the café," "The café provided a sense of community in country towns," "The social centre was the café," "The café was a place where people could meet, speak freely, and do business."[119] Greek cafés in Ipswich were certainly a social focus; the relationships and sense of community that surrounded them indicate that these were great gathering places. Local residents remember that even though the city had at least ten Greek cafés during the 1940s, every shop was full on Saturday nights, particularly after the 'pictures' came out, and people could walk town trying to find a seat. For journalist, Sally McInerney, the Greek café's role as a meeting place was its most important function.[120] Even today, in inner-city areas, the legacy of the kafeneion as 'third place' is evident in the slogan of the Coffee Club, a prosperous café chain that is the dream child of three Brisbane-based Greek-Australian businessmen; "Where will I meet you?" reflects the essence of the kafeneion as it has existed from the beginning of coffee consumption. It seems likely that the

Greek café's role as a meeting place reflects the influence of the male proprietor's social background in the kafeneion.

While the importance of the kafeneion is evident in early 20th century Australia, when it firmly established its role as a contact point through which new immigrants found jobs and accommodation with other Greeks, few historians connect the evolution of Australia's Greek café with the kafeneion as a food outlet; most locate the genesis of the café in the 'oyster saloon' and connect the kafeneion instead with a movement towards organised Greek community.[121] It was, however, the kafeneion's function as a gathering place, as distinct from the Parisian café's sense of sophistication or the Italian espresso bar's technology, which the Greeks brought to their shops in Australia. The essence and function of Greek cafés indicate that they were indeed first rate examples of Oldenburg's 'third places'.

American Food-Catering Technology

In addition to the influence of the kafeneion as a social model, café names like the Marathon, Parthenon, Paragon, Ellisos, and Olympia and, often, the face behind the counter, reflected their proprietors' Hellenic origin. But little else about Greek cafés was Greek. In other respects, the Greek café was a marriage of American food catering ideas and British-Australian taste. Janiszewski and Alexakis go so far as to describe the Greek café as "a 'Trojan Horse' for the Americanisation of Australian eating habits."[122] The United States was a major destination for Greeks prior to 1924 and many of Australia's Greek food caterers, or their relatives, had

Conomos notes that Mullumbimby in northern NSW had an oyster saloon as early as 1906. A posed photograph taken inside a café in Mullumbimby in 1923 celebrates the remodelling of the town's first Greek café, which was renamed the Marble Bar Café because the milk bar's new counter and façade were made of marble. Behind the bar, which boasts no fewer than four gleaming soda fountains, Milton Samios (left) serves two customers with ice cream sodas in elegant, stemmed glasses (see Aliens of the Tweed and Brunswick for further details).

State Library of Queensland Image No. 41448.

Maureen and Vera worked as waitresses at Londy's Café in Ipswich in the late 1940s and early 50s. Londy's boasted a milk bar that served ice-cream sodas and malted milks in a variety of flavours and Maureen recalls that soda fountain drinks and icy-cold fresh fruit drinks were particularly popular with young people. Sodas consisted of syrup and carbonated water dispensed from a fountain hooked up to compressors and pumps underneath the shop. This photograph shows the syrup flavours available: lemonade, lime, sarsaparilla, strawberry, passion fruit, pineapple, ginger ale, ginger beer, and kola.

previous experience in America. Given the kinship structures that gave rise to the chain migration phenomenon, it is to be expected that American food-catering ideas would find their way to Australia and spread quickly. The original proprietor of Newcastle's Niagara Café, for example, had been to the gold diggings in California before he settled in Australia and opened the café in 1898. He had seen the Niagara Falls, from which the café derives its name, and he had experienced hamburgers, milkshakes, ice creams, and other American delights firsthand. Some 113 members of the Karanges family can trace their history to the Niagara Café and many of these went on to establish their own cafés and milk bars.[123]

An American influence is evident in Australia's Greek shops even before the turn of the century. The 19th century oyster saloon or 'parlor' is the first evidence of the popularisation of American food catering ideas – reasonable prices, sit-down and takeaway service, women's lounges, and provision for families all suggest an American influence. The soda fountain, which appeared in the second decade, and the milk bar of the early 1930s, however, are unmistakably American, as are café names like Niagara, California, Monterey, Hollywood, Astoria, Golden Gate, and New York.[124] While it is difficult to know precisely who introduced soda fountains and milk bars to Australia, two things are clear. The innovative technology derived from American ideas and it was the Greeks who popularised their use in Australia.

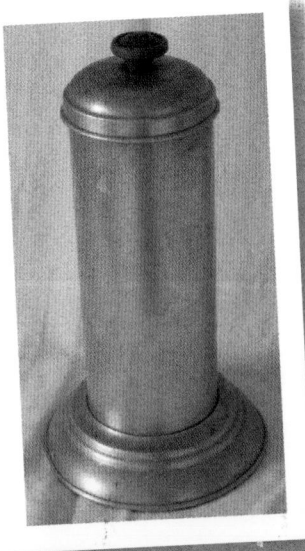

Soda Fountains and Ice Cream Sodas

Soda fountains originated in the American drug store. They made effervescent drinks by injecting water with pressurised carbon dioxide. Flavoured essences were added to make sodas and the addition of ice cream produced ice cream sodas.[125] Australian food historian, Michael Symons, claims that an American introduced the soda fountain to Australia in 1921, but Janiszewski and Alexakis argue that Greek café proprietors imported American soda fountains possibly as early as 1910.[126] They identify three Greeks, who had five shops in Sydney during the 1910s. Having come from America, the three men established the 'Anglo-American Company', and their shops, which were based on the American drug store soda bar, introduced the soda fountain to Sydney consumers.[127] Sodas are associated with the 1950s, but even as late as the 1970s, the Regal Café in Ipswich sold ice cream sodas that were still made with carbonated water piped up from a machine in the cellar. Raspberry and lime were the most popular flavours and were commonly known as Raspberry or Lime Spiders. When Coca Cola became popular, this was supplied in cans for ice-cream sodas, which were called, of course, Tarantulas.

Milk Bars and Malted Milks

Joachim Tavlaridis, an immigrant from a Greek community in Turkey, introduced another new form of drink consumption to Australia. Mick Adams, as Tavlaridis was known in Australia, did not derive his idea for a milk bar from Greece, or even from Turkey; his shop too had its origin in the drugstores of America. On November 4th 1932, Adams opened what many consider to be Australia's first modern 'American-style' milk bar, the Black and White 4d Milk Bar in Martin Place, Sydney. A black and white mechanical cow on display with its calf in the milk bar window was milked by a milkmaid, producing a continuous flow of white liquid. The 'milk' so fascinated passers-by that police were called because they were stopping traffic. Five thousand customers were served on the day the milk bar opened and all proceeds were given to charity, a tradition that Adams repeated annually. The shop's enduring success was partly due to the promotion of milk as a health drink by the NSW Board of Health and the NSW Milk Board in the early 30s, but the Black and White Milk Bar's popularity caused milk consumption to skyrocket. Adams opened another five Black and White Milk Bars, including one in Brisbane.[128] Locals remember that it too had a mechanical cow in the window.

Milkshakes are recorded as early as 1890. These were "an iced drink made of sweetened and flavoured milk, carbonated water, and sometimes raw egg, mixed by being violently shaken by a machine specially invented for the purpose."[129] The product made at the milk bar evolved to a sweet, frothy mixture of milk, syrup, and ice cream, which was aerated by placing it in a large metal cup under a simple milkshake machine.[130] The milk was ladled from tall stainless steel canisters stored under the milk bar and the syrup was ladled from glasses stored under hinged lids in a bank of syrup containers. For decades, the most common flavours were vanilla, strawberry and chocolate, and the addition of malt extract produced a malted milkshake. The drink was poured into a tall, stemmed glass and the bubbly surface sprinkled with nutmeg from a shaker available on the counter. Customers sucked the milkshake though a paper straw as they perched on bar stools at the counter or slid into side cubicles. The balance of the milkshake was left in the metal cup from which customers topped up their glasses, but as the years passed, the glasses mostly disappeared and the milkshake was served in the metal cup. Plastic straws and paper cups gradually replaced the original version and a plastic lid became necessary because customers were more likely to take the drink away than to drink it in the shop. Hot malted milks were also popular at one time.

Adams is widely credited with introducing the milk bar to Australia, but the exact origin of the milk bar in Australia may never be known. While some suggest that Adams may even be credited with having created the milk bar concept – basing it on the American drugstore practice of 'quick stand-up or bar-stool bar trade' but placing the emphasis on the milkshake – and that he introduced the concept in England as well, others claim it was Kytherian-born George Sklavos who opened the prototype for these new shops in Australia. Sklavos opened the American Milk Bar in Fortitude Valley, Brisbane, in 1912, modelled on developments he had seen in America. Further, Janiszewski and Alexakis record a primitive version of both bar-style vending and a shaken milk drink being sold as a 'milk shake' by a Greek in Sydney as early as 1910, and they refer to other non-Greek enterprises, which fit the description of a milk bar and which may also have preceded Adams' shop.[131]

Elemental 'firsts' are elusive and trying to locate them is, arguably, futile, but the Greeks undoubtedly played a major role in firmly establishing the American-derived milk bar within Australian culture. According to Conomos, an electrically-refrigerated milk bar, which chilled water, milk, and ice-cream, and was equipped with malted-milk mixer, soda fountain, fruit-juice extractor, and ice-cream maker, was a feature of the new-style Greek café that appeared throughout Australia during the 1910s.[132] Clearly, the Greeks employed American food catering ideas in their popular food outlets decades before McDonalds invaded Australia. American confectionery, or candy, and ice cream, known in American as a delicacy, were also popular items in Greek cafés.

Ice Cream and Sundaes

Ice cream was enormously popular in America at the turn of the century and 'took off' in Australia during the 20s. It can be considered as yet another American influence that Greeks popularised through their cafés. Many proprietors made their own ice cream until after the Second World War, when new dairy treatment methods like pasteurisation stopped small businesses from making their own.[133] Constantinos Karanges, recalling the ice cream in his Niagara Café (Newcastle), claims that their ice cream was made on the premises from gallons of cream – "not like the frothy stuff you buy nowadays."[134] Childhood memories can be particularly sweet, but 'café kids', whose fathers made ice cream in big mixers on the café premises, claim that it was the best ice cream in the world, that they have never tasted anything

A representative from Peters Ice Cream presents proprietors, Mr and Mrs George Kallinicos, with a cheque to cover the installation of a new milk bar in their Ritz Café in the 1960s.

like it since that time, and that they would be millionaires if they had that recipe today.[135] But proprietors stopped making their own ice cream. Peter Londy claims that American MPs monitored the standard of hygiene in cafés in the towns where their troops were stationed, and to avoid having to check the quality of the ice-cream in Greek cafés, they insisted that proprietors stock only Peter's Ice-Cream if they served US forces. The army couldn't stop cafés from making their own ice cream, but American GIs were forbidden to patronise shops that did not conform to the standard.[136] MPs were stationed outside if necessary. Londy's, like many other cafés, never made their own ice-cream again. Signs advertising Peter's Ice Cream can be seen in many of the photographs of Greek cafés reproduced here.

Frederick A. B. Peters, an American from Michigan, founded Peters American Delicacy Co. Ltd. in Sydney in 1907. An associate company was formed in Boundary Street, South Brisbane, in 1927, and by 1930 Peters manufactured and sold ice cream throughout the country.[137] Following the early use of ice-and-salt refrigeration, Peters adopted what was viewed in 1934 as a bold new policy of supplying and installing thousands of "power ice holding cabinets" in retail outlets throughout NSW. Since refrigeration was required to create a mass market for ice cream, when these cabinets were installed in Greek milk bars across Australia, the ice cream industry flourished.[138] Some Greek cafés traded under the name of Peter's & Co. to cash in on the ice cream company's popularity.[139] Peter's and Co. is written on the hoarding above a shop in the main street of Kyogle and inlaid in bronze in the footpath in front of the doorway, suggesting that this shop was, at some point in its history, a Greek café.

In a pre-supermarket Australia, cafés were the primary retail outlet for the ice delicacy. Proprietors used ice cream in milkshakes and ice cream sodas, causing both to brim with white froth, and no dessert would be complete

the advent of pre-packaged goods, supermarkets, and convenience stores, Greek cafés played a considerable role in supporting two of Australia's major primary industries.[140]

The Ice Cream Sundae consists of ice cream with fruit, and sometimes jelly, topped with syrup and nuts and in some cases adorned with a wafer. Served in a silver dish or a glass boat, it was a favourite in Greek cafés and milk bars. Legend has it that an American drugstore owner invented the sundae in the 1880s to circumvent the law regarding what could be made on the Sabbath. Sunday, in Puritan tradition, was a solemn day; swings were chained, reading was banned, and theatres were closed. Ice cream sodas were also deemed illegal, but mixing syrup with ice cream was not. The drugstore owner's new formula followed the letter of the law and was called a Sunday because it solved the problem of making a delicious treat for his customers on Sunday. A change of spelling then appeased objections to the dessert being named after the Lord's Day. Sundaes became so

without it. Maureen remembers that at Londy's Café in Ipswich during the 40s, popular desserts included sundaes, banana splits, waffles, parfaits, jelly, and fruit salad, all of which were freshly-made and served with ice-cream. She also remembers growing up in the country town of Coominya in the 30s and enjoying the Saturday afternoon ritual of walking to the local café for a penny ice cream. In a hot, dry climate, the ice-cold sweetness must have been heavenly to children and adults alike.

Because ice cream was made from natural products, dubbed "gifts of Nature" in the 1930s, and because Peters emphasised the importance of purity and hygiene in the manufacturing process, ice cream, like milk, was considered a health food. This added to its popularity. Since Peters Ice Cream was made from 83% cream and milk and 16% cane sugar, and remembering that Greek cafés were a primary retail outlet for ice cream before

Sundae dishes from the Regal Cafe.

popular that customers started requesting them during the rest of the week. The new dessert's fame spread far and wide; it soon became a classic and is now sold internationally.[141]

Sundaes with names like 'American Beauty' and 'Mexican Banana Split' reflect the sundae's American origin, but Australian proprietors invented names for their own variations of these popular desserts. A favourite at Londy's Café, for example, was the 'Aeroplane Special' – a three-scoop sundae with two horizontal triangular wafers for wings and a vertical one for the tail.[142] The Sydney Café served the Kiss Me Quick and the Summer Joy Special. At the Austral Café in Murwillumbah, NSW, a 'Tutti Fruiti' consisted of a single scoop of ice cream served with fruit salad and whipped cream. The addition of nuts produced a 'Nutti Fruiti'.[143] The Peach Melba was created from canned peaches and two scoops of ice cream with strawberry syrup, whipped cream and nuts. It appears, however, that while Dame Nellie Melba was Australian, the Peach Melba was the creation of a French chef working at a London restaurant in 1893.[144] The demand for American-style sodas, milkshakes, and ice cream sundaes increased during the war years, when American troops stationed in Australia craved the foods of their homeland. The influence of US troops also explains how Australians came to love donuts, Coca-Cola, and hamburgers.

Confectionery

American-style hard sugar confectionery is a further American influence that leaked into Australian culture via the Greek café, because most Greek cafés had an extensive front confectionery counter. Confectionery can be seen piled around the proprietors in many of the photographs reproduced in this book, and in some, like the one of the Regal Café on the cover, the confectionery counter is signed as a 'Candy Bar'. While the English call it 'sweets' or 'sweeties' and Americans call it 'candy', sugar confectionery is traditionally known in Australia as 'lollies'. Loose lollies were stored in square glass jars on the counter and on shelves along the wall – also known as a pantry – as well as being kept in compartments under the glass counter. They were weighed on a set of scales, which sat on the confectionery counter, and were sold in white paper bags. Some cafés pre-weighed popular varieties to speed up transactions in busy times. Confectionery like Cowboy Chews and Texas Chews clearly indicate an American influence, but Australian confectionery was also sold. In Ipswich, sales reps for big Australian companies visited cafés and proprietors also placed orders with the local firm, Johnson's Confectionery Company, which operated on the corner of Bell and Union Streets. Apart from loose lollies, confectionery was sold in boxes and tins, and chocolates came in blocks, boxes, and tins.

A particular association between movies and confectionery formed in the early decades of the 20th century, and this is likely the result of a similar association in America, but some Australian classics especially spring to mind in relation to Australian movie

Allens and MacRobertson's lolly tins.

In 1934, Dalby had five Greek cafés, all of which were viable businesses. Café staff, including Milton Samios and his son, Jim, stand behind the confectionery counter of the Paragon Café in Cunningham Street, Dalby, in 1936. They are dwarfed by piles of chocolate bars on the counter, an assortment of loose lollies under the counter, and a huge array of boxes and tins of confectionery, as well as some ornaments or toys, which may also have contained confectionery, on the bottom shelf.

State Library of Queensland Image No. 41450.[145]

audiences. Boxed confectionery, such as the Aussie classics, Minties, Fantales, and Jaffas, was especially popular with theatre crowds, and confectionery counters in cafés that traded beside picture theatres, such as the Ritz Café and the Wintergarden Milk Bar in Ipswich, would be swamped with customers during interval. Fantales had film stars' biographies on the wrappers and it was fun to play a game of 'guess who' in the moments before the curtains drew back and the lights went down, and no visit to the 'flicks' would be complete without one or two Jaffas to roll down the sloped, wooden floor during the movie. Local resident, Dot Kennedy, remembers one occasion when a theatre patron, having finished his loose lollies, blew up the white paper bag like a balloon and popped it

Boxes of Bex and Vincents powders and Aspros are piled on the shelves behind the counter at the Metro Café. Vasiliki Stathis is pictured with her cousin and a local waitress.

between his hands. The explosion brought applause and cheering from the audience. A long-suffering and cranky usher also came running in his direction. But this particular usher had a harelip, and after he burst out, "Who bob bab baber bab," the audience was rolling in the aisles too.

Cigarettes and 'medications' like Throaties and Irish Moss, Bex and Vincents were also stocked at the confectionery counter. Proprietors remember that customers did not always come for toasted sandwiches and coffee, malted milks, or mixed grills; some came for their daily 'fix'. They ordered a Bex or Vincents, which staff normally served with tonic water or a soft drink. Bex and Vincents were the equivalent of Panadol on today's supermarket shelves and many Australians used them as a pick-me-up throughout the day. The products were not made in capsules and sold in handy blister packs, but consisted of an amount of bitter powder folded inside a piece of paper. Bex was a white powder; Vincents was pink. The powder was unwrapped and the paper creased to make a channel so that the powder would slide down onto the back of the tongue. Panadol replaced Bex, Vincents, and Aspros because evidence suggested that certain ingredients could make the stomach bleed if taken over long periods of time.

Hamburgers and Takeaways

Already popular in the United States, the hamburger was introduced to Australia through the US military forces in the 1940s. The American version was the meat patty, although Australian cafés and snack bars eventually elaborated on this to include steak burgers, egg and bacon burgers, and the 'lot', which included thickly-sliced pineapple and beetroot. Greeks proprietors agree that a 'proper' hamburger had to have beetroot.[146] The hamburger was one of the most popular items in Greek snack bars like Tony's in Ipswich, where Jim Pavlakis made generous, tasty burgers that are still remembered today. In 1972, they cost only 15 cents, but hamburgers have enjoyed enduring popularity. A young man fondly describes the hamburgers at his favourite café – a Greek snack bar in Goodna on the outskirts of Ipswich – before it recently changed hands: "The hamburgers were great because the bloke made them with love. He made them like he was going to eat them himself."[147]

Sadly, this ongoing link between the Greek café and popular American foods contributed to its eventual demise. In time, fast-food chains like McDonalds replaced family-run businesses, and Greek cafés like the Central Milk Bar and

In an age when most Australian households have a freezer with ice-making facilities, a refrigerator, an Esky, an air-conditioned car, and, increasingly, an air-conditioned home, and most shopping centres and workplaces are air-conditioned, it's difficult to imagine the impact that an ice-cold drink had upon earlier generations of Australians. The ongoing popularity of Icy Cold Fruit Drinks is evident on the mirrored signs behind many café counters, where they accompany the café's name, as in the case of the Regal Café. Although not necessarily of American origin, fruit juice was ladled from a milk canister kept ice-cold in the milk bar.

Café in Ipswich were forced to transform into takeaway outlets in order to survive. Maria, who worked in several Ipswich cafés before retiring at the end of 2004, set up the Central to sell hamburgers in 1985. In comparison with her time at the Regal in the 50s, Maria notes that takeaways were 'a big seller' at the Central. Hamburgers were particularly popular, as were hot chips.

into a bucket of sugar, to which water and citric acid were later added.[148] Joanne, who was a teenager when she worked at her father's Ipswich café in the mid-70s, recalls that icy cold, freshly-squeezed fruit drinks were still one of the Regal's most popular items in 70s. The Regal's electric juicer survives today, the fluted dome in the centre now worn to a burnished copper colour.

Greek cafés evolved at a time when many Australians did not yet enjoy the benefits of electricity, so by selling cold drinks, they made a major contribution to the Australian way of life. In 1850, ice was harvested in America and shipped to Australia to cool food. Writer, William Kelly, gives us a glimpse of what an ice-cold drink meant to Australians in this quote from 1853: "It was not until I

Icy-Cold Fresh Fruit Juice

Another extremely popular item on the Greek café menu, and one that many proprietors recall with pride, was homemade, icy-cold, fresh fruit juice. This was made from freshly-juiced fruit to which water, sugar, and syrup were usually added, although it was mostly sugar according to some who grew up in cafés. One 'café kid' recalls her father sitting in the kitchen after closing time grating oranges

Frank Hurley. Albert Street Showing King George V Monument (nla.pic-an23478002). Photograph courtesy of the National Library of Australia.

Jim Bellas did not own the Star Milk Bar at the time this photograph of Albert Square was taken, but the Statue of King George on horseback was directly in front of his shop. Brisbane City Hall was built on a vacant block of land between Ann and Adelaide Streets, which was called Market Square after the nearby fruit and vegetable markets in Roma Street. City Hall, completed in 1930, was set back from Albert Street, and the narrow strip of land in front was named Albert Square. Following the death of King George V in 1935, Albert Square was widened to include Albert Street and renamed King George Square.[152] *The Star Milk Bar was eventually demolished to make way for further redevelopment to King George Square, and Jim was given only 28 days to vacate his shop.*

came to Victoria, and got half baked in the dry, roasting, hot winds of the country, that I became fully indoctrinated in the virtues of ice." What a transition from breathing the parched Australian dust to "sucking the frigid essence of a brandy-spider through a straw."[149] By 1893, most Australians could afford an ice chest, and within a decade, ice carts went door to door on a regular basis. In the 1920s, prosperous families owned kerosene, gas, or electric fridges, and electricity had reached most suburbs.[150] For many Australians at that time, however, especially those in rural areas, and for those who endured hardship during the depression years to come, electricity, fridges, and cold drinks 'on tap' were luxuries they could only dream about. But Greek cafés, with their electrically-operated milk bars, had ice-cold drinks all year round. Even when most Australians had electricity, a brief stop for a cold drink when you were in town shopping or transacting business was a welcome respite, especially in outback towns, and travellers relied on cafés for cold drinks.

Jim Bellas, who owned the Star Milk Bar in Albert Street, Brisbane, claims that his shop was the first to sell fresh fruit juice in Brisbane and, in the late 40s at least, had "the best name in fruit juices in town".[151] Jim's shop offered orange, lemon, fruit cocktail, pineapple, and mango juices, all of which he made by hand from produce procured at the Brisbane fruit and vegetable markets, which are now situated at Rocklea but were at that time in Roma Street. The Star Milk Bar traded opposite Brisbane City Hall so the markets were nearby. Jim juiced hundreds of boxes of oranges a year and people still say of his firm handshake – "Oh Jim, you're squeezing oranges again." He also bought mangoes by the thousands, all of which he peeled, sliced, and stored in plastic bags. Jim had a deal with a nearby ice works to store the sliced fruit so that the Star Milk Bar had mango juice all the year round. Jim says he made 50 gallons of juice every morning.

'Good Ol' Aussie Tucker'

And now to British taste – the third and final facet of this singular union that is the Australian Greek café. Isolated incidences of Greek cafés serving Greek food would undoubtedly have occurred. There is evidence that some Greeks served Greek sweets; baklava and kataifi appeared in Sydney in the 1930s and baklava and galaktoboureko were on the menu in Ion Nicolades' Legend Espresso and Milk Bar in Melbourne in 1956.[153] But in the main, traditional Greek foods like souvlaki, moussaka, dolmades, tzatzizi, and galaktobouriko, which can now be found in Greek restaurants and even on supermarket shelves, did not emerge from behind closed doors until the late 70s.[154] Some Greeks

OUR MOTTO:
CIVILITY
SERVICE
SATISFACTION

SYDNE[Y]
MEALS A[T]

DINNER MENU
Soft Drinks, Tea or Coffee included with all Meals

SOUP

....

FRIED FISH
Mullet — 4/6
Bream
Whiting
Mackerel — } 4/9
Rock Cod
Schnapper
Barramundi

GRILLED FISH
Mullet — 4/6
Bream
Whiting
Mackerel — } 4/9
Rock Cod
Schnapper
Barramundi

Tomatoes 9 Xtra

STEAK
Grilled Steak — 4/6 5/6
Steak and Eggs — 4/9 5/6
Mixed Grill — 4/9
Mixed Grill and Eggs — 5/9
Pork Fillet — 4/9 5/9
Pork Fillet and Eggs — 5/9
Pork Chops — 4/9
Pork Chops & eggs — 5/9

Onions 9 Xtra

EGGS
(Plain or on Toast)
Fried Eggs — 3/9
Poached Eggs — 4/-
Scrambled Eggs — 4/-

Rissoles
Lamb's Fry

CUTLETS
Lamb Cutlets
Lamb Cutlets and Eggs

HOT JOINTS
Roast Mutton
Roast Lamb & Mint Sauce
Roast Pork

POULTRY
Roast Chicken

COLD LUNCHEONS
Combination Salad — 3/9
Mutton and Salad
Ham and Salad — 4/6 5/6
Ham and Eggs

SAUSAGES
Sausages and Potatoes — 4/- 4/9
Sausages and Onions — 4/9
Sausages and Eggs
Sausages, Eggs and Onions — 5/9

SEA FOODS
Crab and Salad — 6/-
Lobster and Salad
Plate of Prawns — 5/3
(Bottle) Oysters — 4/9
Boiled Haddock

SWEETS

Y CAFE
ALL HOURS

DUNN & CO.
Nicholas St., Ipswich
Phone 38

LIGHT REFRESHMENTS

SODA FOUNTAIN DRINKS

Lemonade	
Strawberry	
Orange	
Pineapple	*7*
Sarsaparilla	
Ginger Ale	
Lime Juice	
Kola	
Ginger Beer	
With Ice Cream	*9*

SQUASHES

Lemon Squash, plain	*8*
Lemon Squash with Ice Cream	*10*
Orange Squash, plain	*8*
Orange Squash, with Ice Cream	*10*

ICE CREAMS
(With any Flavour)

MILK BEVERAGES
(With Ice Cream, 1d. extra)

Malted Milk (any flavour)	*10*
Milk Shake	*10*
~~Iced Coffee~~	
~~Iced Chocolate~~	
Egg Malted Milk	
Double Malted Milk	*1/3*
~~Egg Flip~~	

SUNDAES

Any flavour	
Aeroplane Special	
Summer Joy Special	*2/-*
Kiss Me Quick	
Banana Split	

DESSERTS

Fruit Salad and Ice Cream	*1/3*
Bananas and Ice Cream	*1/-*
Jelly and Ice Cream	

STRAWBERRIES
(When in Season)

Small dish	~~X~~
Large dish	~~X~~

MORNING AND AFTERNOON TEAS
(With Tea, Coffee, or Soft Drinks)

Hot Buttered Toast	*1/9*
Ham Sandwiches	
Tomato Sandwiches	
Cheese Sandwiches	*2/3*
Mixed Sandwiches	
Cakes	

TOASTED SANDWICHES
(With Tea, Coffee, or Soft Drinks)

Ham	
Tomato	*2/9*
Cheese	
Mixed	

PIES

Pie and Vegetables	*2/3*
Double Pie and Vegetables	*3/3*
Pie with Tea or Coffee	*2/9*
Double Pie with Tea or Coffee	*3/6*

ON TOAST

say they served 'Aussie tucker' because they "wouldn't have made a penny" otherwise. Others say they would have been lynched if they had served something like spinach pie. Con Castan, president of the Solomos Society of Brisbane claims that serving Greek food "was inconceivable until about 20 years ago . . . no self-respecting Australian would touch ethnic of any kind."[155] Greek cafés catered instead for the British-Australian predilection for steak, chops, fried eggs, fish, chips, plain boiled vegetables, sliced bread and butter, and meat pies. This is clear in menus like the one from Ipswich's Sydney Café from the 1950s. Perhaps the lack of 'ethnic' food in Greek cafés helps to explain Symons' failure to mention the influence of Greek immigrants in his book about the history of eating in Australia. Even under the heading, "Multicultural Society," he makes no mention of the Greeks (222-4).

Many Ipswich residents remember that Greek proprietors dished up large serves of food, and proprietors explain that loaded plates were intended to keep customers happy so that they would keep coming back.

Symons was warned that a book about food in Australia would be exceedingly short for several reasons: Australians 'ate' rather than 'dined', the women could not cook, the men knew nothing of the art of good eating, and, even in the 1940s, preserving good old-fashioned English cooking seemed to be the "gastronomic mission of Australia."[156] Symons claims that an Australian stereotype emerged as early as the 1850s. He – and the stereotype is male, as Australian stereotypes mostly still are – had basic eating habits, derided complementary foods arranged on a plate, valued quantity and rapid consumption over quality and subtle combinations of flavours, and wanted nothing more than a slab of meat, simply cooked. Popular expressions like 'hop in for your chop' and 'two, four, six, eight, dig in don't wait' reflect this Australian attitude toward food, not to mention a larrikin penchant for rhyming slang.

Mixed Grills

It was precisely this fondness for wolfing down copious quantities of cheap, simple food that ensured the popularity of the Mixed Grill, which Symons attributes to Greek café proprietors.[157] The Mixed Grill is served on a large plate and consists of a variety of grilled meats – a steak, a chop, two sausages, and a rasher or two of bacon – accompanied by a couple of fried eggs, two halves of a large grilled tomato, and two slices of white toast, with lashings of Worcestershire Sauce readily available. This kind of dish still holds a strong attraction, particularly for young Australian males. A 20-year-old man recently remarked, "Mixed Grills are a mad idea. Every kind of meat you can get all on one plate. How good's that? It's like . . . Heaven."[158] The Big Breakfast served in contemporary cafés comes closest to the concept of the Mixed Grill, except that it is accompanied by American hash browns, a serve of English Spinach, and perhaps a serve of Turkish bread. Many Ipswich residents remember that Greek proprietors dished up large serves of food, and proprietors explain that loaded plates were intended to keep customers happy so that they would keep coming back. It is evident from the Mixed Grill that the proprietors of Greek cafés and their customers had little concerns about heart disease and cholesterol during the 30s, 40s, 50s, and 60s.

Fish 'n' Chips

Many cafés maintained the seafood menu typical of the early Greek oyster saloon, specialising in takeaway fish and chips and creating an enduring association between Greek immigrants and fish shops in the Australian imagination. Many Australians will recall the luscious, salty smell of the warm bundle that was fish 'n' chips wrapped in newspaper as Greek fish shops sold them. Rather than unwrapping the bundle, people

The Sydney Café in Nicholas Street, Ipswich, is widely recalled for Harry's delicious fish and chips.

often tore a hole in one end, turning the bundle into a container. Staying warm inside their newspaper cocoon, the chips were drawn out one at a time and stuffed into hungry mouths. Although customers savoured these fish and chips, scratching around in the bottom of the bundle to find that last chip hiding in a corner somewhere, they did not always get what they bought. Some 'café kids', even now reluctant to disclose their fathers' secrets, admit that while the cold battered fish displayed in the fish counter wore different labels, underneath the batter it was all the same fish. "It was one of the tricks of the trade."[159]

Proprietors are proud of their reputation for cooking great food and their fish stories are among those told with the greatest pride. Now, fishy tales are notoriously prone to exaggeration, but I hope none of these whoppers is too far from the truth. Because his father was part of a network that extended beyond Ipswich, Peter Londy boasts that Londy's Café always had fresh fish. It arrived in Ipswich by train, shipped in boxes packed with ice, and was often freshly caught. It was so fresh, in fact, that on one occasion, when a fussy customer asked Peter if the fish was fresh, a big cod flicked its tail and broke the front display window. I raise my eyebrows at this tale, but Peter's wife, Mary, says, "No, that's absolutely true." And wives are not usually complicit in their husbands' fishy yarns.[160]

Ipswich's Sydney Café was also renowned for its fish and chips. According to Harry Tanos, their shop had a licence to buy 10% of the fish from the Brisbane Fish Market during the Second World War and was one of the few shops still selling fresh fish at that time. The Sydney even sold cooked fish to other cafés like the Capitol Café, a non-Greek establishment further up Nicholas Street. Fish was shipped to Ipswich by train and Harry would go around the corner to the railway station with a trolley to fetch it. In 1958, the Tanos brothers bought a station wagon and then Harry drove to the markets twice a week. Harry recalls that on Fridays he commonly peeled five 150 pound sacks of potatoes and cleaned and cooked 600 pieces of fish. Given that Peter did a similar trade at Londy's, the people of Ipswich must have consumed over a thousand pieces of fish on Fridays during this period. Harry remembers, however, that after a severe cyclone, a Catholic archbishop granted special permission for Catholics to eat meat on Fridays because of the resulting fish shortage. "And that," says Harry, "was the end of it. If it was alright one year, it was alright the next."[161]

Don Risson was a produce merchant who delivered potatoes and onions to most of the cafés in Ipswich for nearly 40 years. He recalls that in the years after WWII, his father shipped Bismarks and Brownells from

Tasmania because these were renowned as "the best 'chippers' in the world."[162] The shipments – 1,500 bags of potatoes each weighing 150 pounds – came from Brisbane by rail because a tax per ton per mile made road haulage too expensive. The potatoes kept well for six months under the shed at Risson's Produce in Nicholas Street. Don recalls that the Greeks bought 60 bags of potatoes at a time, and this would last them about five weeks.

Most cafés had electric tumbling machines to peel the potatoes and many eventually had mechanical chip-cutters, although others still did the chips by hand. For almost a quarter of a century, Maria hand-cut all of the chips sold at Tony's Snack Bar and the Central Milk Bar. Maureen Reinke, who worked for Maria for a time, remembers that Maria peeled and hand-cut her chips and always used clean oil. Maria had other secrets too. With arguably as much experience at buying, chipping, and cooking potatoes as anyone in Australia, Maria advises, "not all potatoes make good chips and not all dirt make good potatoes."[163]

The wide but simple range of foods offered on Greek café menus for most of the 20th century verifies Symons' observations about plain food and British taste. Peter Spathis recalls the meals at Ipswich's first Greek café, which he bought from John Black about 1917 and owned until 1933.

Don Risson from Risson's Produce was known to the Greeks as 'The Potato Man'. Don and his red Bedford truck were a familiar sight in Ipswich as they delivered potatoes and onions to most of the cafés on a regular basis. Risson's Produce operated in Nicholas Street from the 1910s until the redevelopment of the CBD in the mid-80s, when the Palmer family bought the business and relocated to West Ipswich. The old slab shed was demolished.

At the City Café, I sold meals, confectionery, fruit, fish and prawns. In one window, I had fruit and in the other I had fish, crabs and other sea foods. I sold both fresh and cooked fish. Meals were ham and eggs, steak and eggs, fried fish, roasts – lamb, pork and veal. Also soup and dessert . . . three course meals . . . charged one shilling and sixpence to two shillings a meal. Tea and sandwiches was a shilling. There was a milk bar too – malted milks sixpence. I had ten tables. I had twin shops – one for meals and fish, including fresh fish, and the other for dinner and light refreshments. It was one shop with two sections. Takings were about twenty pounds per week.[164]

Similarly, Maureen describes the food she served at Londy's Café in the 40s and 50s as "meals that you normally find on an ordinary menu. It was just straight out Australian meals".[165] Londy's maintained a seafood menu – fresh fish, prawns, cooked fish including whole whiting – and included a wide variety of other meals: steak and eggs, mixed grill, pork fillet, pork chops, all served with chips and salad or 'vegies', and toasted sandwiches. Breakfast was mostly tinned baked beans on toast. Joanne recalls that, while toasted sandwiches was the primary takeaway order in the 1970s at the nearby Regal Café, a pie with chips and gravy was considered the specialty of the house. The Kentrotis' renowned gravy was prepared to a secret recipe, now revealed as the juices of the roasts thickened with tomato paste. Maria made the pies at the Regal with the aid of a huge rolling pin brought out from Greece.

When Ipswich residents recollect their attraction to local cafés, they almost invariably refer to the quantity and price of the food that Harry Londy, George Kentrotis, and other Greek proprietors served, and their favourite orders are consistent with those listed above. Many note that different cafés were famous for different foods. Dot Kennedy explains that she went to Londy's for dessert – their Banana Split was especially memorable – she headed to the Sydney if she wanted fish and chips, and if she wanted toasted sandwiches then the Regal Café was the place to go.[166] Foaming ice cream sodas, icy-cold fresh fruit drinks, frothy malted milks, mouth-watering sundaes, massive mixed grills, meat pies with peas and gravy, fish and chips wrapped in newspaper, and hamburgers so big that they barely fitted into the customer's hands feature prominently amongst the memories of those who recall the heyday of the Greek café in Ipswich. Along with toasted sandwiches – supposedly first made in Australia in the mid-30s by Hope Gibson in his coffee shop using his wife's iron – the menu indicates the British heritage of the Greeks' newly-adopted homeland and reflects the ongoing influence of American innovation.[167] Greek food was not on the menu.

Rather than trying to introduce the Australian palette to Greek dishes and Mediterranean ingredients, Greek proprietors quickly discerned what their customers wanted and gave them plenty of it, whenever they wanted it. They adhered to this simple business principle, along with a policy of cheap prices and warm hospitality, for decades. Even in the 1970s in Ipswich cafés, milk shakes were still made in stainless steel containers and sucked through paper straws, fruit salad was still home-made, and traditional Greek dishes were still nowhere to be seen.[168]

In addition to the contemporary elevation of coffee to an art form, several differences in eating options between Greek and contemporary cafés are worth mentioning. In the first instance, menus painted on glass suggest that the fare was more permanent than that offered on the chalkboards of today's café. Next, syrups, jellies, fruit salad, waffles, orange and lemon drinks, and sodas were made on the premises; there were no bottled drinks, tinned fruit, or pre-packaged products, other than confectionery and tobacco, until later years. In addition, when customers ordered a menu item in the 40s, two slices of white bread, soup, tea or coffee, and dessert in the form of steamed puddings made in jam tins – not milk bar items – were included in the price. Finally, cafés did generally not sell cakes. Of course this was not always the case: the Garden of Roses in Brisbane had continental cakes; the Paragon Café in Katoomba had a pastry cook, who trained cooks from other Greek cafés;

The Kentrotis' renowned gravy was prepared to a secret recipe, now revealed as the juices of the roasts thickened with tomato paste.

Many Australians had vegetable gardens in the middle decades of the 20th century, but while Australians grew carrots, lettuce, and tomatoes and raised 'chooks' in their backyards, Greek Australians grew basil plants, zucchini, okra, avocadoes, and eggplants in theirs. Some even had olive trees and fig trees smuggled into Australia from Greece by new immigrants. Pictured is a thriving crop of okra in Jim and Athena Bellas' suburban garden. Jim is 86.

Cominos' Café in Cairns had a cake/bakery department; Ion Nicolades' Legend Espresso and Milk Bar in Melbourne sold baklava and galaktoboureko. Most, however, left it to bakeries and cake shops to provide cream puffs, chocolate éclairs, vanilla slices and the like. Jack Stathis of Ipswich's City and Metro Cafés explains, "If a customer really wanted cake, I suppose I would have gone to the bakery and got one for him, but no, we didn't sell cake. The money was in toasted sandwiches."[169] The variety of cakes served in contemporary cafés – cheesecakes, mud cakes, flourless chocolate cake, Pavlova, orange and almond cake, cheese strudels, Tiramisu, Jaffa Cake, Danish pastries and so on – suggests a shift in Australian eating habits and/or locale and specialisation.

The Mediterranean Diet

While Greeks did not serve Greek food in their cafés, along with other immigrants they did eventually change what Australians ate and the way they ate it. The Greeks used 'different' ingredients to make traditional dishes in their homes and suburban neighbours often sampled the food created on the other side of the fence. Several of the immigrants interviewed for this book recall being farewelled by their mothers over half a century ago with this advice: "Don't tell Australians how to run their country and take food to your neighbours." Even though Greek food may not have been served in cafés, it may, by this means, have appeared in Australian kitchens far earlier and far more often than is realised.

Even in their role as proprietors, Greeks influenced Australian eating habits, despite the fact that they did not serve Greek food in their cafés. Anglo-Australian waitresses and deliverymen, for example, were often treated to a taste of what was being eaten in the kitchens of Greek cafés. Ivan Schostakowski, who had a bread run for Anthony's Bakery in Rosewood, delivered bread to Jim Pavlakis' shop (Tony's Snack Bar in Ipswich) and often had a meal there. Ivan remembers the first time Jim poured olive oil over the salad he served with Ivan's Mixed Grill: "I never saw anything like it," says Ivan, "but I loved it and I've eaten salad that way ever since."

Regular customers also had the opportunity to experience Greek food that was not on the menu. Ipswich proprietor, Harry Tanos, now 85, recalls a particular farmer who was a regular at the Sydney Café. The farmer habitually complained about hares, which had reached plague proportions and were causing problems on his property. Finally, Harry, who had come from a poverty-stricken country where anything that could be eaten was eaten, said, "Well then, kill the bloody things and eat them." The farmer was aghast at this suggestion, but on his next trip to town obliged Harry with a bag full of dead hares. Harry stewed them in a traditional Greek style and thoroughly enjoyed them. On the farmer's next visit, Harry gave him some of the stew. The farmer was even more aghast at the thought that Harry expected him to eat it, but he gave it a try and decided that it wasn't too bad.[170]

In the 21st century, it is hard to imagine a time when basil, garlic, yoghurt, olives, and olive oil were not routine items in Australian shops and kitchens, but Maroula Tanos remembers how difficult it was to procure the ingredients for Greek dishes. In the early 60s, she had to purchase olive oil from a chemist and could only get yoghurt through the Greek Club. Sometimes she would have to go to three shops before she could find a lemon. Because these foods were not available in shops, many Greeks grew and/or made their own. These foods were also foreign to the Australian palette and to the Australian imagination. One man recalls that, as a child, he gave his schoolmate a sample of his mother's home-made yoghurt, which was suspended in a cloth above the kitchen sink. His mate spat it out and yelled, "What did you give me rotten milk for?"[162] Another relates an occasion when a friend had just eaten, with great relish, a Greek dish she had enjoyed in his home on several previous occasions. When she asked about the unique flavour, the woman was told it contained olive oil. She promptly vomited. Australians were appalled at the thought of cooking with olive oil because they did not consider that it was food. It must have been difficult for immigrants to accept this ignorance of foods which had been staples in European countries for centuries.

One Christmas Day, before he married Maroula, Harry was celebrating with a group of Greek friends at a swimming hole. They had built a fire and were preparing to cook souvla – pieces of meat threaded onto a skewer – over the flames. A carload of Australians came along the road and yelled 'BLOODY WOGS!' as they passed. When the car returned some time later and slowed to a halt, however, Harry and his companions expected the worst. The Australians got out of the car. The ringleader sniffed the air, inspected the proceedings, and demanded to know what it was called, this strange new food that smelled so good. When Harry explained, the man replied, "Oh, we thought it musta been some bloody wog ritual." Harry shakes his head: "They knew nothing. . . nothing."

Maroula Tanos remembers how difficult it was to procure the ingredients for Greek dishes. In the early 60s, she had to purchase olive oil from a chemist and could only get yoghurt through the Greek Club.

Italian immigrants had similar problems. Ipswich councillor, Charlie Pisasale, is the son of Italian immigrants. As a child in Ipswich in the 1950s, he worked for McMahon's, a local soft drink manufacturer. Charlie recalls Frank McMahon asking him one day about the 'new food' called spaghetti; Frank wanted to know whether or not it grew on trees. "And he was deadly serious," says Charlie. Charlie's lunch was also the focus of unwanted attention. He recalls schoolmates ridiculing his 'frog sandwiches', which were the result of Charlie's insistence that his mother put his char-grilled green capsicum between two slices of bread "like the other kids had." Charlie recalls that it was not until he married in the late 60s that he came to see his 'ordinary' Italian fare, through his Australian wife's eyes, as something desirable.[172]

Ivan also delivered bread to a gang of single Italian immigrants, who worked for a company called Transfield, which had the contract to take powerlines west from Swanbank. The gang's Italian cook asked Ivan if he could get hold of some 'hard-baked' bread – 20 per day and 40 on weekends. Ivan arranged for the bakery to overcook their Vienna loaf especially to the cook's requirements. When he saw the Italians break off thick chunks of the bread and dip it into olive oil, Ivan commented that Australians always sliced and buttered their bread so that they could make sandwiches. An Italian worker replied, "Australians bloody fools." Fifty years on, Australians have adopted a wide range of breads, as well as the practice of breaking and dipping bread on occasion. And in the light of knowledge about heart disease, they commonly use alternatives to butter.

Australians also ate a more limited variety of fish than the Greeks. Harry Tanos claims that in earlier days his customers wouldn't eat anything but mullet when ordering fish. According to Harry, the mullet tasted like kerosene because of the pollution at the mouth of the Brisbane River, where the fish were caught. Although his customers complained about this, they refused to eat other varieties. In later years, customers came to accept whole grilled whiting, gar, bream, plaice, and other kinds of fish. One Ipswich resident remembers that he was fishing with some Greek mates as a young man, when one of them pulled an octopus ashore. To the non-Greek Australian, octopus was as inedible as toadfish and sea cucumber, but one of the Greek boys seized it and dashed it on the rocks in preparation for cooking. His Greek mates explained that octopus made good eating if you bashed them on a rock as soon as you caught them to prevent the ink from fouling the flesh. They then cooked the 'delicacy' and ate it. Anyone who has sampled calamari at Brisbane's Greek Club will agree – the Greeks know a thing or two about cooking the fruits of the ocean.

As a reflection of the kafeneion, Greek cafés were the great gathering places of their communities. They employed American food-catering ideas like the soda fountain and the milk bar and popularised American foods like ice cream and hamburgers. Because proprietors catered to British-Australian taste, they did not serve Greek food. The Mediterranean diet is now so much a part of the Australian lifestyle, however, that Greek restaurants are popular, take away outlets sell Greek dishes, supermarkets stock traditional Greek ingredients, and suburban kitchens employ basil, garlic, oil and yoghurt – the kinds of ingredients Greeks have used for centuries – on a regular basis. The subtle influence of Greek immigrants played a significant role in this; as friends and neighbours, they eventually changed the face of Australian cuisine.

CHAPTER FIVE

Daughters of Aphrodite: Café Brides

'I will introduce you to your fiancée.' Vince handed her a bouquet of gladioli and said, 'Your future husband.'

* * *

They looked at each other in silence.[173]

A woman was among the first Greeks to settle in Australia. Katherine Crummer (nee Aikaterini Plessos), the wife of an army officer, arrived in 1835.[174] Greek women were also part of the Ipswich community in its early days – records show that Mrs Asica Matton, born in Greece in 1855, was a widow and a shopkeeper in Ipswich when she was naturalised in 1903.[175] The story of chain migration that produced the Greek café phenomenon, however, overwhelmingly concerns single men, 'male pioneers' who came to Australia to make their fortunes before returning to Greece.[176]

Australia's first 'oyster saloon' was established by a man. Men sponsored male relatives and fellow countrymen in the subsequent exodus to Australia. The kafeneion is a men-only establishment, and it served in Australia as a meeting point and labour market for male immigrants. Australia's early Greek cafés were generally owned and operated by men, although a handful of Greek women, like Mrs Asica Matton, did own shops. Men prepared food, cooked, waited on tables, and washed up in cafés all across the country, and for the first two decades of the 20th century, even female employees were rare.[177] Though few Greek immigrants originally contemplated settlement, once they became established in catering businesses, many of these 'male pioneers' did not return to their homeland as planned. Sweethearts arrived from Greece, some men married Australian women, others married by proxenia, and the 1920s saw a shift from a Greek community dominated by single men to one dominated by the family.[178] As the 20th century progressed, women played a significant role in the unfolding story of Australia's Greek café.

The tendency for women to follow rather than lead the pattern of Greek migration in the 20th century produced several interconnected effects and these caused many Greek women to feel culturally isolated. Husbands may have already spent 20 years in Australia and were constantly mixing with the public. As a result, they knew many people in the local community and often spoke impeccable English.[179] Young brides, on the other hand, spoke no English. With husbands at work in their cafés all day and most of the night, these women had limited companionship and an even more limited social life. In Ipswich, for example, Elpiniki Black of the Australia Café led a lonely existence as one of only eight Queensland Greek women living outside of Brisbane in 1916. Elpiniki, who had been married just four years at the time, saw little of her husband, John, since he typically worked long hours in the café. In search of companionship during the evenings, Elpiniki would push their baby in a stroller to the café, where she helped John until they closed up at midnight. They then walked home together.[180]

While Greek men often married Australian women, especially in the early days when few single Greek women lived in Australia, Greek women were less likely to marry Australian men, so at home they spoke only Greek. Also, if these women didn't work in the front of cafés because of language difficulties, they had even less opportunity to mix with the Australian public. These factors meant that women were even less likely to speak English well. Allied with the language barrier and domestic responsibilities that kept women at home, the fact that Greek social and cultural occasions revolved around men and the male-dominated tradition of the kafeneion exacerbated the

Vasiliki and Nick Stathis' wedding photo was taken shortly before the couple came to Australia around 1927. Vasiliki, who was known in Australia as Bessie, was only 16 when she married 25-year-old Nick. The couple was sponsored by Bessie's mother's uncle, who had a café in Toowoomba. Her first two children were born while Nick was working in the Toowoomba café. When Nick's brother arrived in Australia, Nick and Bessie moved to Brisbane as the brothers went into partnership in a café in South Brisbane. In 1938, when his brother returned to Greece, Nick took over the City Café in Ipswich, which was at that time owned by the relative who had sponsored their immigration.

problem.[181] Most of the older Greek women, who were born in Greece and married café proprietors in Ipswich, have poor English or very strong accents. Older women who are the children of an earlier generation of immigrants and who grew up in the family café, however, speak English well. I noticed that 'café children' who are now in the 70s often speak English noticeably better than most Anglo-Australians their age.[182]

When proprietors sought Greek wives, they often married by proxenia. According to Conomos, this involved a family friend, called the proxeniti, selecting a prospective bride from among the women living in Greece or those who had already come to Australia. If the prospective groom approved, the woman would be approached with an offer of marriage. Photographs could be sent back and forth – although men often sent photographs that were 20 years out of date, and some even sent pictures of American movie stars – but much depended on the judgement of the proxeniti charged with making a suitable match. Marriages conducted in this fashion could proceed with great speed. The process left little room for romance, but, according to Conomos and most of the women interviewed for this chapter, the marriages were lasting and happy ones.[183] With their husbands and children, these women created the iconic Greek shopkeeping family. The popularity of Mark Mitchell's stereotypical characterisation of 'Con the Fruiterer' and his wife Marika springs from the widespread recognition of this iconic status

Many of the women whose stories of café life in Ipswich are recorded in this chapter were born in Kythera, a small island to the south of the Peloponnesus. Kythera is renowned as the magical island of love because Aphrodite was conceived in the foaming sea nearby. Aphrodite is known as the goddess of love because of her beauty and because she possessed a magical girdle that made everyone fall in love with the wearer. Kythera's reputation as a mythical land of love also arises from a tryst that the lovely Helen later kept on the island with her Trojan lover, Paris.[184] Many Kytherians who opened cafés in Australia returned to their homeland, the mythical island of love, in search of brides. While the stories of Aphrodite and Helen continue to enthral us when they are retold even centuries later in art, literature, and film, the women of Kythera, latter-day goddesses who were borne across the sea to Australian cafés, will still amaze you with their stories.

Allied with the language barrier and domestic responsibilities that kept women at home, the fact that Greek social and cultural occasions revolved around men and the male-dominated tradition of the kafeneion exacerbated the problem.

Vasiliki's Story

Kytherian-born, George Kentrotis, left Fratsia in 1925, when he was 21. He returned from Australia at the age of 53 to find a wife. Vasiliki was a beautiful 25-year-old from Fratsia. She had an aunt who used to tell people's fortunes by tipping the dregs of their coffee cups out onto a saucer. Vasi recalls that when she was a teenager, her aunt 'read' her cup and told her that she would one day marry an old man and travel far across the water. Her aunt was right. George and Vasi were married in Greece on the 13th of October, 1957, and she sailed with him for Australia.

Vasi remembers everyone's surprise at her agreeing to marry such 'an old man'. So why did young women like Vasi leave their families, their country, their language, and their culture to travel to the other side of the world and marry 'old' men they had never met? The answer lies in a lesser-known aspect of chain migration, the flipside of the Australian Greek café phenomenon, which is dealt with at length in Chapter Twelve. Because so many men had migrated to Australia or America, there was a devastating lack of men in Kytherian villages like Fratsia. Even if men were available, there was no one to provide the bride's dowry. According to several respondents, Greek sons were responsible for setting their sisters up in houses as a kind of dowry before they themselves could marry – the groom simply arrived with a suitcase and moved in. Villages depleted of both sons and prospective grooms therefore left a generation of women who faced the prospect of never marrying or having families.[185] Kythera, the birthplace of the goddess of love, had become a place of abandoned houses and childless women.[186] Vasi says she was very happy to marry George because he was rich by Kytherian standards; she would have her own house and be able to help her family.

Like many Greek women her age, Vasi had little schooling. She was only eight when WWII began and she did not go to school from then on because the teachers were in the army and the schools were closed. In days filled with bombing and other dangers, Vasi's job was looking after elderly people, sometimes hiding them in the woods from German soldiers. The pounding of distant guns was sometimes heard on Kythera as the Germans bombed passing ships. The people were very poor. They waited. Eventually shoes and clothing and huge tins of jam washed toward the shores of Kythera and the people would scoop them out of the sea. One day they noticed increased activity around the docks. The Germans were leaving. The next day Australian and English troops parachuted onto the island and all of Kythera celebrated. After the war, however, many people left because they could not face the prospect of being invaded again. Vasi never learned to read or write, but when her three children were old enough to go to school, she acquired enough English to handle money and serve in the Regal Café with George. Unfortunately, after the business closed down, she had little contact with people and lost much of her English.[187] George died when Vasi was only 49, which exacerbated her language difficulties, as does the fact that some of her grandchildren speak no Greek.

During the time that Vasi and George had the Regal, Vasi's work did not end at the door of the café. She kept a large 'chook house' in the backyard of their inner-city home and killed and dressed 15 chickens at a time for the café, where they were served with roast vegetables. Fortunately, George's bride was also a keen cook, because some weekends George would invite 30 people home for a meal. The row of tables would stretch from the enclosed rear verandah outside Vasi's kitchen, through the archway, across the dining room and into the sitting room to end near the front door of their old Queenslander. As one Ipswich resident recalls: "Georgie was a kind little man – always nice to people and nice to kids." He was a great host and Vasi is a great cook. Vasi also remembers making wine from the grapes they grew in the backyard of their home by treading them in a vat underneath the house. Her backyard is still a patchwork of well-tended vegetable beds that produce spinach and tomatoes for her table, although the drought has reduced their capacity. Her lemon tree is indispensable, but the olive tree near the fence still refuses to bear any fruit.

Helen's Story

Vasi's story is not unusual; many Greek women involved with Ipswich cafés were married by proxenia. Vasi's sister-in-law, Helen Kentos, has a similar tale to tell, except that Helen was born in Townsville, the daughter of a Greek who had migrated to Australia earlier in the century. Helen's father had a confectionery shop in Townsville during the depression, and although she still remembers with longing the tantalizing dark chocolates with walnuts on top that her father made in his confectionery shop, she claims that never got to eat a single one. After school was out, the local Greek children went straight to Greek school to learn how to read and write Greek. Helen and the others would be ravenous as they walked from the public school to the Greek school, so they would dawdle past Mr Marendy's café, twice if necessary, because if the proprietor saw them, he would invite them in for milkshakes. These they drank from white, stemmed glasses as they perched on stools at the milk bar.

Helen's father later had cafés in Roma and Mullumbimby, but it was in his fruit shop in George Street, Brisbane, that Helen met John Kentos. On his annual visit to Brisbane from a café in Orange, John saw Helen working at her father's business and asked a matchmaker to inquire about marriage. Helen, however, having set her heart on a tall, dark, handsome Adonis for a bridegroom, heartily refused the proposal. On John's visit the following year, he asked again, and was again refused. The day before John was to return to Orange, Helen remembers that she was bent over the laundry tub while her grandmother washed her hair. As her grandmother poured the rinsing water over Helen's head, she was uttering a Greek blessing that translates roughly as a prayer that she might perform this act in preparation for her granddaughter's wedding day. Helen's father stopped at the laundry on his way to the Greek Club and he said, "Look, Helen, the man wants an answer." Helen says that to this day she does not know what possessed her, but she said, "Well, alright then." As her hair was towelled dry, Helen thought, "Oh, no. What have I done?" But it was too late; her father was gone.

When the family lived in Townsville during the depression, Helen was the eldest of five children, including twin sisters, and the sales from their father's confectionery shop were all the family had to live on. When the shop burned down, her father worked in Mr Marendy's café.

These they drank from white, stemmed glasses as they perched on stools at the milk bar.

At the betrothal party, which took place the following week, Helen saw the four Kentrotis brothers – George, Jim, John, and Peter – lined up at the side of the room. She didn't know which one was 'hers'. Her fiancé returned to Orange the next day, and although Helen saw

The Kentrotis brothers, were very similar in appearance, but they did not conform to the image of the tall, dark and handsome Adonis of Helen's dreams. John is not in this photograph, in which Vasi's husband, George, Peter, and Maria's husband, Jim, stand behind the counter of the Regal Café.

him during the week prior to their wedding, and even went to the pictures under the watchful eye of a chaperone, her impression of being married in this way is that it was like "getting into bed with a total stranger." "But," she adds as she relates John's early death, "John was the love of my life." Helen and John were married in 1950.

Greek women in Brisbane found it difficult to work in family cafés because their shops were likely to be situated some distance from their homes, making movement between the two spaces difficult. But in rural towns like Ipswich, women and children often worked in family cafés at various times during the day because they lived within walking distance and could move easily between their home and the shop.[188] Most of the Ipswich proprietors lived only a couple of blocks from the city centre. In the 1950s, Helen Kentos and her husband, John, owned the milk bar beside the Wintergarden Picture Theatre in East Street, and lived in rooms at the back. After they installed neon lights, mirrors, and a juke box, business thrived and, like most proprietors of cafés close to picture theatres, Helen and John kept particularly long hours. For Helen, these hours persisted seven days a week every week except for Christmas day and Easter. When asked to recall the worst thing about café life, Helen, who vividly remembers hanging nappies out at two o'clock in the morning with the aid of a lantern, says, "Oh, the endless longing for sleep."[189]

This photograph was taken on board ship only minutes after a bride arrived from Greece to marry Helen's uncle, the man without a hat near the centre of the photograph. Helen's mother is on the right with a young child on her hip and the bride is third from the left. One can only imagine what she was feeling.

Because cafés were too busy to accommodate young children, women mostly worked in the family café after their children were old enough to start school. Harry Londy's children went to the shop when school finished, and after dinner his wife, Theodoroula, took them home. When the Londy children were older, Theodoroula stayed at the café after they went home, working until ten or eleven o'clock at night.[190] Conomos records the lives of Greek women who worked alongside their husbands from 5am until midnight, sometimes washing and ironing until 2am the following morning, without ever having a holiday. While waiting to prepare coffee and toast for the rush that would come at interval and when picture theatres closed, they attended to household tasks like mending and ironing. They were also likely to work until a few hours before babies were delivered. Antigone Andronicus of the Club Café in Toowoomba recalls being in labour while she was serving, with her husband urging her to be patient until the pictures came out. Antigone left the café at midnight and her daughter, Gloria, was born at 4am.[191]

Other women left their children, for short periods, in the care of nannies. Some, however, saw little of their babies.[192] When Helen and John had their first child, Helen began providing baby items for friends and customers through warehouse contacts, finally opening a baby shop across the street. After a full day in the baby shop, she would cross to the milk bar and help John until the theatre trade finished, they had fed those returning from dances in Brisbane, and it was finally time to close up for the night. One day, when both lanes of traffic in East Street screeched to a halt, Helen glanced outside to see her 18-month-old daughter, at that time in the care of her father in the milk bar, standing in the middle of the street. Helen recalls with sadness accepting her mother's offer to raise the baby in Brisbane. Until Helen's children reached school age, she saw them only on Sundays.

Maria's Story

Maria Pavlakis was 29 yrs old when she left Greece in 1956 to live with her sister, whose husband had a café in Mareeba. Because relatively few Greeks lived in Mareeba at that time, and Maria couldn't speak English, her mother considered that Maria still had little hope of finding a husband and having her own house. To remedy the situation, Maria's mother, who was still living in Greece, arranged for the Kallinicos family in Ipswich to invite Maria for a holiday and organise a meeting between her and Jim Kentrotis,

a man 17 years Maria's senior. Jim was in partnership with his brother, George, at the Regal Cafe. Maria refers to this tradition of arranging marriages by 'proxenia' as "going on the market," and it is interesting that having one's own house, rather than falling in love, emerges as the primary issue when talking to Vasi and Maria.

Maria went to Ipswich on holiday in 1958. She stayed with the Kallinicos family and helped out at their shop, the Ritz Café, in Bell Street. When she was introduced to Jim, Maria remembered having seen him as he was leaving Fratsia for Australia in 1936, when she was nine. She agreed to the marriage. Maria and Jim married in 1958, and the reception was held in the Ipswich Trades Hall, with the Regal Café doing the catering and the café waitresses serving meals. Maria says, "I come to Ipswich for a holiday and I make my roots here and I stay forever." That so many Greek marriages in Australia were organised under similar circumstances demonstrates the significant fact that Greek cafés were not just a meeting point and a labour market for early male immigrants; they were also a site through which marriages were facilitated. For the Greek community, they were links in an effective network that stretched across state and even international boundaries.[193]

Maria worked in her husband's café until her two children were born; she was the dishwasher. The Regal also had three cooks, four waitresses and two counter staff at that time. Maria sponsored her brother, Jim Pavlakis, when he decided to come to Australia in 1960. According to Maria, Greeks had to have been living in Australia for five years before they could sponsor a relative, and they could only sponsor blood relatives. Jim's godfather, a very close relationship within Greek families, was therefore unable to sponsor him. Maria had only been living in Australia for four years at the time, but she remembers that the Mayor, Mr Finimore, came to her house one night and naturalised her so that she could sponsor her brother. Jim worked at the Regal Café with the Kentrotis brothers and when Tony Veneris was murdered in 1962, he bought Tony's Café.

Maria helped out with Jim's new business. She remembers the first time a customer ordered a steak. In her capacity as dishwasher, Maria had never had to cook a steak before, so she invited the customer behind the counter and he showed her how it was done. Her husband died in 1979 and the following year, she bought the building which housed the nearby Central Milk Bar and Café, built by a non-Greek proprietor, Bernie Smith, several decades earlier. When Maria took over the business with her son, Bill, the Central's regular customers stopped patronising the café. Maria feels that this was because of a misconception that 'Dagoes' had forced 'Aussies' out of business. She recalls two occasions, however, when she gave food to hungry men who had no money. The first never returned to pay for the meal, but the

> *Maria had never had to cook a steak before, so she invited the customer behind the counter and he showed her how it was done.*

second not only returned with the money, but he also encouraged his workmates to end their boycott of the café and business soon boomed.

For 25 years, Maria started work at the Central at around 4am, often not leaving until 1am next day. The hours were long because many jobs could not be done while the café was open; the filter in the exhaust fan over the deep fry unit, for example, was best cleaned while it was still warm but not in use. Reflecting on her life in the café trade, Maria says, "I enjoy all my life in Ipswich. I walk to the mall, everyone know me." After a moment's reflection, she adds, "It is different now – now people don't talk."[194]

Vasi, Helen, and Maria married three of the Kentrotis brothers. None of them knew the men they agreed to marry, but all of them were happy during their brief married lives. All of them said they had good lives with their husbands. And Maria grew misty-eyed as she told of his death. "I have good life with my husband. But," Maria shrugs her narrow shoulders, "I lost him." The Kentrotis brothers died within 12 months of each other and these women have been widows for nearly 30 years.

Maroula's Story

Not all Greek women entered marriages without any prior romantic feeling. Harry Tanos leased the Sydney Café in Nicholas Street, Ipswich, with his brother Christopher in 1951. Harry remembers that when he returned to Greece in 1962 to find a wife, he had 16 prospective brides to pick from, and he wanted Maroula. Maroula recalls that she had the option of marrying a wealthy man who had a coffee plantation in Africa. "I would have been treated like a queen," she says, with a glance in Harry's direction. "I always dreamed of going to Africa for the diamonds, or India for the rubies. But no," says Maroula, "I clicked with Harry and I got a milk bar."

They smile.

The Other Story

Because the labour women and children contributed partially explains the success of Greek cafés, women's involvement can be viewed from different perspectives: as an unusually equitable distribution of labour in terms of gender, as the exploitation of women, as slavery. While historians acknowledge that some male immigrants in the early part of the 20th century lived a life of virtual slavery, the young men who 'served their apprenticeships' went on to own their own cafés.[195] This was not the case for married women. In an era when many women were confined to the private sector, Greek women behind the counters may be viewed as a more equal distribution of labour, but a feminist analysis is more likely to read the situation as excluding women from the realm of value because they were not paid for their work. Speaking of the role wives and children played in cafés, Brisbane historian, Effie Detsimas, whose father had the Day Dawn Café in Queen Street and the High Hat Café in the Valley, says it was "a lot of work and no pay most of the time."[196] Most, though not all, of the women in this study spoke in terms of 'my husband's café', and the kind of work they performed arguably resulted in them occupying a different, and subordinate, position from the men with whom they worked, as is evident in some of the experiences shared earlier.[197]

Sadly, marriage by proxenia did not always produce the happy results that women like Vasi, Helen, and Maria report. It was an arrangement that could potentially lead to young women being cut off from their families to live like slaves in cafés on the other side of the world. Another woman who 'married into' a Greek café was a 24-year-old Athenian, the eldest of seven children. Her aunt proposed a marriage in 1947. The prospective groom was the 40-year-old brother of an acquaintance, who owned a Queensland café. Recognising the opportunity to provide a future for herself and her siblings, the woman accepted her aunt's proposal. She was married within a month of arriving in Australia, but she worked in her future brother-in-law's café from the day after she arrived and was never paid for her work.

The woman recalls the 1940s and 50s as being an exhilarating time, when towns bustled with social activity. Several picture theatres operated within walking distance of her brother-in-law's café – many people went to the pictures several times a week – and local dances were held regularly in the Town Hall. Her face lights up as she recalls the women who came into the café during this period. Before and after the evening session at the pictures, at interval, and after the dances, the café was alive with the sound of women in full-skirted taffeta dresses with yards of tulle underneath that rustled and swished as they walked, shimmering satin shoes that clattered on the café floor, and frocks of frothy material, as light as sea foam, that floated between the tables and made no sound at all. In an era of wide patent leather belts, marcasite claps, and narrow waists, long, slender gloves, black glass buttons, and hail spot fascinators, this woman never went shopping for clothes or accessories. Because she never went to a dance. Whenever she needed clothes, her husband bought them for her, which was source of amusement for the 'girls' in the local department store, especially when he went to buy a bra, because his English was "not so good."

The couple later had their own business and people who knew the town in those days recall that the woman's husband was a sociable fellow, often visiting other cafés and stopping for a chat, while she was left to run the business. One customer remembers going into their shop and nodding to the woman's husband, who was reading a newspaper on the front steps. The man called out to his wife, who was busy working in the kitchen, to come out and serve.

> *The prospective groom was the 40-year-old brother of an acquaintance, who owned a Queensland café.*

None of the woman's siblings came to Australia.

She did not see her mother again for 30 years

And she claims that she did not inherit her home when her husband died, because she had no children.

CHAPTER SIX

Serving Time Behind Bars: Growing Up as a Café Kid

Greek cafés were family business, and from an early age Greek children learned to work behind the milk bars and in the kitchens of their families' cafés. Amid hissing soda fountains, bags of potatoes, the smell of fish, and a steady stream of customers, they played their games, ate their meals, did their homework, and entertained their friends.

The presence of children in Greek cafés was not just a matter of 'kids' who were hanging around because they needed to be under adult supervision. The labour children contributed, even from a young age, was a significant part of family businesses. The family as an institution has played a vital role in financing and staffing small business in Australia, and Greek cafés are no exception.[198]

Most Greek cafés kept prices low to attract a wide section of the community, and, especially in the early days, proprietors relied on sponsored relatives, wives, and children to make their cafés viable. Even in later decades, many cafés depended on the unpaid labour of women and children, and this was the only reason some survived as long as they did. Also, when reliable, honest workers were hard to get, children were often used out of necessity.[199]

One of the earliest family-run businesses was Peter Comino's Oyster Saloon in Mackay. Comino started the business in 1906 and his wife and two children arrived from Greece to join him in 1913. After only one year, Kaliope Comino was taken out of school to work full-time in the shop, serving at tables and behind the counter, when she was only nine.[200] Some children were scrubbing the shop floor at the age of five, but selling lollies and cigarettes at the confectionery counter, for many 'café kids', proved the best training ground for café work.[201] Julie Nichles, of the Crown Café in Brisbane, learned to work a till at nine or ten years of age. Standing on a fruit box, she took the customer's docket and money and worked out the correct change – cash registers did not calculate automatically in those days. By the time she was 14, Julie was in charge of the busy milk bar, making sodas, milkshakes and sundaes.

Each of the second generation Greek-Australians interviewed in this project worked in their family's Ipswich café. On an average evening in the 60s, when the Regal and Ritz Cafés would be jam-packed with families out window shopping, café staff needed all the help they could get, and the kids pitched in. Children were not paid for their work and many worked full time after finishing high school.

The Kentrotis family owned the Regal Café. Like the families of most Ipswich Greek cafés, they lived close to the town centre, so the children walked between home, the café and Blair State School. Joanne helped her parents, George and Vasi, from 7.30am until it was time to head off to school. She returned to the shop after school finished. Joanne also worked during the school holidays, particularly

from the early 70s, when her parents were getting older, and she worked full-time at the café after finishing high school, when her responsibilities included taking orders, serving meals, and doing the banking. Her brother, Bill, started helping his parents when he was about seven years old and continued to work after school and on weekends until he went into the construction industry.

While Joanne and Bill worked in the shop, their younger sister, Marianne, had a different kind of job. Her task was to 'work on the lollies', which meant that she had to make sure she smuggled enough lollies home from the café for the other two. It is interesting that 'café children' relate memories of not being allowed to help themselves to café food. Emmanuel Cominos, whose father had a big café in Cairns, recalls that if he wanted an ice cream, he had to go to his father and ask, and his father would give him the money so that he could go to the relevant counter and purchase the item like any other customer.[202]

As a small child, Bill worked mostly 'out the back', often in the company of his Uncle Jim, with whom he was great mates. Standing on a box beside Jim, Bill helped with the washing up. Chipping the potatoes was another of the jobs they shared. Having climbed up onto a pile of boxes with a bucket of potatoes, Bill could tip them into the electric potato tumbler, which was housed downstairs. When the machine had taken the skins off, he retrieved

the potatoes from a chute at the bottom of the machine and hauled them by the bucket load up the stairs into the shop, where he and Jim cut them into chips by hand. The pair would do two 150 pound bags of 'spuds' every second day. Bill remembers dragging a stinking, half-rotten bag of potatoes toward the tumbler, loudly protesting all the while that he refused to put his hands into the bag. "Son," said his father, whose poverty-stricken Kytherian childhood had left him with a deep appreciation of the value of food, "there's some good potatoes in there." Bill also cleaned and crumbed fish ready for freezing, and he remembers that his hands smelled like fish for three days afterwards.

Many café proprietors did not drive, especially those who lived close to their shops as did most of those in Ipswich. Some businesses, like Risson's Produce and Berry's Smallgoods in Nicholas Street, made regular deliveries to the café – like many of Berry's customers, Bill remembers the delicious, smoky smell of Berry's hams. At other times, someone had to fetch goods for the café. Someone in the family owned a Mk2 Zephyr utility, which was parked in front of the café for this purpose, but because George never had a drivers licence, fetching produce for the café on foot was a job that often fell to Bill. He feels that from the age of nine he was always walking around town with a box of something or other in his arms. He collected boxes of lettuce and tomatoes from a supplier in Ellenborough St and fish from a supplier at the top of town, who sold wholesale to the Regal. A milkman, who pulled up in front of the café, brought milk inside in a ten-gallon milk can, from which he filled the café's four-gallon canisters. Bill helped his dad lift these in and out of the milk bar. Orange and lemon drink was also stored in these containers and batching up the popular drinks from fruit juice, flavoured essence, and sugar was another of Bill's jobs.

Life was very similar for the children at the Ritz Café in Bell Street. George and Demetra Kallinicos, who were relatives of the Kentrotis family, had three sons – Minas, Manuel, and John. They too washed up or served behind the counter after school and on Saturday mornings and school holidays. The Ritz Café was next door to the Ritz Picture Theatre, and the last five minutes before intermission was a particularly busy time at the café. Manuel remembers the flurry of activity as he and the other children helped café staff to roll hot chips in newspaper ready for the onslaught that was to come. Manuel recalls, "There were certainly times when we would have liked to go and play, but we had to work in the café. We didn't know any different; that was just the way it was." Like most other cafés, the Ritz operated seven days a week. Manuel recalls that this dropped back to only six days in the 1960s, although Sunday, their day off, was usually spent cleaning the café.[203] Peter Londy and Jack Stathis belong to an earlier generation of 'café kids' and they too worked in their families' cafés before school. Jack and Peter noted that, while their older brothers were able to attend university when they finished high school, they were given no option but to work at the café.

In the middle decades of the 20th century, children whose families owned Greek cafés had less leisure time than most Ipswich children. Café kids were expected to work in the shop when they were not at school, so their lives were perhaps more like those of Australian farm children, who helped their parents with the milking and were responsible for poultry and the like. At this time, sport was a favourite childhood activity, as it is now, and Bill, a keen cricketer, remembers feeling that as a café kid in the 60s he missed out on a few things, especially on playing sport. He and his father clashed when Bill wanted to play cricket. Sometimes he would "duck off" to play hockey, trying to get back to the Regal before he was missed, but this was not so easy to accomplish with a cricket match. Prior to WWII, Jack Stathis, who was a young boy in the City Café, recalls that his father, Nick, had a similar position on sport: "If you've got energy left over, you can put it into the shop."[204] This suggests a significant difference between Greek and non-Greek Australians' attitudes to sport and the relationships between work, sport and masculinity.

Even though café families worked all year round for much of the 20th century, closing only on Christmas Day and Good Friday, Greek picnics are fondly remembered as rare occasions when families would leave the drudgery and hard work of café life behind, if only for a few hours. The Kentrotis family occasionally took the train to Shorncliffe, where they set up tables by the sea and were soon joined by other Greeks. Vasi, of course, packed plenty of Greek food. George would announce that he was "going to the office" and soon returned with bottles of Bulimba and XXXX. The adults sat together laughing and talking and eating all day while the kids played and swam. Sometimes, during summer, the Kallinicos family went to Margate, where George erected a shelter that he had had custom-made. Tyre tubes roped to the top of the car were ready for use in the water. Manuel remembers one week-long holiday at the beach in the mid-60s. In winter, they often went to Lowood shooting ducks, pigeons and hares, from which their mother would make a traditional stew.

Knowing that he or she was somehow different from Anglo-Australian children was another aspect of the Greek-Australian child's life. Many café children recall their parents being called 'dagoes' and being told to go back where they came from, particularly by regular, usually-friendly customers, who had had a few drinks. Several remember their fathers bodily throwing these inebriated 'regulars' out of their cafés.[205] One day, a drunk from the pub in Nicholas Street came into the Ritz Café. When he became particularly abusive, calling Manuel's father a 'dago' and other similarly derogatory terms, George asked him to leave the premises. The drunk refused and the abuse continued. Manuel says, "My father was not a big man, but he was tough. He leapt the counter and laid into the man with the lump of four by two that he kept under the counter for dealing with disturbances." According to Manuel, the drunk returned with a policeman, who listened to both sides of the story then said, "Mr Kallinicos has the authority to beat the crap out of you in his own café. I never forgot that."[206]

Some 'café kids' were called 'dago' at school and were involved in fights on a regular basis. Jack Stathis claims that he had to fight someone every day of his school career for calling him 'dago', 'wog', or 'greaser'.[207]

Andrew Tanos of the Sydney Café.

Bill and Effie Kentrotis with their mother, Maria, and their Uncle Jim.

He was so accustomed to this form of abuse that one day, when a teacher told Jack, who was a dayboy, to give a boarder an instruction, and the boarder replied, "You can't tell me what to do; you're just a day. . ." Jack immediately launched his assault. What the boarder had been trying to say was, "You can't tell me what to do; you're just a day-goer."[208] Helen Kentos recalls offering the shelter of her umbrella to a classmate on the way home from school. The boy said, 'dago' and spat on her. Helen is still astounded by this because the boy was Russian, but in an evolving multicultural landscape, alliances between and against ethnic groups are to be expected.

Manuel has similar recollections of his schooldays. He particularly remembers one science class when a boy "from a well-known, well-respected family" started abusing him within hearing of the teacher, calling him a "greasy dago". The teacher did nothing and when Manuel asked if he could shift, the teacher replied, "No, you sit there." This attitude was not always the case. Jack's brother, Jim Stathis, punched a boy at school one day because, when Jim was dressed in his cricket whites ready to play, the boy said, "Dagoes can't play cricket." The child was concussed, so his father appeared at school next day and Jim was hauled before the principal and the child's irate father. When Jim recounted the event, however, the father didn't want to take the matter any further, declaring, "I thought I had raised my son better than that."

Other children, like Jo and Bill Kentrotis and Marina Londy, report having no trouble fitting in. While food had the potential to single out migrant children – Charlie Pisasale's 'frog sandwiches' being a prime example – many Greek café kids, took 'Australian' café food for school lunches and did not encounter this problem. The Kentrotis children's lunches were more interesting than vegemite sandwiches, but Bill recalls that his lunch fascinated his schoolmates, who wanted to try it and usually liked it. His 'Greek' lunch only enhanced Bill's popularity.

Vasi, who still loves to cook, packed Bill's lunch with meatballs, pastitso – a spaghetti pie with spaghetti set in custard with cheese on top – spinach pie, and semi-circular pastry parcels with silver beet, egg and cheese inside, folded, crinkled at the edges and deep fried, which were Bill's favourite. "But," says Bill, "I'd have killed for a jam sandwich." Bill especially remembers the popularity of his mother's seratigano, a rolled pastry dropped into hot oil and dusted with icing sugar, which is used for weddings and special celebrations among the Greek community. This he swapped for jam sandwiches. Even Bill's teachers delighted in raiding the Greek sweets in Bill's lunch. His favourite teacher, Mrs Wallace, who taught Bill in grade one, would let out a shriek of delight and swoop on the flaky pastry dripping with sticky syrup in his lunch box: "Billy, is that what I think it is?" Vasi sometimes sent a plate of baklava along to school for Mrs Wallace.

Helen Kentrotis is married to one of Bill's three cousins who are all also called Bill. Helen remembers that Greek-style school lunches were especially interesting during lent, when she was denied meat and dairy products. "Our mothers, determined to make us good little Greek orthodox children, would fill our lunchboxes with olives and tarama sandwiches – trendy now, but try explaining the salty fish egg concoction spread between thick white bread to your Aussie friends! . . . Our mothers would try different ways with lentils and vegies, all the while calling us 'tourki' (Turks) if we so much as looked sideways at a steak!"

Bill often visited his Uncle John, who owned the Wintergarden Milk Bar and lived near the General Hospital. Bill remembers John's garden. At that time, many Australians grew grapes and vegetables and raised 'chooks' in their backyards, but Greek Australians grew unusual produce like orca, zucchini, eggplant, and broad beans. Vasi had a huge fowl run in her backyard, from which she supplied all of the Regal's chickens, which Bill helped kill and clean. "That was another one of my jobs," he recalls. "All of the chooks at the Regal came out of the backyard of number 39."

Effie is Jim and Maria Kentrotis' daughter, a cousin to Joanne and Bill. She remembers little of her early years at the Regal Café, where her father was in partnership with George, but has vivid memories of the time her mother worked at Tony's Snack Bar with her brother, Jim Pavlakis, and later at the Central Milk Bar. Effie recalls that as a seven year old, she couldn't wait to start using the cash register at Tony's. She had to climb up on to the fridge door handles to reach the numbers, but was soon able to serve customers. Weekends and holidays for Effie and her brother, Bill, were always spent in the shop, even Christmas Day. "Tony's Café was probably the only shop open," says Effie. "Everybody came in for drinks, cigarettes, bread, and milk. One Christmas was so hot we sold every single drink in the shop. Even the McMahon's stubbies went."

Effie's brother, Bill, remembers that Christmas too. It was 1971. He was 12 and the temperature in the shop was 41 degrees. Bill's job was to stack fridges, serve customers, and control the crowd. When the shop overflowed, he took orders from customers waiting outside the shop and ran back to the kitchen to place the order. This went on all day until he finally finished up at nine o'clock. Another Christmas also stands out in Bill's memory. It was many years later. He was short of hot chips, so he decided the fairest thing was to limit customers to two dollars-worth each. The shop was full of customers waiting patiently for their two dollars-worth of chips, when someone came in and ordered five dollars-worth. Bill explained the situation, but the customer became irate. Finally, Bill said, "I don't need this." He threw all the chips in the rubbish, shut the shop, and went home.

Unlike most Ipswich 'café kids', Bill took over the family business. After leaving school in 1977, he turned up for work at the Central Milk Bar every day, seven days a week, guiding the shop through Ipswich's boom times and slumps, until his first holiday in 1995. Then he cut back to five days a week. Bill took his daughters to the shop with him during their school holidays. Marissa and Olivia would leave with Bill at the crack of dawn and come home late at night exhausted. They specialised

Mrs Wallace, who taught Bill in grade one, would let out a shriek of delight and swoop on the flaky pastry dripping with sticky syrup in his lunch box.

in clearing tables, with Bill struggling to explain that it was rude to hover around the table watching every mouthful and asking if customers were finished yet. Bill's wife, Helen, believes that growing up in a café had a positive impact on 'café kids' and, while she and Bill strive for a better life for their girls, she is glad they had a taste of shop life, even for those few years. Bill finally closed the doors of Central Milk Bar in March 2006 after nearly 30 years. He no longer had the energy to keep it going and someone came along with supposedly better ideas for running the shop. After six months he handed back the keys, but Bill is definite that he will not take the café on again. He's done his time.

The experience of Andrew Tanos of the Sydney Café is unique among the stories of Ipswich café kids. The hectic pace in a Greek café could not accommodate babies and toddlers, so when children were very young, most women stayed home with them. Because families lived within walking distance of their shops, mothers could also leave children with baby sitters and walk to the café to help out during busy times, or take children to the café at night during slower periods. The family and staff at the Sydney Café, however, lived in the rooms above the shop, so for Christopher's son, Andrew, the café was a playground and he spent his early childhood years riding his tricycle around the block. "That was my backyard," says Andrew. "I used to envy kids who lived in a real house . . . but that was the only life I knew . . . there were always lots of people around . . . it was noisy."[209] The only occasion when Andrew was not allowed in the shop was when meetings across the road at the Trades Hall adjourned to the café so participants could have a meal. His recollection is that, with the exception of Christmas Day, the Tanos family worked for 11 years without a holiday.

For most second generation Greeks, Greek was their first language and most Greek children in Ipswich went to Greek School with other café kids early on Saturday mornings at the Central Methodist Church. Manuel Kallinicos and Bill

Kentrotis remember this. It does not seem to have been very popular with the children and they recall that it didn't last long.

Despite the hard work and lack of time for sport, which is so much a part of the Australian childhood, Bill believes his early years at the Regal Café instilled sound life values. He learned the value of hard work, but he also came to appreciate the importance of family. For Bill, the worst thing about his childhood was seeing how hard his father worked. George left home at four o'clock each morning and worked until midnight seven days a week. He suffered from arthritis and his legs were so badly bowed that he walked with a trademark limp. Bill saw his father at the café, but he was never really able to spend time with him.

But life in a Greek cafe was not all hard work and no play. When asked to recall the best thing about growing up in one, most respondents, especially the men, immediately remember a particularly positive aspect of life for a café kid. "Well," says Jack Stathis with a boyish grin, "you never went hungry."[210]

CHAPTER SEVEN

Fun and Games: Good Times and the Greek Café

Happiness is like coke – something you get as a by-product of making something else

– Aldous Huxley[211]

Although they existed primarily to sell food, Greek cafés became involved in people's lives. The activities that took place inside them were therefore not restricted to over-the-counter exchanges of meals and money. Also, because Greek cafés were woven into the social fabric of Australian culture, when the winds of change blew through communities like Ipswich, life changed for café proprietors too.

The next three chapters look more closely at aspects of café life, in particular, the good times associated with running a café, the difficult times cafés shared with their communities, and the extraordinary years of the Second World War. First, practical jokes and the exploits of SP bookies are highlights of this chapter, which focuses on happier aspects of café life, including relationships between café proprietors, and interactions between proprietors and the local community.

For locals and for travellers passing through, Greek shops are more than just somewhere to grab a quick bite. The Central Milk Bar in Ipswich, for example, trades mostly in takeaways and drinks, but because it has occupied a site in the centre of town for several decades, it has, on countless occasions, also been a source of information, especially for people from out of town. When Maria Kentrotis retired in 2005, she had worked at the Central for over a quarter of a century. Maria routinely arrived by four o'clock to get the milk bar ready for business by six. On one occasion, she was disturbed by a semitrailer driver pounding on the front door. It was five o'clock. On his way west, the driver had missed the Ipswich bypass and had been circling the CBD trying to get out, when he saw Maria preparing for the day's trading. She directed the truckie to the highway and later told local politician, Paul Pisasale, to do something about the signage, which he did. Not only was Maria the only one around at that time of the morning, but in her role as café proprietor, she knew her hometown well. Interestingly, when I visited the Central to talk to Maria's son after she retired, a motorist came into the shop with a street directory to ask Bill for assistance.

Staff at the Central: (from right) Bill Kentrotis with his mother, Maria, Maria's brother, Jim, and his wife, Lumbrini, Maria's sister-in-law, Vasi, and Vasi's granddaughter, Melissa.

Jim Kentrotis enjoying a well-earned break at the back table of the Regal Café.

In addition to helping visitors with directions and local information, proprietors knew how to look after local customers. Harry Tanos at the Sydney Café sold a particular brand of cigar, which was so expensive that no other Ipswich café stocked it. Only two customers ever bought these cigars – a man from Scott's Foundry and one from Faulkner Motors – but Harry stocked the cigars just for them. "Those cigars cost about two shillings each," says Harry, "but they would last them all day." People also made a habit of stashing their belongings in Greek cafés. In Ipswich, many regular customers were country people who, on their weekly trips to town, formed close relationships with particular proprietors. Harry remembers the weekly visits of a particular farmer whose wife had recently died.

The widower used to pack his dirty clothes in a suitcase and bring them into town each week for his sister to wash. He habitually left the suitcase with Harry while he did his shopping, returning at the end of the day to collect it and take it to his sister's. One day, the man had come in and left the case as usual, but another customer, who came later in the day, asked Harry to mind a suitcase full of new tools, which he had just purchased and did not want to lug around town while he finished his business. Harry agreed, of course, and stowed both cases in the kitchen. Each man returned as planned and collected his case.

On the same day of the following week, the second man walked into Harry's shop, holding a suitcase aloft and demanding, 'Who left this here? He's pinched me brand new tools and left his dirty, old clothes.' It was not long before the farmer turned up and wanted to know who had stolen his clothes. Between frying fish and cooking steak and eggs and making endless rounds of toasted sandwiches, Harry sorted the problem out. Leaving things with café proprietors or staff was not an unusual occurrence. Maureen, who was a waitress at Londy's Café in Ipswich during the 1940s and 50s, was often asked to mind suitcases for men while they went next door to the North Star Hotel. One man, who enjoyed a round or to with his mates at the bar, used to leave his wallet with Maureen so that he could not spend the entire contents of his pay packet. People trusted the proprietors and staff of their favourite café.

In another demonstration of how cafés served local people, a woman who worked in a nearby shop used to bring the meat for her family's evening meal into the Sydney Café. Harry would roast it and she would collect it on her

way home from work. Try getting a café to do that today. If nothing else, health regulations would not permit it. Another challenge Harry faced on an almost daily basis arose because the North Australian Hotel was situated directly across the street from the Sydney Café. Country people often drank at the pub, but because they didn't like to drink alone, they wanted Harry to come across the street and have a drink with them. But Harry had too many customers. And too many friends from out of town.

Greek proprietors appear to have had an equally benevolent relationship with the community as a whole. Jack Simos of the Paragon Café, for example, supported the Katoomba community; he was a foundation member the local Rotary Club, and the Paragon Café hosted the club's meetings for 55 years. Also, Peter Cominos explains that each year his father donated 1% of the takings of their shop – an extraordinarily large café in Cairns – to the local Ambulance Brigade. His customers 'posted' their dockets in a box at the front door as they left the café, and at the end of the year Mr Cominos totalled the dockets and worked out the percentage. In addition, behind the waitresses in a photograph of Londy's Café in Ipswich is a sign urging customers to support the Currumbin Beach Surf Lifesavers Building Fund Appeal by purchasing a souvenir badge for the price of a shilling. But perhaps the best-known story of generosity belongs to Mick Adams of the Black and White Milk Bar in Sydney. On the day that the milk bar opened, Adams donated the entire proceeds to the Dalwood Health Home for Children. He had served 5,000 customers. This donation became an annual promotional event marking the milk bar's anniversary.

At other times, Greek proprietors gave food to people who were unable to pay. Vasilia Corones

The Metro Café, Londy's Café, and the Regal Café worked to a Sunday roster so that families occasionally had time together.

of the Corones Hotel in Quilpie remembers people's struggles during the depression:

> Once, the bank manager lent us money of his own because he couldn't do it from the bank. We couldn't help ourselves, let alone anyone else, but still people wanted food and we gave them food. We gave free food to people in need. Sometimes, we'd let them roll out their swag in a corner of our hotel somewhere. We couldn't turn them away. People didn't have any money.

Elpiniki Black has similar recollections of Gero Black, one of the earliest café proprietors in Brisbane, and Helen Kentos believes that she would be a millionaire if she could collect on the IOUs her husband received at the Wintergarden Milk Bar in Ipswich during the 1950s.[212] Harry Londy was known to give food to coalminers during the prolonged strikes that plagued Ipswich from time to time. This repeated generosity and community-mindedness may have stemmed from proprietors' impoverished backgrounds and from the fact that many cafés were becoming established during the depression years, a time when many people experienced hardship.

The relationships between café proprietors was quite complex. When they were 'strangers' to each other, they often treated Greek cafés as 'the opposition', even though both were aliens in a foreign land.[213] When they were related, however, they often cooperated in significant ways. Most of the café proprietors in Ipswich were related because a good number of them came from Kythera, and Maria remembers no competition. The Metro Café, Londy's Café, and the Regal Café worked to a Sunday roster so that families occasionally had time together. Maria recalls those times as "golden days." She says:

> *The Sunday we have closed we gather all in one house and we have (she laughs) ball. Oh, you never know what it was because – all the children. By then they have some more families. We gather all and the most we gather in Mrs Stathis' house – she loves entertaining. It was lovely days. Yes!* [214]

Jo Stewart from the Regal Café, on the other hand, notes that there was always rivalry between Kytherian cafés. Greeks are passionate about their food and proprietors had definite views about who made the best chips, the best ice cream, the best mixed grill, the best toasted sandwiches, and so on.

Despite this, café proprietors cooperated in ways other than the roster system. The 'grapevine' proved an effective means of communication between the Greek cafés in Ipswich. Proprietors phoned each other when 'the potato man' arrived to see if others wanted him sent around, and when the Health Inspector put in appearance at one café, word quickly spread to the others. The same applied to price inspectors during the war. Jack Stathis from the Metro and Harry from the Sydney also mention that proprietors agreed on prices. On one occasion, when a salesman travelling through town claimed that prices in Ipswich cafés were the cheapest in Australia, Mick Londy called the local proprietors to a meeting, at which all except Nick Stathis agreed to add threepence to the price of their meals. Also, Peter Londy describes the way owners accessed the best fish and fruit through café connections in other towns. He recalls that his

father was part of a much bigger café network extending well beyond Ipswich, which enabled Ipswich cafés to access fresh fish and fruit from Maryborough, Brisbane and the South Coast. Even if there were no good fish at the Brisbane fish markets, there would always be fresh fish at Londy's Café in Ipswich.

Greek weddings provide further evidence of the close relationships between the Greek families, particularly those who were related. Jim Stathis recalls the way proprietors worked together on his wedding day. In the lead up to the wedding at St Paul's Cathedral, 250 guests had been invited, but only 200 had accepted. Knowing that most people would come, whether they got around to an RSVP or not, Jim's family catered for 250 guests. When 300 turned up to the reception at the Trades Hall, there was not enough food.[215] The bride and groom arrived and were detained in a side room while the local cafés got to work making extra meals. Jim recalls this occasion with great pride and gratitude.

Fun and Games

Cafés meant hard work, but there were plenty of occasions when Greek and Anglo-Australian staff made time for fun. Lily was a local Ipswich girl, who started working for the Stathis family at the Metro Café in 1955. She was 16 years old. Lily loved the years she spent in the café and when asked to recall what, specifically, was good about them, she responds, "What wasn't? I had a whale of a time." As she poses with Jack, Mrs Stathis, and another waitress for a photograph behind the Metro counter, Lily's cheeky grin suggests that she has always known how to enjoy herself and, although Mrs Stathis ran a tight ship, Lily and the other staff had a lot of fun when she was not around.

Lily particularly remembers 'mucking around' in the kitchen with Peter, a relative of the Stathis family. Pumpkins were prepared in great quantities for roast meals. Using big chopping knives, the staff peeled them and then chopped them into halves, quarters, and then into eighths. One of Lily's favourite games was to stab a chunk of pumpkin when Peter wasn't looking and, with a flick of the blade, throw it across the table at him. If Peter was quick enough, he would catch it on his knife with a swift upthrust of the blade and flick it back. Talking to Lily, it is difficult to decide whether to include her experience of café life in the chapter on fun or the one on hardship, because one day Peter missed the pumpkin and Lily's hand was impaled on the blade.

Another memory, and one that still brings a twinkle to Lily's eye, is of tricking Jack Stathis into cooking her tea. Staff members normally made their own meal at a time that was convenient, but on this occasion, Lily wrote an order for grilled pork fillet, a 'coupla' chips and some salad on her order pad and passed it through to the kitchen, where Jack was the cook. He made up the order and called it out to her. "Thanks, Jack," she grinned and she sat down and ate it. Predictably, water fights were another of Lily's favourite pastimes. The Metro Café was not the only café in town where staff knew how to turn the hard work and drudgery of café life into fun.

> One of Lily's favourite games was to stab a chunk of pumpkin when Peter wasn't looking and, with a flick of the blade, throw it across the table at him.

One Greek man whose family owned a popular Ipswich café was particularly fond of practical jokes. On one occasion the gentleman in question – let's call him 'The Joker' – had been playing preffa, a card game best described as three-handed bridge, with two other local Greek proprietors. Cafés at this time bought sides of pork with the tails still attached, and when one of the men, a rotund fellow, got up to leave, 'The Joker' grabbed a pig's tail, evidently prepared for the event, and furtively hooked it onto the back of the man's trousers. 'The Joker' and the other player watched the man walk out of the café with the curly tail swinging behind him. They stifled peals of laughter until he was out onto the street and heading back to his own café. Rumour has it that the tail went swing, swing, swing, swing, all the way home.

After a triumph like this, it was not long before 'The Joker' struck again. Greek cafés often had amenities beneath the shop, and on one occasion when a cook was showering in a cubicle underneath the café, 'The Joker' hit upon an ingenious plan. Proprietors made syrups to lace the top of their ice cream sundaes – strawberry syrup consisted of boiled strawberries enhanced with bright red food colouring. 'The Joker' poured the glistening, red, strawberry syrup carefully between the floorboards directly above where the cook was showering. As the red fluid ran down the cook's body and circled the drain, the poor man assumed he was haemorrhaging. Believing that he was not long for this world unless he found help immediately, the cook burst from the shower to find 'The Joker' leering at him from behind the syrup bottle.

Encouraged by the potential of the basement facilities, 'The Joker', and doubtless those around him, also derived great pleasure from the occasions when he set fire to a roll of newspaper and ushered wisps of smoke under the door of the toilet when it was engaged. This was followed by tongues of flame and shouts of "FIRE! FIRE!" The victim would rush out of the toilet with his pants around his ankles and fall, once more, into the hands of

'The Joker'. Other issues cropped up in the café from time to time, which required 'The Joker's' special touch. A situation arose concerning a man who had reason to be in the café on a regular basis and was stealing eggs, also on a regular basis, by smuggling them out inside his clothing. Everyone knew he was doing this, but no one confronted him. So, one day, as the gentleman was leaving the shop, 'The Joker' accidentally on purpose bumped into him, causing a sudden and inexplicable explosion of eggs on the floor around the man's feet. The situation was resolved.

Other happy memories arise from cultural differences between Greeks and Australians. Greeks often congregated at cafes, generally in the last booth; visitors would be fed and very animated discussions would take place. As each spoke over the others, the conversation grew louder and louder until customers asked what the trouble was. They were told that it was just 'the oldies' deep in conversation about the old days. At other times, staff would teach Aussies to say filthy Greek words, telling them that they were greetings – words they should teach their mothers and sisters – and this resulted in considerable hilarity. At other times language confusion was unintentional. One woman remembers her mother's story about a lady who came into the shop and very quietly pulled her to one side to ask for tampons. The proprietor had no idea what the woman wanted, so she proceeded to repeat the word over and over, inquiring of the shop in general if everyone knew what this 'tampons' was. She thought the customer very rude when she turned and quickly walked out of the shop.

Drunks

In the 40s and 50s, pubs were as plentiful as Greek cafés in central business districts. Pubs and cafés were often next door to or across the road from each other, and between them, they catered for just about everyone in town. But being close to a pub had it downside. Pubs, at one time, had to observe six o'clock closing. In what was called 'the six o'clock swill', patrons made a mad dash for the bar in the final minutes before the bar closed, and were often well under the influence when they hit the streets looking for a meal. A Greek café, the only establishments that were open in the evening, was usually only metres away. When pubs were permitted to open later, their patrons were likely to come for meals in a similarly inebriated state at any hour of the night.

The Metro Café was across the road from the Palais Royal Hotel and local waitress, Lily Burke, recalls that drunks would roll in from the Palais until the café closed at about 11pm. "They were a nuisance," says Lily, "because they never knew what they wanted, but you had to be nice to them." Lily recalls that she would look up to see an unsteady gentleman weaving his way across the street and say, "Here we go again." Maureen, who worked at Londy's Café next door to the North Star Hotel, claims that drunks drank the black sauce to sober up.[216] Many cafés had Worcestershire Sauce on the tables and two slices of white bread were usually provided with meals. One Ipswich resident confirms that when he came in for 'tea' after a session at the pub he would pour black sauce over the bread and eat this while he waited for his fish and chips to cook.[217]

Drunks also put salt in the sugar as a prank, but while refilling sugar pots and sauce bottles was a nuisance, it wasn't the worst of it. "Sometimes," says Maureen, "they would buy a bottle of oysters and just go glug, glug, glug and drink them down. And if they ordered a greasy meal – a mixed grill or something like that – they'd be sick all over the table and we'd have to clean it up." On several of these occasions, Maureen retrieved customers' false teeth, which she cleaned and put aside for them when they returned. "If they were game enough," she adds. Maureen also speaks of an Irish customer who would leave his belongings with her before going into the North Star so that he would not lose them; he was invariably drunk when he came back for them.[218] Peter Londy notes that hungry drunks would often leave their shoes or watches with café staff as surety when their money had already run out in the pub.

Like many of the Greek proprietors, Con, Nick Penglis from a fruit shop further up Nicholas Street, and a man named Pappas enjoyed a weekly game of preffa.

Gambling

Playing cards is an integral part of the companionship and entertainment in the kafeneion, and many Greek proprietors in Ipswich were great card players. Don Risson, 'the potato man', commented that when he delivered produce it was not unusual to find several proprietors sitting in the back of a shop drinking Greek coffee and playing cards. In those days, proprietors used to take the day's takings home with them when they closed up for the night, and some of this money would change hands during late night card games. One local resident remembers that Tony Veneris, for example, had a regular poker game with three other men on Tuesday nights. The game started when the cafés closed and commonly finished around 2am, and a café's takings could grow or shrink considerably depending on how the cards fell. Ipswich's famous gambling story, however, belongs to the Sydney Café.

The Sydney operated in Nicholas Street and was originally two shops with a connecting door – one side was a milk bar and the other was a fish shop – but because of a winning casket ticket, proprietor, Con Honianakis, was able to renovate, removing the wall to

George Penglis in his Uncle Nick's Dodge truck on the family's Raceview farm in 1945. Nick was one of losers in the famous card game that still has the town talking.

make one big shop. Like many of the Greek proprietors, Con, Nick Penglis from a fruit shop further up Nicholas Street, and a man named Pappas enjoyed a weekly game of preffa. The trio had a tradition. Each week, the losers would pay for a casket ticket on behalf of the group. The price of the ticket was about five shillings and sixpence. On this occasion, Con won the game and the other two surrendered the money for the ticket, which Con bought in his name. The ticket won first prize – 6,000 pound, which was a considerable sum of money in the late 1940s. Con, however, refused to split the winnings with Nick and Pappas, so they took him to court. The pair won the case, but they were unable to collect their shares because of a 100-year-old gaming act forbidding the collection of money on a card game. Con died of a heart attack in the café soon after.[219]

SP Bookies

The spaces above the City and Ritz Cafés were originally used as function rooms, but when they were no longer viable, proprietors turned them into billiard parlours. George Kallinicos renovated the function room at the Ritz during the 1950s and operated it as a billiard parlour until 1968. According to George's son, Manuel, the parlour was not a rough area, but it seemed to attract that reputation and never became the family venue that was originally envisaged. Manuel remembers that his father had a "lump of four by two" under the counter, which he would take it out at the first sign of trouble: "If there was a ruckus overhead, Dad would race out of the café and up the stairs. You'd wait. Then silence. And down he'd come again."

Billiard parlours were popular in the 40s and 50s; at least five operated within about 200 yards of each other in the centre of Ipswich during this time. In addition to billiards, a game of two-up could be had in many billiard parlours, some of which had a raised section in the ceiling to allow the pennies to 'fly'. In others, patrons played a version of two-up with dice on a billiard table. The billiard parlour at the Ritz was accessed via steps at the side of the café, and, although Manuel and his brothers were forbidden to go upstairs, they sometimes managed to sneak past their father. Manuel remembers that Cribbage and Five Hundred were favourite games, but on Saturday afternoons, the lazy, golden air in the billiard parlour rang with the sound of the races being called over the wireless.[220]

In the days before television, congregating in billiard halls or pubs to listen to the races and have a bet or two was a national pastime. Before the government established the TAB, however, the only way to gamble legally was to place a bet at the track, where the bookies had to pay a fee to be registered. Australians, on the whole, felt that this did not constitute 'a fair go', and viewed the illegal SP bookie as a reasonable solution. SP stands for 'Starting Price' because the price was determined by the odds at the start of the race; punters didn't know what the odds would be when they placed their bets.

According to older residents, everyone knew who the local bookies were and where to go or who to ring in order to place a bet. SP bookies usually operated from their homes and punters simply rang them from the pub or the billiard hall. At other times, people operated from a corner of the pub on commission, taking bets and phoning them through to the bookie. One man who operated as an SP bookie claims that someone ran a book in nearly every railway workshop, mine, pub, billiard room, and milk run in Ipswich during the 1950s. At least one of the Greek café proprietors in Ipswich took bets for him. The man adds that punters had to be known to the bookie, or the man on commission, or have someone to vouch for them, but, in his view, racing people were reasonably honest and he carried few bad debts. Because he was operating outside the law, he could not, of course, sue punters who failed to pay, but he could 'blackball' them so that no one else would take their bets. No one wanted a reputation like that.

One resident explains that 'if any' was a term employed in case you couldn't get to a phone in time to place a bet on the next race; it meant that if there were any winnings, these were to be placed on the next race. Sometimes cash was collected after the last race. At other times, bets were 'squared' at the next opportunity. This was often on Mondays, or in the case of the railway workshops on payday. Another resident explains that he saw envelopes pass from hand to hand in all sorts of venues with barely a word being spoken – people knew what they owed or were owed and they 'paid up' or distributed the winnings accordingly. Describing the way that SP booking worked, local resident, Alf Colless, explains that "It was an honest system. Everyone had to rely on everyone else being honest. And they were."

Not only was betting with an illegal SP bookie a common practice, but many people also operated as SPs during hard times just to survive. Shirley (not her real name) is an Ipswich woman whose grandfather set up as a bookie for this reason just after the war. After a win on the casket, however, he had the "big idea" of going into SP booking full-time, and took over from another operator. His "big idea" paid off and he was soon "the town's biggest SP bookie." His son joined him and it became a family business. Shirley's grandfather had two phone lines installed in his home, and these were attended by his daughters-in-law. "My mother and my aunt weren't gamblers or drinkers or anything," Shirley adds. "They were just ordinary, respectable housewives." Both phones rang all day on Saturdays. Shirley, who was only about five at the time, was taken to the pictures every Saturday afternoon so that she would not be in the house while this illegal activity was taking place.

Most residents seem of the opinion that 'everyone' cooperated to allow the illegal gambling system to operate. Summing up the prevailing attitude, one Australian claims, "I'd say the majority of people took SP booking and two-up as a national pastime, but you had to be careful not to get caught, that's all."[221] Shirley claims that police understood and even the girls at the telephone exchange pitched in. They would cut off phone lines to her grandfather's house if a call came through to the effect that Brisbane police were on their way. Otherwise, if a raid was scheduled – and every now and then someone had to be 'caught' so that the police were seen to be doing their job – the bookie would hire someone to be on the premises so that an arrest could be made. Usually an old drinker would volunteer. The bookie would pay the fine of one guinea as well as the hiring fee, which sometimes amounted to a few bottles of beer. If you were convicted three times, then you had to go to jail, but most bookies avoided this. Shirley's grandfather gave the business away when Shirley's mother was arrested. He became a registered bookie.[222]

On Saturday afternoons, lookouts, often children, were posted outside pubs and bookies' houses to keep an eye out for the police. The lookout was called the 'cockatoo'. At a signal for the cockatoo, the evidence would disappear. SP bookies devised ingenious ways to hide evidence of punters' bets. Some used slates or wrote them on the wall in chalk. One man kept his tickets in empty milk bottles in the fridge of his billiard saloon. These were painted white on the inside and were always sealed with a foil top bearing the current date. The Greek café proprietor who took bets for Shirley's grandfather in Ipswich was careful never to hold any written evidence in his shop.

The ex-bookie remembers that the proprietor either memorised the details or phoned them straight through to him.

Shirley recalls incidents when police raided her grandfather's home. The tickets were never up in the manhole, she recalls, because that was the first place the 'coppers' would look. Sometimes they were in an old corset or under a false bottom in the wardrobe. After a hectic day, Shirley's grandfather, his sons, and daughters-in-law always shared a roast dinner on Saturday nights. On one occasion, the cockatoo sounded the alarm as Shirley's mother was about to serve dinner. When the police appeared, they conducted a thorough search, even checking the contents of the oven. Shirley smiles, "But they didn't check the stuffing inside the roast turkey, did they?"

Esther Brewer

A Queensland Times article from the 1970s celebrates some of the odd characters who used to frequent Ipswich streets. Here, local personality, Vic Loetzsch, recalls people like Nobby Keogh, who wore an overcoat tied at the knees with old neckties, Fairey Brown, who was always accompanied by six dogs, and Alf Harper, whose 90-year-old father chased him around their furniture store with a walking stick. There was Lennie Staples, the mad barber, Jackie Harrold, the one-armed swimmer, and Darkie Simpson, the morgue attendant, as well as an assortment of characters with intriguing names like Whistling Annie, Puppy Pie, and Sago Rice. But none comes close to a larger-than-life character mentioned by almost every person interviewed for this book – Esther Brewer.

Esther Brewer was a cook at the City Café in Brisbane Street and Esther "was a legend." These are the words of Yvonne Hawkins, who worked at Whitehead Photographic Studio uphill from the City Café, and this legendary status is undisputed. I was unable to find a photograph of Esther, and perhaps that's just as well; larger-than-life characters should never be reduced to the confines to a two-dimensional page. "She was the cleanest girl I ever knew," says Yvonne. The building that housed Whitehead's studios overlooked the laneway where Esther hung the café's laundry, and the items were always snowy white, even the mops. Yvonne recalls the café proprietors saying that Esther was the cleanest and the best worker they ever had. Don was often on the receiving end of Esther's meticulous cleaning regime when he delivered 'spuds' to the City Café. Hearing him come through the back door, Esther would sing out, "Don't you bloody well drop that down on my clean floor!" And there was hell to pay if he did.

Nola worked at Whitehouse's Café; she confirms that Esther ran the cleanest kitchen in town, but her strongest memory of Esther is her lipstick: "It was the reddest red you can imagine." And local resident, Dot Kennedy, remembers that Esther wore a leopard skin coat everywhere. "She was a larrikin," Dot adds. The 'larrikin', a much-loved Australian archetype, is usually male. Perhaps it was the larrikin's audacious behaviour, anti-authoritarian attitude, and unfailing sense of humour that set Esther apart from other women of her time. Arnold Dull, who delivered milk to Ipswich cafés, says that Esther as the funniest lady he ever met. When I ask him to elaborate, Arnold chuckles and offers nothing more. But his response is understandable when one considers some of the anecdotes surrounding the mysterious Esther Brewer and the joy she brought to the streets of Ipswich. Harry Tanos remembers that people would wave and call out to Esther as she drove down Nicholas Street in her utility.

On Saturdays, Esther often packed the ute with local kids and headed to the river for a swim, shouting the kids a milkshake at Harry's café afterwards. But the form of transport for which Esther is best remembered is her bicycle. On Sunday nights, when people used to walk the streets looking in the windows of department stores like T. C. Beirne and Cribb and Foote, the Salvation Army band would play on the footpath at Cribb and Foote's corner (now McDonalds). The Salvos in Ipswich have always had a large band and the bandsmen struggled to read their music, play their large brass instruments, and stop themselves from falling off the footpath onto the roadway. Esther, not known for reverence or a serious disposition, would come down Brisbane Street on her bicycle and whiz around the corner doing 50mph, keeping as close as possible to the gutter so that she would alarm the poor young bandsmen balancing on the edge of the kerb. And to see Esther come sailing down Brisbane Street on her way to work with her feet on the handlebars and her skirts up around her ears brought such merriment to bystanders that even today her name is never spoken without a smile.

The other aspect people recall about Esther is her passion for wrestling. Whenever she could, Esther went to the wrestling in Brisbane's Festival Hall and was often glimpsed in the front row when bouts were televised. According to Yvonne, Esther's enthusiasm sometimes got the better of her and she would reach through the ropes and grab a wrestler's legs. With her red lips, her leopard skin coat, and her whizzing bicycle, Esther ran a spotless café and had a larrikin sense of humour. But the name of Esther Brewer is perhaps still imprinted on the memories of people who lived in Ipswich during the 1940s and 50s because, like Princess Di, Grace Kelly, and Marilyn Monroe, Esther never grew old – at least not for the people of Ipswich. Accounts of what became of the fun-loving lady larrikin vary, but the most popular tale among the locals is that Esther went off to America with Killer Kowalski, a wrestler who won the hearts of women in Japan, Malaysia, Hong Kong, South Africa, and Australia, before he retired in 1977. But whatever became of the legendary Esther Brewer, no doubt she continued to bring a little of the sense of joy in just being alive for which she is so fondly recalled by the people of Ipswich.

CHAPTER EIGHT

Hard Luck and Health Hazards: The Tough Times

Police investigating the murder of an Ipswich café proprietor, found battered in his station wagon, have detained a young man. The victim was Antoine Theodoros Veneris, 48, of Quarry Street, Ipswich, a Greek. He has a wife and a five-year-old son, Theodore. They believe he had been robbed of about 100 pounds.

Brisbane Telegraph,
Friday April 6th, 1962

Early immigrants arrived in Australia with little more than the address of a kafeneion and the clothes they stood up in. The hardship they endured is related in earlier chapters. This chapter focuses on the stories of day to day hardship that was part of café life for Ipswich proprietors and their staff as the 20th century progressed, as well as some of the tough times that Greek cafés shared with the Ipswich community.

Café kitchens were a hive of activity. Produce boxes and old utensils lined walls and floors, stacks of dishes waited to be washed up – a never-ending job for café staff – and the entrance was a continual flow of waitresses moving back and forth with orders. Fish was frying, steaks were sizzling, and soup or boiling vegetables were simmering in big, black pots on wood-fired stoves. Those who worked in these kitchens remember that the heat was terrible. Cooks were a lather of sweat; their clothes were soaked and they wiped perspiration from their glistening faces with towels hung from their aprons specifically for the purpose.[223]

These kitchens were prone to accidents because kitchens are dangerous places and because health and safety regulations in the mid-20th century were a mere shadow of what they were to become in the 1990s. If the front of the shop appeared calm and under the proprietor's control, in the kitchen, pots of boiling water and hot fat pushed the temperature up, wood fires spewed soot into the stifling air, huge knives and electrical appliances were an ever-present danger, and the pressure of a shop full of hungry customers escalated the pace of activity and frayed the tempers of tired and overworked staff.

Photo courtesy National Museum of Australia, Canberra.
Noelle Sandwith's drawing, Greek Café Kitchen, captures something of the primitive conditions under which many proprietors and cooks worked. The drawing was made in a Greek café in Moree, NSW, in August 1952.

Kitchens sometimes caught fire – according to Jack Stathis, the kitchen at the Metro caught fire in 1963, when a toaster was left on, and Bill Kentrotes recalls that the Ritz kitchen caught fire too. It seems that these kinds of incidents were sometimes the catalyst for cafés closing down. When the kitchen at the Stathis family's Metro Café caught fire, the owners refused to renew the lease on the building, so the Metro closed down. Health Department inspectors presented another problem, when they demanded changes that were not economically viable for proprietors.

Health Inspectors

Although food-catering in earlier times was not subject to the stringent regulations that govern café practice today, health inspectors were a problem for Greek proprietors, whose main aim in life was to sell big serves of cheap food that would bring customers back – everything was plain and simple and prices were as low as possible. Inspectors often had a different agenda. Men like Bob Rogers in Ipswich regularly visited cafés to check that the floor had an impervious surface, that a wash hand basin was situated between the toilet and the shop, that it was supplied with soap, and so on. At the Sydney Café in Ipswich, fish was a 'big seller' and proprietor, Harry Tanos, sold a serve of fish and chips wrapped in newspaper for ninepence. But Harry had an on-going battle with health inspectors over the way the fish was wrapped.

The health inspector insisted that Harry use white paper to wrap the food because newspaper was unhygienic, but at ninepence a serve, Harry couldn't cover the cost of the fish and chips and the white paper. And he couldn't afford to put the price up. In frustration, he took the health inspector out onto the footpath and pointed to several of his customers, who were eagerly devouring chunks of battered fish and hot, salty chips. The Sydney Café was next door to T. C. Beirne, one of the town's two department stores, which had big shop windows with deep sills at about knee-height. It was the habit of many of the Sydney's customers to perch on Beirne's window sills with their fish and chips spread out on the footpath between their feet. Grit from Nicholas Street, which was at that time the main road between Brisbane and Toowoomba, drifted onto the footpath and into the customers' meals.

"See that," said Harry. "What difference does it make what I wrap them in?"

"I can see your point, Harry," the inspector agreed, as the pair turned to go back inside. "But it's the law. You still have to wrap 'em in white paper."

Inspectors also finally insisted upon upgrades to the Sydney Café's kitchen, where soot from the coal stove caused problems in the area of general cleanliness. Unfortunately, the building did not belong to the Tanos family and the owners did not want to sell. To make major renovations to someone else's building without a long-term lease was a financial risk the Tanos brothers were not prepared to take. This led to the family closing the business in 1961 and moving to Brisbane. With profit margins so small, and kitchen work so hazardous, it is little wonder that proprietors rang around to warn each other when the inspector was about – especially in a town like Ipswich, where nearly all of the café owners were related, although the Sydney Café was one of the few businesses not owned by Kytherians.

Accidents

Fires were not the only source of accidents. For Lily, a fun-loving waitress at the Metro Café, one Saturday morning particularly stands out in her memory. Lilly laughs as she recalls that day, although it was not very funny at the time. The Bundamba races were on, the café was busy, and Jack and Harry were cooking flat out. Lily took an order for "crumbed pork fillet for four and two halves," which meant meals for four adults and two children. A bell rang to signal that it was ready. Lily put the four adult meals on a tray with a pot of tea. This she balanced on one hand, while she held the two 'halves' in the other. The kitchen at the Metro had an 'in' door and an 'out' door and as Lily was backing out of the 'out' door, the tray caught on something, tipping the steaming contents of the teapot down the front of her uniform. She remembers little of the events that ensued; the following is largely pieced together from onlookers and other staff.

Lily ran out of the front door of the café and raced up the street flapping her uniform up around her stomach trying to get cool air onto her body. In shock, she rounded the corner into Bell Street and headed towards the railway station, raking the blistered flesh on her belly with her long nails. Café staff and customers set off in 'hot' pursuit, but none was able to catch her. Townspeople reported seeing the waitress heading down the street with strings of skin draped from her fingernails, but Lily was nowhere to be found.

Some time later, Harry heard someone whimpering in the storeroom at the back of the café and, suspecting that it was Lily, called the ambulance. Lily went to hospital with third degree burns. She grins, "I got a hernia from 17 years of lifting milk cans out of the café's milk bar too." If Lily's experience of café life is a mixture of pain and pleasure, there can be no doubt about the events that took place in the Veneris family's lives.

Tragedy

Kytherian immigrant, Tony Veneris, started work in Ipswich as an employee at the Ritz Café in Nicholas Street. He soon leased a shop of his own and married 22-year-old Crystallie (Doris) Canaris. Tony was 32 and his career as a café proprietor in the new land of opportunity was off to a good start. When the bank took over the building, Tony bought a block of shops at the bottom of Brisbane Street and opened Tony's Café. In 1956, their son, Theo, was born. Doris' father, a fisherman from the island of Castelloroso, had died of pneumonia in Townsville when she was five years old. Like Doris, Theo was five when his father died.

In the early hours of the morning on April 6th 1962, Doris answered a knock at the door to find police and family friends on the doorstep. Doris had been anxious that Tony was late home – he normally closed the café about 11pm – but the tragic news that Tony had been found murdered in his car nearby seemed so bizarre that she could hardly take it in. He had been shot in the head at close range with

GREEK CAFE PROPRIETOR BATTERED
MAN HELD ON IPSWICH CAR KILLING

LATE EXTRA

3-STATE FORM GUIDE TODAY

Police investigating the murder of an Ipswich cafe proprietor, found battered in his station wagon, have detained a young man.

THE FAMILY NEWSPAPER
TELEGRAPH
32-0101. BRISBANE, FRIDAY, APRIL 6, 1962. 44 PAGES—4d. (Air Freight Extra)

The victim was ANTOINE THEODOROS VENERIS, 48, of Quarry Street, Ipswich, a Greek. He has a wife and five-year-old son, Theodore.

- They believe he had been robbed of about £100.

Detectives recovered the money under a house at East Ipswich and found a Gladstone bag abandoned nearby.

They also found a sharpening stone, which they believe may have been used in the attack in a car in the East Ipswich area.

GET FIT

NO single sport — say the experts—provides a truly balanced development for all parts of the body.

This can be acquired only by regular participation in a number of carefully selected sports.

But for most of us this is impossible.

Tomorrow, the Telegraph will publish the first of six charts telling you how to get fit—and keep fit— for an outlay of only 11 minutes of your time each day.

This is 5BX, the scientifically designed Canadian plan for physical fitness—an easy to follow program without the aid of gimmicks or elaborate equipment.

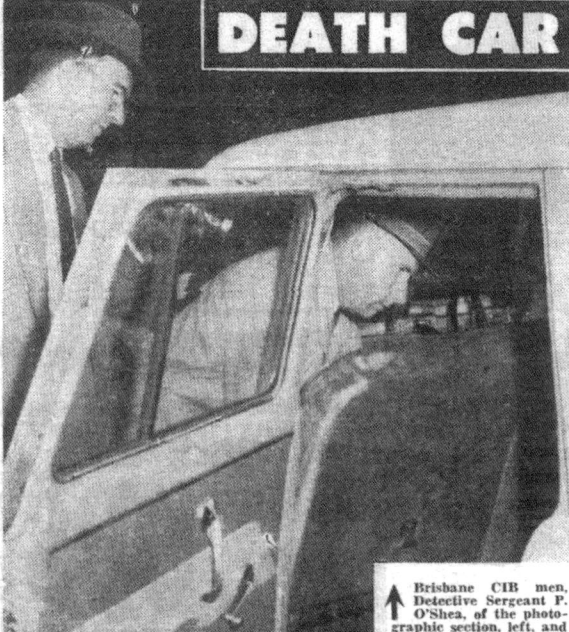

DEATH CAR

HEADLIGHTS FULL ON

Detective Sergeant J. Kerr, of Ipswich, was told that Veneris left his cafe and snack bar in Brisbane Street, Ipswich — the city's main street — at 11.15 last night.

At 12.5 a.m. Detective T. J. Wightman and Constable A. Allwood, who were on patrol, noticed that the headlights of a green station waggon which was parked in Garden Street, Ipswich, near Thorn Street were burning.

This was about three-quarters of a mile from Veneris's cafe.

They found Veneris badly battered at the back of the head, slumped across the front seat of the car.

Police believe Veneris still was alive then, and died in an ambulance on his way to Ipswich Hospital.

Check on cafe customers

Senior police were called and immediately began checking on Veneris' movements last night.

They obtained some information from his wife, Doris, and made inquiries about cafe customers, including those who were last to leave last night.

About 3.15 a.m. they went to an Ipswich house and later took a man to Ipswich Police Station for questioning.

Police have recovered a blood-stained man's coat.

The car was found near an Ipswich Council works depot only about 300 yards from Veneris' low-set green-and-white weather-board house.

Tyre mark and bloodstain

At the area where the car was parked police found an 8ft. tyre mark in the mud on the edge of the road and a 3in. bloodstain.

Rain could have washed away footprints that may have been made in the mud beside the road.

Detective Sergeant P. O'Shea took photographs of the area where Veneris' car was found, and of the car, and Detective C. P. O'Brien examined the car for fingerprints.

Man, 21, being questioned

Police have been told that about £20 of the £100 that was recovered was in silver, and the rest in notes.

Police today were questioning a 21-year-old man who was dressed in a pyjama coat and shorts.

Detectives E. A. Little and T. J. Costello are helping Ipswich Police Chief, Inspector W. J. Garvey, Detective Sergeant Kerr and Detective Wightman in the investigations.

Detective Sergeant J. Ryan and Detective C. Bopf, of the Brisbane CIB, went to Ipswich to help local police.

● Army service, P. 3.

Brisbane CIB men, Detective Sergeant P. O'Shea, of the photographic section, left, and fingerprint expert, Detective Constable P. C. O'Brien, examine the car in which Veneris was attacked. Constable M. J. Soden, of Ipswich, stands guard at the murder scene, at the corner of Garden and Thorn Streets, Ipswich.

Another £1000 for nothing

Telepix No. 9 appears today on Page 28 and again you can win £1000 for NOTHING.

You can send as many entries as you like and extra papers can be obtained from your newsagent or from the Telegraph.

There's always a payout in Telepix. If the top prize is not won, £100 will go to the nearest-to-correct entrant.

The result of Telepix No. 8 will be published tomorrow.

Thugs stab 4 dancers

LONDON, Thurs. (AAP): Twenty young thugs burst into a London youth club last night and stabbed four youths and beat up several others in five minutes of terror.

One, Victor Green, 18, was wounded in a lung. The others were less seriously hurt.

CITY FORECAST:
FINE
MAX. NEAR 77

Printed and published by Telegraph Newspaper Co. Pty. Ltd., 93 Queen St., Brisbane, at that address. Registered G.P.O., Brisbane, for transmission by post as a newspaper.

GIRL TOP RAF BASE OFFICER

SHIRLEY GOTT

LONDON, Thurs.: Group Officer Beatrice Barnett Parker today celebrated the news that she is to be Britain's first woman commanding officer of an RAF station staffed mainly by men . . .

She went out and had a new hair-do and bought some chic new civilian suits.

Blonde, 5 ft. 8 in. tall Group Officer Parker (her rank equals a colonel, naval captain or air group captain) is not daunted by the challenge that faces a woman in command of men.

"I've been in the Air Force since the day war broke out in 1939, and I think my experience of how men and women can work together will be absolutely invaluable," she said.

Group Officer Parker will take up her appointment as new C.O. at Spittlegate Base, Lincolnshire, on April 16.

Do men take easily to women commanders?

Group Officer Parker— aged 50 but looking a young 38—smiled innocently.

"I think my job will really be a question of common sense and knowing the psychology of how people work," she said.

"After all, we are all, whether men or women, part of the Service."

Group Officer Parker wears a pearl ring on her right hand.

"I'm all for marriage," she said. "It's just that it doesn't happen to have worked out for me."

She also wears glasses over her Air-Force blue eyes.

a .22 rifle. The day's takings, which Tony always carried in a Gladstone bag, were missing. Within hours, a rifle, a little over 100 pounds, and other identifiable articles from the bag were discovered at the home of the man Doris had suspected of the crime. The man, who regularly delivered meat to the café, shot and robbed Tony to pay some debts. He too had a young child.

One resident recalls that Tony's murder was the first time anything like that had ever happened in Ipswich. The story repeatedly made front-page news in *the Queensland Times*, the *Telegraph* and the *Courier Mail* over the next months, indicating that crimes of this nature were unusual at that time. The man Doris suspected was jailed for Tony's murder, but Doris says, "What good is that? It won't bring my husband back. It won't give the boy back his father." She hopes he has ulcers so that he cannot enjoy his food. "What worse punishment is there than that?" she asks. Everyone knew Tony Veneris because he was a café proprietor, and Doris recalls that St Paul's church was packed out for his funeral. A friend counted over hundred cars in the cortège.

"Personality plus, my husband was," says Doris, "Personality plus."[224] Doris and Tony had been married just 15 years.

Determined that her son's childhood would not be overshadowed by his father's death, Doris did not tell five-year-old Theo that Tony had been murdered; she told him his father was away on business. Theo did not learn about the murder until he was in high school. Then, when he was 40, he found a stack of old newspapers in a wardrobe at his family home. Yellowed and brittle with age, the papers featured one story in particular. Many times it was on the front page. "It was like reading a book when you already know the ending," Theo says, "but this was my father and mother they were talking about. It was really chilling."

Ironically, when he was a young man, Theo applied for a job at Cribb and Foote's hardware on the site that had once been the Ritz Café where his father had started work as an employee so long ago. "Fifty kids applied for that job," Doris says, "and they all had their mothers with them." But Theo went alone, having told his mother that if they asked him why he should get the job he would say, "I am willing to work hard and make money for the company." Theo got the job. He has now been in the hardware business for over 30 years and still follows his mother's advice, which was, "You don't want to make millions; just enjoy your life. And always treat people with respect."

The Great Flood

After Tony's death, Doris opened a book exchange and began Ipswich's first Coffee Lounge & Art Gallery in one of the shops beside her husband's café. She sold Tony's to Jim Pavlakis, who had been working in the Regal Café with the Kentrotis Brothers. Jim ran the café, thereafter known as Tony's Snack Bar, until he returned to Greece in the mid-80s. During this time disaster struck again, but on this occasion it was to affect a significant proportion of the homes and businesses in Ipswich. In January 1974, floodwaters inundated the city, rising to levels that had not been seen since 1893, and the block of shops that Tony Veneris had bought over 20 years before disappeared beneath the rising floodwater. The shops were submerged beneath 30 feet of water for five days.

Theo helped Doris evacuate the books in the exchange before the murky floodwater swirled in. When the water subsided, they shovelled

mud out of the shop and began the massive task of cleaning up and moving the books back in. Doris is now in her 80s. She still loves books and has a particularly soft spot for Phantom comics. Doris still opens the book exchange from Monday to Friday, working whatever hours she feels like. "People go out of their way to say hello to me," she says, "because I make them feel welcome."

While Doris and Theo were rescuing books from the rising floodwaters, Jim and his sister, Maria, were busy at Tony's Snack Bar. Maria's daughter, Effie has vivid memories of that day: "We had to remove all the electrical equipment to Mum's house. The shop was under water for two or three days. The Regal was still open so all the cold stuff was transported by car or foot to dad's shop." Some of the produce in Jim's cold rooms must have been left behind because Theo remembers a luxuriant crop of tomatoes that sprang up in the rich river silt behind the shops after the massive cleanup that followed.

When tragedy devastated the lives of Doris and Theo Veneris in 1962 and floodwaters inundated Tony's Snack Bar in 1974, these were landmark events that touched Ipswich people's lives in significant ways. Accidents and health inspectors, on the other hand, were difficulties that Greek café proprietors and their staff faced on a daily basis. Few customers realised the difficulties migrants had to overcome, even in the post-war period. As a bride coming to an Ipswich café in the 1950s, Maria had to teach herself to speak English, particularly as she became a proprietor herself.

While a lot of Greek women tried to learn English, many stayed in the kitchens, where language was not such a problem. But language was not the only difficulty Maria had to overcome. Greek currency was organised on a decimal structure, so when Maria came to Australia, she had to cope with a completely different mathematical system.

In those days, 12 pennies made a shilling (otherwise known as a 'bob') and two shillings was a florin (24 pence), a pound was 20 shillings and a guinea was one pound and one shilling (that's 21 shillings). And that's not counting farthings and halfpennies, threepences and sixpences. Maria says that in the early days she would lie in bed at night and think back over some of the day's transactions. Sometimes she cried herself to sleep, tortured by the knowledge that she had probably short-changed a customer, or the proprietor, through her inexperience. Those of us who remember the arrival of decimal currency will have some idea of Maria's bewilderment. When I tell her that I had difficulty coming to terms with two pennies equalling two cents and three pennies equalling two cents and four pennies equalling three cents, when decimal currency arrived in Australia to the tune of *Click Go the Shears* on the 14th of February, 1966, she laughs and throws her hands up in the air. "Oh," she says, "the best day of my life."

CHAPTER NINE

'Oversexed, Overpaid, and Over Here': Wartime

It was wonderful, here was all these men [...] with flowers, manners, cigarettes for Mum, chewing gum, chocolates, taking you out to restaurants, we couldn't believe all this.[225]

The Second World War was a hard time for many Australians. The battlefront deprived families of husbands and fathers, many of whom never returned, and civilians lived with limited supplies of food, clothing, petrol, and other necessities.

It was also an extraordinary time; there were blackouts, air-raid drills, rubber and aluminium drives, and casualty lists. But it was the sudden influx of American servicemen with their cash, confectionery, and charm that made the Australia of the war years seem like a foreign country. For many young women and children, life improved during the 1940s. Some Australians remember the war years as "just one great pack of fun."[226]

Many greeks in food service industries were spared conscription, but many also joined the ranks of the Australian Army. Jim Bellas, later of the Star Milk Bar in Brisbane, was conscripted, and George Kallinicos enlisted prior to taking over the Ritz Café in Ipswich. George had worked in several cafés and his officers prized his culinary skills so highly that they snaffled him for the officers' mess and refused to let him see active service.[227] For those who served behind café counters during the war, however, rationing and the presence of American and Australian soldiers presented significant challenges.

Rationing

Petrol rationing had been in place since 1940, but in 1942, when Australia was in the grip of the Second World War, Prime Minister, John Curtin, announced that 'a season of austerity' had arrived:

> *The civilian population can learn to discipline itself; it can learn to go without [. . .]. The cost must be paid now – not by the invading enemy, but in equipping our fighting men so that they will hold Port Moresby and Darwin, so that they will hold this Australian bastion for democracy, and finally, wrest the initiative from the enemy.*[228]

Australians learned to change the habits of a lifetime as food and clothing went first to those fighting at the front. Civilians were issued with coupons that limited the quantities of basic goods they could purchase. Money was now longer enough for purchasing tea, alcohol, petrol, sugar, butter, tobacco, milk, meat, flour, and the like; people needed ration coupons as well. Neighbours swapped coupons, and Australians even packed food parcels to send to 'the mother country'.

Newspaper advertisements encouraged Australians to support troops by being thrifty and exercising patience when stocks were unavailable: "Vegemite fights for the men up north [. . .] If you are one of those who don't

Photo courtesy of Mimmo Cozzolino. Page 100.

need Vegemite medicinally, then thousands of invalids and babies are asking you to deny yourself of it for the time being;" Wrigley's chewing gum is not available because it helps "our fighting men in easing tension and as a moral builder."[229] Magazines printed recipes for 'meatless dishes', Austerity Potatoes (supplemented with breadcrumbs), Austerity Fruit Cake (without eggs or butter), and Wartime Cream Buns that used egg powder and mock cream.[230] People grew their own vegetables. They kept chooks. When clothing rations were also introduced in 1942, mothers cut down their old dresses to fit their children, turned the collars of their husbands' shirts, and used old flour bags for handkerchiefs.

Penalties applied if shopkeepers sold goods without the appropriate coupons, although one Greek café proprietor in Ipswich, a renowned 'ladies' man', found it impossible to resist selling butter to his girlfriends when they ran out of coupons. The government also appointed price-fixing inspectors to ensure that shopkeepers didn't take advantage of the situation by overcharging on goods that were in short supply. Knowing that unfamiliar customers might be inspectors checking that they were charging correct prices, Greek proprietors often undercharged unknown customers, just in case. Jack Stathis of the City Café in Ipswich, who was barely in his teens when the war finished, had to go to court for overcharging on matches. A box of matches cost a penny halfpenny (1½ pennies), but customers could buy two boxes for tuppence (2 pennies). Jack inadvertently charged a customer threepence for two boxes. He was fined five pounds.

Inspectors also checked that goods were weighed correctly. Most grocery items, at this time, were not pre-packaged and shopkeepers bought flour, sugar, tea, and the like, in bulk. Sugar came in 40 pound bags, for example, and butter in boxes that held 50 one pound blocks. Wooden chests and sacks with rolled-down tops would be lined up at the back of shops. Shopkeepers would scoop out the contents, usually to within a shake of the required amount, and after weighing them, pack the goods for their customers. Loose lollies sold by this method in Greek cafés were subject to weight checks.

Supplies of luxury items like alcohol, cigarettes, tobacco, chewing gum, chocolates, and nylon stockings were so limited that people often couldn't get them even if they had ration coupons. Confectionery and cigarettes were made available to shops by quota once a month, although not all shops could get a tobacco quota. As Jack explains, "If you couldn't get a tobacco quota you may as well shut up shop." Jack's family moved from the City Café across the road to the Metro Café, which another Greek, George Andrews, had opened after the war. George was able to secure a cigarette quota because he was a serviceman.[231] Jack suggests that the shortage of tobacco was good for teenagers, because they didn't smoke as much, but he says that some people tried smoking sawdust. Athena Bellas recalls that girls coped with the lack of nylon stockings by painting their legs with a product they bought from the chemist and finishing off the look by drawing 'seams' up the back of their legs with eyebrow pencils.

Long queues formed whenever word got around that a shop had stocks of luxury goods, because there were long periods when they were not available at all. Jack explains that café proprietors kept cigarettes and chocolates hidden under the counter so that customers had to ask for them. "You saved them for regular customers," says Jack. "You had to look after them no matter what." Julie Nichles, whose family had a café near the Treasury Building in Brisbane during the war, remembers the highly-prized Lucky Strike cigarettes, and she notes that her father also hid these when they came in because he was

The government appointed price-fixing inspectors to ensure that shopkeepers didn't take advantage of the situation by overcharging on goods that were in short supply.

Photo courtesy of Mimmo Cozzolino. Page 126.

keeping them for certain customers. Despite the best efforts of government officials, there was, as might be expected, a black market in luxury goods, and Conomos claims that some Greeks sold tobacco and confectionery at inflated prices on the black market.[232]

Paper was also in short supply during the war, and was among the materials sought by Boy Scouts, who collected anything that could be recycled. Cafés were required to wrap fish and chips in white paper, but since this was scarce, they cut the paper into 12 inch squares, placed the fish and chips on these, and then wrapped the bundle in newspaper. These they bought cheaply from the Telegraph or Courier Mail offices when they went to the fish market in Brisbane. Older Australians remember that at the height of the war, they had to take their own wrapping paper or plastic bowls to the butchers to buy meat.

Soap was also harder to get during the war years and Jack's brother, Jim Stathis, recalls that their father used old fat to make soap for use in the café. In an earlier Australia, when caring for the environment was yet to become a global issue, 'recycling' needed no promotion. In pioneer huts, on outback properties, and during the depression, Australians routinely kept, reused, and remade old tins, packing cases, and produce bags. Recycling was limited only by the imagination and Australians took pride in the thrifty use of resources. They called it 'making do'.[233] Wartime scarcity meant that people had to be especially ingenious at the art of recycling. Nick Stathis made the soap for the City Café by adding caustic soda to old fat that had been used for frying fish and chips. He poured the mixture into old cans, a further example of re-use, and when it was set, the can was punctured with holes and hung under the tap ready for washing up. Jim believes that most cafés did this. The homemade soap used on the café's kitchen floor was so strong it would sometimes take the colour out of the bottom of shoes.

Yanks

When the Japanese bombed Pearl Harbour in December 1941, the Americans joined the war and Australia became one big American army camp. Newspaper columnist, Neil Groom, cites a Brisbane City Council brochure, which claims that 750,000 US servicemen passed through Brisbane during World War Two, but a Courier Mail article reporting on the closing of the US Pacific Air Command at Brisbane Airport, dated 1st February 1947, claims, that 2,290,757 Americans passed through Brisbane between 1942 and the end of the war.[234] United States Air Corps personnel began to arrive in Amberley soon after the Americans entered the war. Up to 1,000 US servicemen were stationed at Amberley and there were more in air fields at Lowood and Coominya.[235]

Photo courtesy of Mimmo Cozzolino. Page 126.

The arrival of the Yanks gave Australians a glimpse of a lifestyle that had previously only existed for most on the silver screen. Unlike Australian 'boys', American servicemen had ready supplies of rare 'luxury' items like chocolates, lollies and chewing gum, stockings and cigarettes, and they were very generous with these supplies. Athena Bellas, a Brisbane girl at the time of the war, remembers that Australian soldiers were only paid six shillings a day and had very basic uniforms, while the Americans had plenty of money and "lovely gabardine uniforms." And when they gave girls stockings, it wasn't usually just one pair, says Athena, but a whole box, and they had "cigarettes to burn." Having suffered from a severely depleted supply of male companions since the war began, girls were suddenly the focus of male attention. Hordes of romantic young Americans with their beautiful uniforms and silver tongues must have seemed like movie stars, and Australian girls could easily imagine themselves dancing with the likes of Robert Taylor and Clarke Gable. Meanwhile, Australian men, with coarse uniforms, little money, and no chocolate, and not renowned for charming manners or witty conversation, hovered at the edges unable to compete.

It appears that the Americans had first chance at everything. They charmed the girls, but they were also served first in cafés while locals waited outside, and had the best seats at the pictures. Local residents, Yvonne Hawkins and Myrtle Fellows, remember that the upstairs area and the front stalls at the Wintergarden Picture Theatre were reserved for American servicemen. Considering that the Wintergarden, built in 1925, seated 2,000 patrons and was packed out most week nights before the war, with standing room only on Saturday nights, many wartime locals queuing outside for the remaining seats must have been turned away. Sharing the wait was a common practice, as people sometimes queued for hours by swapping their place in line with relatives.

Image published in Hollywood and the Great Stars, Crescent Books, New York, page 200.

Yvonne remembers periods when sessions at the flash new Ritz Theatre were booked out by American servicemen.[236]

War was an exciting time for many children. Because Ipswich was so close to Amberley, fears of the city being bombed changed children's routines considerably. They spent less time in classrooms, only going to school for half the day, and were constantly distracted by air-raid drills. Yvonne went to West Ipswich State School. She remembers carrying a cushion, a rubber peg, and ear plugs right through the war. In the event of an explosion, children were to put the plugs into their ears and bite down on the peg to stop their teeth from shattering.[237]

Up to 1,000 US servicemen were stationed at Amberley and there were more in air fields at Lowood and Coominya.

• A drawing of the theatre from the opening program.

Image published in Robyn Buchanan's "Old Theatre Put on the Ritz" Queensland Times: Lattice & Lace Column, 2nd May 1986.

In addition, there were cartridge shells to souvenir, camps to invade, and training routines to spy upon. Convoys and platoons streaming past and planes flying overhead were regular occurrences.[238] Julie Nichles has vivid memories of sitting on the counter her father's milk bar opposite the Treasury Building watching parades go past and Jack Stathis recalls watching "thousands of soldiers riding on horses down Brisbane Street" from the footpath outside his family's City Café in Ipswich. When they passed, Jack says, the street was covered in horse manure. Also during the war, a low-flying aircraft spooked a horse that was pulling a cart in Brisbane Street, and the driver, a Greek who owned a shop near the North Ipswich end of the town bridge, was killed. And as if all this excitement was not enough, the streets were suddenly awash with American soldiers whose pockets were full of lollies and money.

According to many reports, the Yanks were especially friendly and generous where children were concerned. Many had children at home. They must have missed them and this is perhaps why they were nice to Australian kids. Born during the depression years, most Australian children had never seen the kind of affluence the Americans seemed to enjoy.[239] One Australian, who was a child during the war years, remembers their generosity: "we'd always say, 'Have you got any gum, Yank?', and they'd say, 'Sure kid.' They had their pockets full of it."[240] Julie Nichles recalls them giving kids comics and magazines, lollies and American chewing gum. She says, "To me [the war] was one big party."[241] Although the Yanks liked Aussie kids, and gave them lollies, kids were not necessarily allowed to accept these sweet temptations.

The children of West Ipswich State School received their daily ration of milk when they marched to a designated building, where mothers doled out cups of hot Milo. Each of the children, about 80 in Yvonne's grade, had a metal cup, which a local man made especially for them from empty condensed milk tins, Yvonne believes. Yvonne's name was written on sticking plaster on the bottom of the cup when she received it in 1942.

Mothers, in particular, often forbid their children to accept chocolate and chewing gum from the Yanks. Yvonne thought the Yanks were "absolutely lovely," but her mother made it clear that Yvonne was not to accept their money, which they sometimes threw from passing convoys, or their 'candy'. Yvonne used to watch the soldiers play a fascinating 'new' game called baseball at the West Ipswich School oval. She talked to them. She took their candy. And she made sure the evidence had disappeared by the time she reached home. Heather Colless was also forbidden to speak to or take 'candy' for these 'strangers'. She reasoned, however, that picking it up off the ground would be permitted as this could not strictly be classed as taking it from them. The difficulty she never resolved was how to get them to throw the lollies to her without talking to them. Unfortunately, the Yanks never worked it out.

The children in Greek cafés were in a key position to benefit from American soldiers' generosity. Jack and Jim Stathis remember that cleaning up the tables late at night in the City Café in Ipswich could be quite lucrative and they fought for the job of sweeping up. The Americans were 'big tippers' and they often left tips under their plates. They also didn't bother to pick up money that dropped onto the floor. If they were inebriated, they were even more likely to leave their money behind in the café.²⁴²
Jim recalls that, as a kid, he would go around the tables of Americans scrounging chewing gum, and he would usually get a handful. And Jack still has American coins and Japanese invasion money, which he picked up in the café.

Julie Nichles recalls the Yanks giving kids comics and magazines, lollies and American chewing gum.

Young Jack Stathis and Jack today with his granddaughter.

When the war broke out, Con Castan was put to work in his uncle's Southport shop. He was about 10 years old. Americans frequented the café and Con's uncle, being an astute businessman, learned all the American ranks and knew how to recognise them. He was able to address new customers correctly, and this made him very popular. Con recalls that the Americans were big spenders and big eaters. On one occasion, an American ordered and ate 10 dozen oysters. Con was not paid for his work in his uncle's shop, but he got chocolate, cigarettes, and chewing gum from the Yanks and was allowed to keep the tips they gave him, which could be considerable.[243]

Australians seemed to have welcomed Americans with open arms. The Yanks were lonely and bored a lot of the time and many Ipswich families befriended them and invited them home for meals, as did families all over the country. Tex Cummins found the friendliness of Ipswich people overwhelming, and at times embarrassing, because they treated him as a conquering hero come to help win the war. This perhaps explains why Australians accepted them taking the best food, being served first, and getting the best theatre seats. When he went into town on leave, people would walk up to Tex and say, "Hey, Yank, come home and have tea with us." He also remembers that café proprietors treated them like kings and he specially mentions the big steaks at the Regal Café.[244]

On the other hand, Australians sometimes found the friendliness of the Americans overwhelming. Ipswich resident, Myrtle Fellows, remembers that she was pushing a pram home one day, when two Americans took control of the pram and fell into step beside her. She tried to assure them that she didn't need their help, but they would not be put off and chatted about their families all the way to her house. "What am I going to do with these two when I get home?" she thought. "Oh well, there's nothing I can do about it now." She says she felt really rotten about not inviting them in for a 'cuppa', but felt uncomfortable inviting two strangers in while she was alone. She adds that the Americans didn't seem to mind and they went on their way saying they would write home about the baby.

> *Australians seemed to have welcomed Americans with open arms. The Yanks were lonely and bored a lot of the time and many Ipswich families befriended them and invited them home for meals, as did families all over the country.*

Boom Time

Wartime presented many challenges to Greek proprietors. Labour was in short supply because employees were sometimes called up, and stocks of meat, sugar, cigarettes, and other commodities were often low. In spite of this, many cafés were continually bombarded with servicemen. When large encampments of Australian or American troops were stationed nearby, soldiers flooded into local cafes and takings far exceeded that of the pre-war years. Business boomed and Greeks were often unable to keep up with the number of customers. Conomos explains that cafés were often packed out as soon as the doors opened in towns close to where troops were stationed. Proprietors had to shut the doors again until the troops were fed and the café cleaned, and when they reopened the frenzy would begin again.[245]

Brisbane was of course flooded with servicemen, but the massive increase in trade was widespread because troops were stationed throughout the country. An army camp established at Redbank in 1939, for example, had an initial quota of 2,500 men. More men were stationed at Wacol, Amberley, Coominya, and Lowood. In small country towns like Murgon, where there were large army camps, coping with a sudden influx of customers was especially difficult with only a handful of staff. Conomos describes one occasion when Theo Comino's Murgon café was inundated

by 400 troops at half an hour's notice. The five staff members were rushed off their feet and every bit of stock was sold. Julie Nichles remembers her father "drooping with fatigue" in his Brisbane café during the war years.[246] Fortunately, on occasions like this, Greek café employees who had enlisted were able to step behind the counter and help out.[247]

In Ipswich, Harry Londy doubled the staff in his café from eight to 16 and had to reduce shop hours to avoid running out of food. In Bundaberg, his brother, Charles, increased his staff from 10 to 17.[248] Harry also faced the problem of procuring enough fish, fruit, and poultry from Brisbane to satisfy the needs of the thousands of Australian and American servicemen stationed near Ipswich. He killed and dressed hundreds of hens behind the shop. Harry's son, Peter, claims that fish was a big 'seller' because meat was rationed. Despite the quota system, goods were bought outside of the quota and butchers, especially, were glad to sell what they had.[249] Nick Penglis won the contract to supply Amberley

Gabriel Penglis (Nick's brother), Vera and Nick, with children, Jim, Ruth and John on their Raceview farm 1945.

Image courtesy of Mimmo Cozzolino page 125.

with fruit and vegetables during the war, a deal which also secured extra petrol rations. The Penglis family grew produce on their Raceview farm, as Nick could not otherwise procure enough produce to supply the RAAF's needs. During the war years, two Italian internees were released into Nick's care to work the farm; he provided them with accommodation, cigarettes and pocket money.

Sometimes, the Americans helped out with supplies. One day, an American officer was told that pork was not available when he ordered a pork chop in a Greek café in Woolloongabba. An American truck delivered two pigs to the café the next day, compliments of the US Army. The officer returned and ordered a pork chop. "When the American guys want pork, they get pork," the proprietor said.[250] The Americans monitored the standard of hygiene in cafés and stopped Americans from going into shops that didn't meet their standards. At the 'request' of American military police, many cafés, including Londy's in Ipswich, were forced to stock only Peter's Ice-Cream.

Price-fixing kept profit margins low. Conomos notes, however, that many Greeks had a flexible price system; they charged Americans higher prices than they charged Australians. One Brisbane shopkeeper admitted to charging four shillings for T-bone steak, two shillings and sixpence for tea and sandwiches, and one shilling for a malted milk, when these items should have been two shillings and sixpence, one shilling and sixpence and nine pence respectively.[251] But business was good even for those who observed price restrictions, because the Yanks tipped handsomely and often told proprietors to "keep the change."

Supplies of crockery, cutlery, and glassware were also stretched beyond their limits in flooded wartime cafés, and café staff couldn't keep up with the washing up. Ipswich resident, Myrtle Fellows, remembers drinking milkshakes out of ripple-topped flower vases during the war years because of the shortage of glasses. The theft of café crockery and cutlery by Australian servicemen was a constant problem. Brisbane writer, Effie Detsimas, believes that a Greek café proprietor invented the steak burger during the war because he could not maintain the supply of cutlery to serve with steak meals. One night, when his shop was packed with impatient troops and staff barely had time to grill steaks, let alone wash up the remaining cutlery, he hit upon an idea:

> *I toasted two slices of bread, pounded some steak, grilled it and put it between the toast with some tomato sauce. I wrapped it and approached the nearest soldier. There you go mate, steak-burger. Easier to eat and won't cost you as much. They knew of hamburgers, but not steak burgers, so it caught on.*

"Not the Americans," Effie adds, because they had well-stocked canteens, "but a lot of the cutlery from Greek cafés ended up at the Australian barracks at Enoggera."[252] Conomos notes instances of provosts with fixed bayonets being stationed outside shops to deter theft.[253]

Fights

While young women and children enjoyed the sudden influx of Americans, Australian soldiers were not so enamoured of their American allies. They resented them 'moving in' on their territory and found their appeal for Australian women particularly aggravating. As one woman put it, "Aussie blokes just couldn't get a look in." Australian soldiers complained that the Yanks were "overpaid, oversexed, and over here." Often, however, this annoyance went well beyond verbal complaint and brawls broke out in the streets. Brawls in Greek cafés were also common because these were popular locations for servicemen on leave. One man, who was proprietor of the Star Milk Bar in Albert Street, Brisbane, during the war, recalls that there were fights between American and Australian soldiers every night. To avoid conflict, some proprietors sat American and Australian soldiers on opposite sides of the shop.[254]

Accounts of violent outbreaks in Brisbane – in particular, the 'Battle of Brisbane' on the 26th and 27th of November 1942 – are well documented, but incidents in Ipswich are less well-known. An Australian soldier was stabbed during a fracas that occurred in a Goodna café. This is recorded by the Brisbane History Group, but Jack recalls an incident in the City Café in Ipswich that is probably not recorded anywhere else.[255] One night, a fight broke out between American and Australian soldiers and the American MPs were notified. The City Café had a large area above the dining room. This had once been a function room, but because of shortages during the war, Nick Stathis had converted the area into a billiard Hall. When the MPs attended the disturbance, they burst into the café, but failed to have any impact on the escalating battle. The MPs, having been raised on a diet of John Wayne films, ten-gallon hats, and sheriff's badges, fired several shots into the air. They put holes in the ceiling of the café. Fortunately, they missed the people who were upstairs quietly playing billiards. Jack remembers another incident in which a soldier rode a horse into the café. According to Jack, "It just about kicked the counter to pieces."

There were 1,500 white Americans and 2,000 African Americans encamped in the Ipswich area and fights also broke out between these groups. Clashes resulted in segregation;

Goodna and Redbank were out of bounds to the latter and African Americans were not permitted in Ipswich.²⁵⁶ Those who transgressed these boundaries were dealt with severely. Myrtle was near Nolan's corner one evening when she saw two American MPs leap from a passing vehicle and bash an African American soldier who was walking along the footpath. They threw him into the vehicle and pulled away. "He never said a word," Myrtle says, "They just weren't allowed past Wacol." Yvonne lived on Denmark Hill and as she was walking to work one morning at about 7am, she found a pile of congealed blood on the corner of Limestone and Nicholas Streets. "It was enormous," says Yvonne, "Someone had obviously been stabbed." She followed an ever-decreasing trail of blood up Nicholas Street in the direction of the railway station. Myrtle and Yvonne also remember a rumour circulating around Ipswich at the time to the effect that an African American soldier had been shot at the back of the Palais Royal Hotel.

The streets of Ipswich are quiet today. People no longer routinely meet on Nolan's corner or congregate in droves outside Cribb and Foote's. They don't queue for hours to buy tobacco or secure a seat at the pictures. Cafés don't shut their doors because they've run out of food or can't fit more customers inside. Showers of candy no longer spray from convoys that take hours to rumble down Brisbane Street. And it is impossible to imagine the footpaths awash with khaki as hundreds of American servicemen chat up the local girls, while Australian soldiers size them up. And yet all of this happened in streets where Ipswich residents walk today. While the Second World War brought some of the toughest years residents have yet had to face, it was probably the most exciting thing that ever happened to Ipswich. In the words of Charles Dickens, "It was the best of times, it was the worst of times, it was the age of wisdom, it was the age of foolishness."²⁵⁷

CHAPTER TEN

One of the Family: Waitressing for Greek Proprietors

We
Were
Family.

MAUREEN SHEPPARD,
A WAITRESS AT LONDY'S CAFE
IN THE 40S AND 50S

Many of the waitresses who worked in Ipswich's Greek cafés stayed with their employers for long periods of time and got to know Greek families well. Maureen Sheppard worked at Londy's Café in the 40s and 50s, Lily Burke at the Metro Café in the 50s and 60s, and Maureen Reinke for the Pavlakis and Kentrotis families in the 70s and 80s. They remember with fondness the years they spent with their Greek employers, who treated them like family. Some waitresses befriended the wives of café proprietors and have maintained friendships with these women decades after their cafés closed and their husbands died.

Some cafés employed surprisingly large numbers of staff. Peter Cominos claims that, before WWII their Cairns café employed an astounding 175 staff; the three-storey café sometimes catered simultaneously for two weddings on the two upper levels as well as supplying a ground floor dining room that seated a hundred customers. Ipswich cafés, however, typically employed 6-8 people – cooks, someone to wash up, waitresses, and counter staff – except for the boom during the war years, when staff numbers doubled. The Sydney Café, for example, had about six staff in the front of the shop with Harry working flat out in the kitchen.

Labour was highly organised according to gender and ethnicity; from the 1920s, cooks were mostly Greek men and waitresses were mostly local Anglo-Australian girls.[258] In Ipswich cafés, Greek proprietors rather than local staff, appear to have tended cash registers. Age may also have been a factor, because Greek wives or older Anglo-Australian women often did the washing up. Helene Marendy and Maria Kentrotis note that washing up was their job in their husband's cafés.

Maureen's Story

Maureen Sheppard was a local girl who started work as a waitress in Londy's Café in 1947 when she was seventeen. The new job offered a slight pay increase over her previous job, which paid 25 shillings a week. Maureen lived near Hill Street in North Ipswich at the time and she cycled to and from work. If she was on the morning shift, she would arrive for work at about 6am to clean the mirrors and have breakfast – always baked beans on toast. If she worked the second shift, she cycled home after midnight because the café didn't finish serving customers until 11pm. While the last buses always waited for the last of the café crowd to head off, waitresses were busy for some time after the doors closed. Maureen was occasionally followed home from work in the early hours of the morning, but she says that a police wagon driven by younger policemen used to "keep an eye on things." The white

wagon, dubbed 'the ghost car' by locals, was always around somewhere and Maureen recalls, "I always felt as if someone was looking after me. I always felt safe." An older sergeant walked the inner-city streets and kept an eye on the North Star Hotel, which occupied the same building as Londy's.

Four waitresses worked each shift at Londy's – two on each side of the café, with particular tables to look after. They wore casual clothes with an apron over the top. Maureen made her own aprons. These had a pocket to hold her order book and sometimes she embroidered LONDY'S across the bib. Customers were seated at a table on arrival, then a waitress took their order, the customers paid the waitress, and she took the money to the cashier, usually a member of the Greek family. This was slightly different from the practice at the nearby Regal Café, where customers took their docket to the counter on the way out, as happens in many restaurants today. Customers did not pay at the counter before they ate their meals.

During their heyday from the 30s to the 60s, Greek cafés often overflowed with customers. Ipswich residents commonly report walking the streets looking for a vacant table on Friday and Saturday nights in the 40s. Londy's was especially busy after the pictures, when toasted sandwiches and coffee were popular, and at lunchtime, when meals or takeaway sandwiches were ordered by families coming into town from the country. Hungry workers from the Queensland Times, at that time diagonally across from the North Star Hotel, added to the lunchtime rush. According to Maureen, eating at Londy's was an everyday practice rather than a treat. She recalls that regular customers often ordered the same thing: "The Vermeer boys, for example, they always had toasted cheese sandwiches and coffee made on milk."

Tucked away in a cupboard at Maureen's place is an old photo album. The thick, charcoal-coloured pages are brittle with age and some hang loose in their padded red leatherette cover, but this album is a wonderful record of a slice of Ipswich life. Developing snapshots in her parents' bedroom with the aid of a red bulb, a blanket across the window, and a towel under the door, Maureen captured images of the Londy family and their customers and staff. These images articulate the kinds of relationships she had with each during the years she spent at the café.

A number of photographs depict 'foreign' customers – Fred and Peter Vermeer, Zyggy Bar and his sister Halina, "Two English Chaps", Len Leong, and friends and relations of each of these, most of whom were also immigrants. This suggests that Greek cafés were possibly a haven for others who had not been born in Australia or whose background deviated from the white Anglo-Celtic hegemony of Australian culture during this period. Notably, Maureen is the daughter of German migrants, which, allied with the fact that Greek staff also had a strong presence in the café, may account for the role Londy's played in the lives of immigrants from other countries.

In addition, since most photographs were not taken at Londy's, but at private gatherings and venues, they indicate that not only did Maureen's customers become friends but also that she was a substitute family, a home away from home, for those who felt isolated in a predominately Anglo-Celtic, often xenophobic, culture. "We had good times when we worked there," Maureen says. "We'd hear people's stories." The Vermeer brothers,

for example, talked about their family in Holland and their plans to bring them out to Australia. When their family eventually arrived, the Vermeers stopped coming because they no longer needed what Maureen and the café provided. Servicemen, who missed their wives and girlfriends, shared photographs of loved ones with Maureen. She recalls, "Quite a few customers [from other countries] seemed to be a bit lonely and wanted to talk and when we weren't serving we were allowed to stand and talk to customers." Well beyond her role as a waitress at Londy's, Maureen helped newcomers settle into the community.

> *Well beyond her role as a waitress at Londy's, Maureen helped newcomers settle into the community.*

Finally, Maureen's photographs depict a social life enjoyed by those who worked at the café – Greek owners, Greek staff, and local staff. She went to local dances with groups that included the children of the Londy family, although she didn't date the Greek boys. She was also invited to their weddings. Some of Maureen's fondest memories, however, are of the Londy Christmas picnics, and these too are documented in her album. Every year at Christmas time, Harry Londy took the café staff to the beach for the day. They drove down in the family cars, and Maureen recalls that the Greeks paid for everything. Her album contains photographs of a beach picnic in 1953 that articulate the group's camaraderie. One of the Greek 'boys' was an amateur photographer, who took shots of members of the group posed on a life savers' reel, as well as group portraits and animated scenes of watermelon fights and waitresses stuffing George Londy into a rubbish bin.

It seems that, at least in earlier days, Greeks loved to pack up a feast and enjoy it with a big group of their family and friends in an outdoor setting whenever they could. Despite the long hours routinely documented in accounts of café life, many of the children who 'grew up' in Greek cafés recall family picnics, books on the history of the Greeks in Australia are littered with photographs of large outdoor gatherings, and Maureen's album is dotted with images of picnic photographs. While the Greek community in Australia was able to maintain many of the traditions of their homeland and, in some ways, a distinct identity within Australian culture, locals like Maureen were welcomed into those traditions.

The album also includes photographs of Maureen and other waitresses at Greek weddings, as well as numerous signed studio portraits given to her by members of the Londy family. When asked why she was invited to family weddings and given studio portraits, Maureen replies, "Well . . ." she pauses and looks at me as if she is lost for words, and then she says simply "we were family." This relationship is evident in other ways. When the Londys made themselves Greek coffee and Greek food like quail served with lemon sauce, or dolmades – mince wrapped in grapevine leaves – they often shared it with Maureen, who says she felt privileged to have it. Maureen also helped one of the Londy boys with language difficulties. During quieter periods, she would sit down with Harry at a café table and use a primitive dictionary with Greek and English words to teach him to speak English.[259]

Maureen thoroughly enjoyed the years she spent at Londy's Café; she formed close friendships with other waitresses, particularly Vera Dawson, who appears in may of the snapshots in her album, and remembers receiving presents from customers when she worked at the café on the day she turned eighteen. Maureen was the inspiration for the original project that resulted in this book. She died on the 12th of February, 2007.

Lily and Maureen

Local girls who worked for other Greek families in later years relate similar accounts of their experiences. Lily Burke was 16 when she started work for the Stathis family at the Metro Café in 1955. Lily lived with three other waitresses in rooms under the Stathis family's home in Limestone Street opposite St Stephens church. She enjoyed her time at the Metro, but she especially enjoyed working the Saturday night shift, when café staff, after being rushed off their feet until late at night, would close the door, clean up the shop, and walk home together.

Working at the café had a significant impact on Lily's life. She learned bits of Greek that still roll off her tongue more than half a century later, especially the swear words, and she was familiar with Greek food long before it appeared on restaurant tables in Australia. Lily also met her husband-to-be at the Metro; Tom came into the shop for a meal, set eyes on Lily, and became a regular customer. Memories of 'mucking around' with younger members of the family stand out as particularly vivid memories of Lily's years as a waitress, and these are related in other chapters, but café life was not all fun and games.

Mrs Stathis (Vasi) was very particular about the way things would be done in her café. She insisted, for instance, that the waitresses wore uniforms. The waitresses in most Greek cafés in Ipswich seem to have worn casual clothes with an apron over the top. Over the course of the 20th century, there were some exceptions. The photograph of the City Café taken in the 1920s (Chapter Three) shows waitresses in a uniform and a photograph of four waitresses from the Regal Café indicates that the girls who worked there during the 1940s had uniforms too. The Metro was one of the few Ipswich Greek cafés where staff wore uniforms during the 50s and 60s. Lily had several models – a red one with a white detachable collar and cuffs, a white blouse with a monogrammed red vest, and a red and white striped one that had

a matching hat, all of which she hated wearing. Vasi and Lily also sometimes clashed because Vasi insisted that the tiles at the entrance to the shop were spotless. Lily's day began with scrubbing these and she says she still hates them, although the shop has housed Action Realty for many years, and some have been replaced with Terracotta tiles. Plenty of other cleaning jobs awaited Lily's attention when the shop wasn't busy. The tables in most Greek cafés had no cloths, so they were wiped clean, but the silverware had to be polished every week.

Girls took the orders at the tables in the Metro, as was the practice in most of the cafés at that time. Lily preferred to sing out the orders to Vasi, who worked behind the counter, or to Harry and Jack, who were cooking out the back, and when the meals came through, she had no trouble remembering who had ordered what. Vasi insisted, however, that the orders be written down on the order pad so that customers could present this for payment at the till. To Lily's mind, this just slowed her down. When she left the Metro, Lily went to work in the railway cafeteria at Shorncliffe.

Maureen Reinke was 27 when started working for Jim Pavlakis at Tony's Snack Bar in August 1972. She worked with Jim for 13 years. When Jim's sister, Maria Kentrotis, bought a nearby shop, Maureen worked for a further four years at the Central Milk Bar. Jim's snack bar was especially busy at night because, since most of the city's Greek cafes had closed by the 1970s, it was the only place open apart from Jimmy Wah's Chinese Takeaway. Having originally been a Greek café owned by Tony Veneris, Jim's snack bar had cubicles and a milk bar.

Maureen recalls that hamburgers were 15cents in 1972, and cigarettes cost 85 cents a packet. Popular meals at that time included steak and salad, hamburgers, and mixed grills.

In this rare hand-coloured photograph, probably from the 1940s, four waitresses from the Regal Café pose for what appears to be a studio portrait. The bodice of their uniform is pale blue, while the skirt, caps and trim are cream with a delicate blue and rose floral print. An inscription on the back reads: To Jimmy from Lorna, Ethel, Audrey and Jean.[260]

In the early 80s, at about the time the mall was built in the centre of town, customers would be ten deep at the counter on Saturdays and Sundays. On Saturday nights, families used to go for walks around the city streets and would often call in for an ice-cream. Taxi drivers also frequented the snack bar, and the girls from nearby Jenyns bra factory, were regular customers. Young people, particularly young men with 'hot' cars, gathered outside the snack bar as part of a Friday and Saturday night ritual that involved lapping the inner-city streets, pausing to drool over each other's vehicles, and lapping once more. Although the 'lappers', as this group has been dubbed over a period spanning several decades, repeatedly attract negative publicity in the local media, Maureen recalls them as a fine bunch of young people. Maria at the Central takes a similar view. The lappers didn't leave until closing time and Maureen says their presence around the café was reassuring. She never feared that troublemakers might bother the staff late at night.

Maureen remembers when Red Rooster opened up in the next block, but does not recall the fast food outlet having a big impact on business at Tony's. When McDonalds opened in the centre of town, however, this "finished them," according to Maureen. Maureen has fond memories of her life as a waitress in Tony's Snack Bar and the Central Milk Bar. She drank Greek coffee with the proprietors, and remembers Maria as a fabulous cook – Maria would bring supper down to the workers at about 7 o'clock. Ipswich people still remember Maureen, 40 years later, as the girl from Tony's. Having worked for Greek proprietors for over 17 years, Maureen recalls them as very hard-working, hospitable people and she was very comfortable in their employ. "Everything they did," Maureen says, "they did well."

The accounts of these waitresses are especially valuable because, during the middle decades of the 20th century, most Australians knew little about immigrants or foreign cultures. In the days before multiculturalism, the predominantly Anglo-Celtic Australian population knew the Greeks simply as 'dagos'.

Several waitresses mention that they had to polish the silverware at least once a week. This included sugar bowls, milk jugs, teapots and coffee pots, sundae dishes, and salt and pepper shakers. Many of these items had the name of the café engraved on the front, as in these vessels from the Regal Café, and the monogram was often painted onto café china. Theft of silver items was such a problem for cafés that Harry Andronicus changed the engraving on the silverware in his Toowoomba café to Stolen from the Club Café.[261]

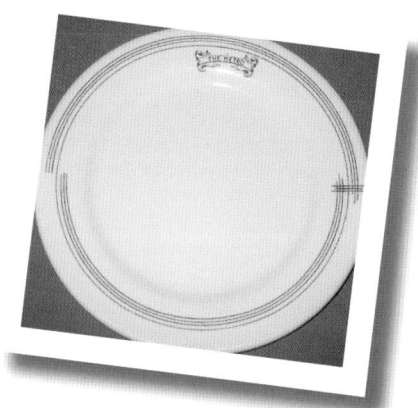

CHAPTER ELEVEN

'Bloody Dagoes': Greek and Anglo-Australian Relations

"Instead of handing the order of the boot to these degenerate and piebald remnants of an ancient glory, we are asking them to come along and join in the fun of providing Australia with cockroach soup, verminised bedding and filthy immorality."

The Truth newspaper,
Brisbane, June 1925[262]

Despite the enormous contribution they made to Australian life throughout the 20th century, Greek immigrants suffered multiple forms of discrimination at the hands of government officials and ordinary Australians.

While that discrimination was widespread, it was temporally and geographically specific, and some Greeks experienced no discrimination at all. Hindsight reveals the unjust nature of accusations made by government officials, and the way Greek immigrants were treated by many ordinary Australians exposes the basis of prejudice in 20th century Australia. Together, these bring another perspective to anxieties about Muslims and refugees in the early 21st century.

The Ferry Report

While much of the prejudice against Greeks operated at a street level, in April 1925, the Queensland Government commissioned a royal inquiry into the social and economic effects of the increasing amount of 'alien labour' in North Queensland. Although immigration policy at the time admitted Greeks to Australia, the *Ferry Report* records Australian racial prejudice at an official level. In that report, Commissioner Thomas Arthur Ferry alleges unhygienic personal habits on the part of Greeks; he found that Greeks had a lower standard of living than other foreigners, that Greek boarding houses were in a "filthy condition," and that some Greek accommodation was "no better than a blacks' camp."[263] How Ferry conducted the research that produced this claim within just two months of the start of the inquiry is unclear, but Ferry also wrote, "The Greek residents of North Queensland are generally of an undesirable type, and do not make good settlers . . . . Their admission to Queensland can be of no possible benefit to the country." Given the extraordinary number of cafés, oyster saloons, and milk bars that Greeks had opened throughout Australia by this time, including, according to Conomos, many in North Queensland, and considering the contribution those shops made to their local communities, Ferry's assessment seems unwarranted and inaccurate.

The Commissioner was referring, however, to Greek settlers from Kythera, Castellorizo, Lesbos, Chios and Athens, who had established restaurants throughout Queensland and New South Wales, when he concluded, ". . . socially and economically this type of immigrant is a menace to the community in which he settles and it would be for the benefit of the State if his entrance were altogether prohibited."[264] In 1981, Doug Anthony, then the leader of the Country Party, spoke at a dinner to welcome the President of Greece on his visit to Australia. Anthony announced that in the pre-war and war years, Australia would not have functioned without the Greek café. He emphasised that wherever you travelled during this difficult period you could get a meal.[265] This is confirmed in Conomos' accounts of proprietors giving handouts to people during the depression and coping with hordes of American servicemen at a moment's notice during the war.[266] How wrong Commissioner Ferry was.

When one considers the number of famous Australians whose parents were Greek immigrants, many of them café proprietors, Ferry's statements seem even more inappropriate: Jason Akamanis, Australian Rules Football player, Prof Manuel Aroney, academic and human rights advocate, Zoe Carrides, actor, Claudia Carvan, actor, Mary Coustas (Effie), Logie Award winning actor, comedian and writer, Michael Diamond, Olympic shooter, Alex Dimitriades, actor, Nicholas Dontas, Northern Territory Minister for Transport, Rebekah Elmaloglou, actor, Nick Giannopoulos, actor, writer, stage, film and television producer, Professor Mary Kalantzis, academic and author, Antigone Kefala, author, Mary Kostakides, broadcaster

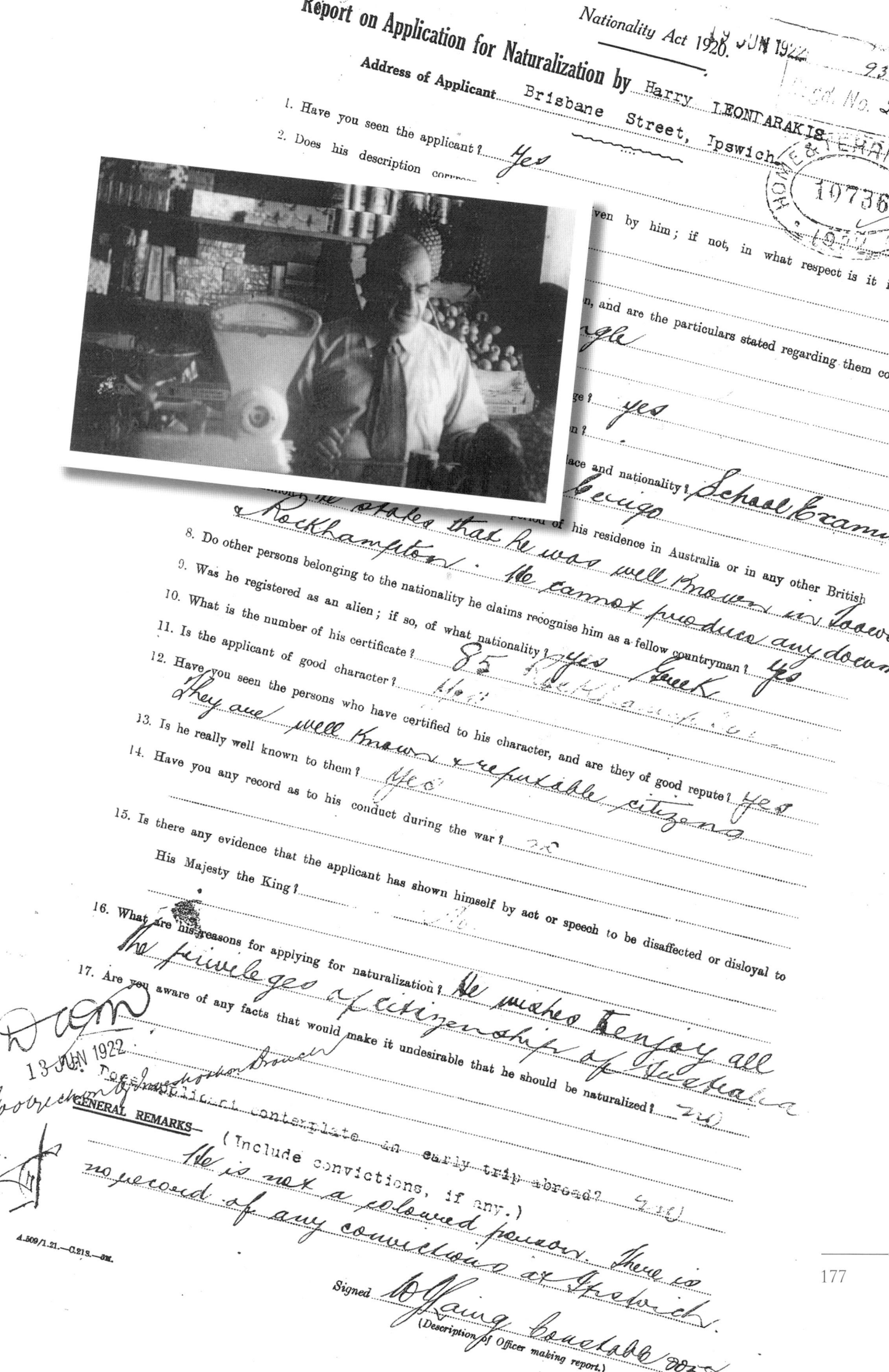

and television presenter, Anthony Koutoufides, Carlton Australian Rules captain, John Lazarou, businessman, Lex Marinos OAM, actor, director, writer and broadcaster, George Miller, film director, Mark Philippoussis, tennis player, Christos Tsiolkas, author, to name a few.

Appearance was part of a general prejudice that reflected the 'White Australia' policy of 1901. The *Truth* newspaper in Brisbane, which was foremost in promoting anti-southern European sentiment, commended Ferry's report on "the hordes of greasy, unwashed, ignorant, illiterate, semi-civilised, and only half-white humans." It stated that Australians did not want the "quarter-caste-looking foreigners" to pour into the country and referred to Greek immigrants in terms of the "menace of a brindle."[267] The processing of applications for naturalisation is a further indicator of official attitudes towards Greek immigrants. Harry Londy, whose café was a focal point of the Ipswich community for several decades, lodged his application in 1922. In it, a police constable notes that Harry is of good character, as certified by "well-known and reputable citizens," but in the final section headed General Remarks the constable writes, "He is not a coloured person." Colour mattered. Greeks with darker complexions suffered greater intolerance and possibly had more difficulty than fairer-skinned Greeks like Harry in becoming naturalised at their first attempt.[268]

Hostility towards Greeks persisted during the 1920s. Greek sailors were referred to as "riff raff" and "scum," and in 1928, the Premier of Western Australia, in a parliamentary speech, referred to Greeks as 'that Fish and Chip Crowd', and in the same year, the Truth made statements such as "the muddy stream that flows to Australia from Greece, Malta and the Levant."[269] Then, in the 1930s, Greeks were summed up by Melbourne geographer, J. S. Lyng, as "the least popular foreigners in Australia."[270] Apart from these kinds of discriminatory statements, which were made at very public levels of society, Greeks experienced racial hatred at the street level too. According to historian and demographer, James Jupp, the general populace did not welcome Greek immigrants.[271]

Although Australia was a young nation when the 20th century began, British identity was so firmly entrenched that fear of anyone whose appearance, language, or customs differed from the dominant British culture was widespread. Despite the popularity of their shops and their standing as prosperous community members, Greeks were tolerated rather than respected. Australians expected them to speak English and to behave like Australian-born citizens. Greek Australians involved in this study repeatedly mentioned that they were abused if they spoke Greek on the street. Harry Tanos recalls comments like, 'He's a bloody dago; he can't speak English. Learn to speak English before you come here.'[272]

Xenophobic feeling in Sydney swelled during WW1 and erupted into riots. Brisbane proprietors faced similar hostility, although to a lesser extent. During an incident that took place in Sydney in December, 1915, numerous Greek shops were damaged as a result of anti-Greek violence. When newspaper reports of

Greece's alleged pro-German sympathies were fuelled by a false rumour that a Greek had killed an Australian soldier in Manly, an angry mob comprised of 300 soldiers and 300 key civilian rioters in an overall crowd of 4,000 people "rampaged" through inner-Sydney streets for approximately two hours, smashing the windows of Greek shops. After that, although Greeks were not interned, they had to carry identification books and notify police of their movements.[273]

Bill Andrews, an Australia-born Castellorizan, relates his father's experience of working in Sydney in the 1920's:

> [T]here was a ... very high degree of prejudice ... and they would always have a chair leg underneath the counter for fear of being attacked because it was the common thing on a Friday or Saturday night, the Australians to go up and have their fill of beer and go up to the Greek or 'Dago shop', as you realize they were referred to those days, order the best of everything and then walk out and wouldn't want to pay, and if they were challenged they were just as likely to beat up the owner so they always have to have underneath something.[274]

In 1922, when one and a half million refugees from the Asia Minor 'catastrophe' accelerated the rate of immigration, fear of foreigners was manifest through violence of this nature.[275]

A census in 1933 revealed that over 99% of the Australian population still identified as British, and there was a strong desire to maintain that identity. During riots in Boulder/Kalgoorlie the following year, Anglo-Australian miners looted and burned Greek, Slav, and Italian shops. The riots lasted two days and involved 1,000 people, two of whom were killed.[276] Such violent behaviour may be explained by the lack of jobs during the depression and the fact that Greek immigrants worked longer hours than many Australians and were prepared to work, and for less pay. But since 'foreigners' were prohibited from working in factories (except during World War 11) – which partly forced Greeks into their own catering businesses – and since the violence in Sydney in the 20s and in Boulder/Kalgoorlie in the 30s was committed against people who were self-employed, it seems that less rational fears, like those concerning colour, religion, language, food, clothing, and other cultural aspects, generated this prejudice. Several factors feature prominently in accounts of discrimination. The attitude toward work on the part of many Greek migrants was different from that of many Australians. Some also had darker complexions and most could not speak English. In addition, Greek names represented an additional form of difference that could incite abuse.

Many Greeks names are long and unfamiliar to the Australian tongue. As a result, the Australian larrikin sense of humour sometimes gave rise to light-hearted forms of name-calling. Jim Bellas remembers the case of a young Greek by the name of Cassimatis who served with him in the army during World

The attitude toward work on the part of many Greek migrants was different from that of many Australians.

War Two. Their sergeant always called the young man "case of tomatoes," which, when pronounced with a strong Aussie accent – "caysa tumarters" – sounds surprisingly Greek. But more often than not, name-calling was not done in jest. The Tanos brothers of the Sydney Café in Ipswich traded under the name, Dunn & Co. to avoid abuse caused by their non-English name. The widespread practice of anglicising Christian names and surnames is a particularly telling aspect of the Greek experience of Australia.

Many Greeks shortened their names – Harry Leondarakis changed his name to Londy, Stratis Galanis became Stan Garland, one of the Kentrotis brothers changed his name to Kentos, Kallos is derived from Kallikeronos, and Megaloconomos became simply Conomos. Others names were translated to their English equivalent – Gianis Mavrokefalos translates as John Black, Dimitri as Jim, and Pappagianou as Johnson. Like the food these proprietors served – steak and eggs, sandwiches, meat pies, fish and chips – and the names of some cafés – *Melba, Britannia, Royal, Empire, Regal, Busy Bee, Blue Bird, Australia, Sydney, Popular* – Anglicised names indicate a determination to avoid friction with locals, who could not pronounce unfamiliar Greek names, and a willingness to forego their own traditions in order to fit into Australian culture. According to Peter Kallos, government officials sometimes changed the names of immigrants when they were filling out their forms because they decided that Greek names were too long and too difficult to spell.

Surprisingly, not one of the Greek Australians with whom I spoke expressed any bitterness regarding this practice, although it should be noted that most male respondents were second generation Greeks. But to change one's name, particularly in a culture that places such importance on the practice of naming, is an indication that the Greeks approached life as aliens in a foreign land with a fierce determination to succeed.[277] When questioned about what it was like for Greeks to not only leave their homes and families behind but to also lose their names, Peter said, "Well, you'd have to know what their life was."[278] He was referring to the terrible conditions on Kythera and other Greek islands, and what migrants were prepared to forego in the hope of finding a better life. Greek immigrants were used to hardship; they were prepared to do whatever was necessary to make Australia their home. If appearance and names formed part of the basis for prejudice in the general population, language appears to be the marker of difference that most often incited abuse, particularly in the form of the words 'dago' and 'wog'.

Greek immigrants were used to hardship; they were prepared to do whatever was necessary to make Australia their home.

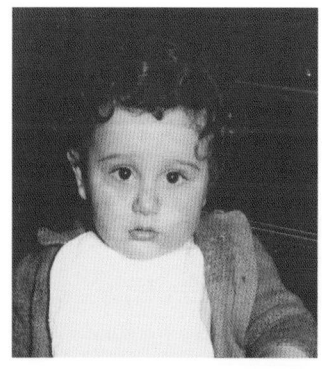

"Speak English Ya Bloody Dago"

Phyllis, an Australian-born waitress at Londy's Café in the late 1920s, spoke Greek fluently and was close to many of the Greeks living in Ipswich at that time. Her daughter, Narelle, who recalls being part of the Greek community from about ten years of age, reports that everyone called the Greeks 'dagos'. Maria Kentrotis began her Ipswich café life in the Ritz Café, married Jim Kentrotis, who was a partner with his brother in the Regal Café, subsequently helped out at her brother's shop, Tony's Snack Bar, and, finally, operated the Central Milk Bar for many years. For Maria, 1972 marked a turning point in the life of Greek immigrants. It was the year Gough Whitlam came to power and introduced the term 'New Australian'. "After 1972 I don't know what happens; I have no complaints after that," says Maria. "Before that, forget New Australians, everybody call us wogs, everybody, we can't walk [. . .] outside to the other shop, we can't walk."[279] The word 'wogs' passes her lips in a whisper of shame. While Anglo-Australians maintain that they meant nothing by the term, it obviously distressed Maria.

One day, a regular customer at Tony's Snack Bar insisted that he was too young to address the café proprietor as Maria, or Mary, as family and friends know her, and asked if he could call her 'Mum'. Maria replied, "Until yesterday, they call me 'dago' so you can call me 'Mum' if you want." She recalls that as a café proprietor she was a maternal figure to many of the boys who frequented the café, but the young man's request after decades of prejudice is a significant memory for Maria. Maria also says that Greeks were called "hungry" because they worked long hours and opened on Sundays when other businesses did not. Greeks were ahead of their time in this respect since, as Maria notes, many businesses now open long hours, some seven days a week.

Constantinos Karanges, whose brother's godfather opened the Niagara Café in Newcastle in 1898, agrees that the Greeks encountered constant racism in the 'early days'. Like Maria, he also notes, "It is very different now, but before Whitlam we were all wogs. You were frightened to speak Greek because people would say, '"If you can't speak English, go back to where you came from'." Constantinos explains that there was no feeling of belonging to their new country. Inability to speak English was a constant barrier: "When you want to express your feelings you can't, because you do not have the right words."[280]

Many older Australian-born people interviewed during the course of research for this book still used the word 'dago', which suggests that the older generation of Australians has still not completely embraced the Greek community. They used expressions like "the wog near the North Star," "the stinkin' Greeks," and "a half a dozen dagoes." Most of them were adamant,

however, that they liked the Greeks and frequently patronised their cafés, and that the term was not intended to give offence. Many said, "We didn't mean anything by it." Narelle confirmed that, although the Greeks were hurt by the word 'dago', there was no animosity between Greeks and Australians in Ipswich because Greeks were very good business people and had a welcoming attitude toward customers. One gains a different impression, however, when speaking with Greek people.

> *They were perfect gentlemen. "But, on Saturday night," writes Effie, "they'd get drunk, and go in there, and abuse the owner. 'You wog. Why don't you go back where you came from?' and so on.*

Most of the Greek Australians I interviewed confirmed that they found the word hurtful, and some continue to do so even when it is used by Greek Australians in comedy shows. Several people added, however, that "you had to listen for the way it was said." They recognised that many times 'dago' was used as a means of identification, familiarity, and even affection, while at others times it was deployed as a derogatory term. An Ipswich resident who grew up in central Queensland recalls a sign over a non-Greek café in Longreach that read, "Shop Here Before the Day Goes". Peter Cominos describes a similar one in Cairns. "It seemed like an innocent sign," he says, "but everyone knew what it meant."[281] Helen sums up her experience: "Not that you were shunned," she says, "but you were."[282]

Even Greek children were called 'little dagos' at school.[283] Arriving in Ipswich in 1922 aged nine, Mick Londy recalls that being called 'dago' made him feel inferior: "It was always there – the prejudice." To make matters worse, language difficulties meant that Mick was always older than other boys in his class.[284] Peter Veneris, whose family had a café in Lockhart, had similar experiences, and he recalls that when his family went into the café business, the term 'dago' changed to 'greasy spoon dago.'[285] Children's experiences of growing up as 'café kids' in Ipswich are elaborated in Chapter Six.

Despite the 'findings' of the *Ferry Report*, the displays of violence recorded by historians like Conomos, and accounts of intolerance given by men and women who participated in research for this book, attitudes towards Greeks varied considerably. One Greek café worker in Charleville during the first decades of the 20th century remembers Australians being angry when he spoke Greek, saying, "Speak English, you bloody dago," but another claims that relations in Goondiwindi were good: "We got on well with Australian customers. It was like one big family."[286] Jupp records a dramatic shift in Australians' attitudes towards Greeks in October 1940, when Greece repulsed Mussolini's invasion unaided.[287] Prior to that, use of the word 'dago', which had begun to disappear, was revived; drunken soldiers abused Greeks, demanding, "Dago, give us a drink. We are fighting for you." Also, Greece's initial policy of wartime neutrality in WWI sparked clashes between café owners and Australian soldiers. Conomos notes that until Greece joined the allies in 1917, drunken behaviour – putting salt in the sugar, refusing to pay, causing fights, damaging cafés – displayed a normally-latent hostility.[288]

Brisbane writer, Effie Detsimas, recalls a story that highlights this latent hostility. The situation took place in a café near North Quay in Brisbane in the 1950s. The café was near the Law Courts and was packed with judges and solicitors enjoying meals every day of the week. They were perfect gentlemen. "But, on Saturday night," writes Effie, "they'd get drunk, and go in there, and abuse the owner. 'You wog. Why don't you go back where you came from?' and so on. On Monday they'd be gentlemen again."[289] Being told to "go back where you came from" was a common rebuke, but, having encountered this perplexing experience several times, Effie asks, "Go back where?"[290]

When you leave a country, you leave it. You might keep your customs, but you make your home in your adopted country. We (migrants) are brought here to be part of the population. When we get here, we are not Greek anymore. We are funny types of Aussies. And we are patriotic as well." [291]

For people like Effie, who have made their home here, Australia is their country and they are proud to call it home. Besides, Effie was born in Sydney.

Some Greek-Australians, especially second generation Greek-Australians, on the other hand, were never called 'dagoes' and never experienced animosity. Because coming to Australia was like being given a new lease of life, some proprietors were even reluctant to talk about the subject because they felt that being called a 'dago' was nothing compared with the benefits they received. Jim Bellas, who owned cafés in the heart of Brisbane between the 1940s and the 1980s, says he does not think Australians were racist toward Greek immigrants. Jim says, "I take my hat off to Australians. I was not trained for anything and had no English at all when I came in 1936 and I was just 16. And now I'm 86 and have a good life. I respect and honour them." Having seen the treatment migrants received at the hands of people in other countries he says, "Australians were too good. I've got no complaints at all. Here, they were wonderful." The only time Jim experienced any trouble in his shops occurred when men were drunk, but Jim waves his hand and says, "That was the beer talking – that's nothing." His recollection of the years he spent in Barcaldine before the Second World War is also that Australians were wonderful – like brothers and sisters.

Athena Bellas was born in Australia and speaks English 'like an Aussie'. She never experienced prejudice either. Raised with a very strong sense of being Greek, Athena says that she is really two people – very Australian and very Greek at the same time. Although she has never lived in Greece, Athena was taught from early childhood that being Greek was a big source of pride, so, as a young person, whenever she heard Australians using the word 'dago' or speaking rudely to Greeks, she just thought, "Oh, they mustn't know about Greece

– how wonderful it is." According to Athena, Greeks were perceived as 'cliquey', which irritated Australians, although she thinks this is only natural with any group of expatriates. She adds that sometimes Greeks spoke Greek in front of Australians just to irritate them, but difficulties sprang from ignorance on both sides. Australian's were ignorant of Greek religion, food, and other cultural practices, as were the Greeks about Australian culture. Because she was brought up in Australia and knew her Australian neighbours well, Athena challenged Greeks whenever they criticised Australians for a perceived inability to cook, for example, saying that they were simply ignorant about Australian food.

Love and Marriage

Even when Greek/Australian relations were good, there were some boundaries that were not easily transgressed. Narelle's claim that there was no animosity between Greeks and Australians came with one qualification: "Unless you wanted to marry one." According to Narelle, a romance developed between her mother and a relative of the Londy family, who also worked at Londy's Café. In 1929, when they wanted to become engaged, the boy was dispatched to a relative's café in Bundaberg and Phyllis to her grandmother's property in New South Wales. According to Jack Stathis, however, Harry Marendy, Jack Cassimatis and George Andrews, who had cafés in Ipswich, married Australians. In the early days of Greek immigration, when few Greek women lived in Australia, it is more likely that Greek men married Australian women than it is that Greek women had Anglo-Australian husbands. Second and third generations were more likely to marry Anglo-Australians – each of Jack's three brothers and his sister has an Anglo-Australian spouse – but it is surprising that many of the grandchildren of second generation Greek-Australians involved in this research married other Greek-Australians and speak fluent Greek. The Greek community in Australia has managed to become embedded in Australian culture and yet at the same time Greeks maintain close networks with each other and a strong sense of Greekness. Con Castan sums it up this way:

> *As soon as I start talking Greek, I behave Greek! People think I was born in Greece. As soon as I stop talking Greek, people think I'm a dinkum Aussie … So I'm both! … I lead several lives – a Jekyll-and-Hyde kind of existence. […] It's a creative tension, not a destructive one … So I'm pretty lucky.*[292]

Marriage, like appearance, names, and language is part of an identity which Greek-Australians negotiate on a daily basis.

Maureen, who worked at Londy's Café, does not convey the impression that Greek families were opposed to a member of the family marrying an Australian girl. Maria, too, saw the main obstacle to her marrying an Australian as her inability to speak English rather than the fact that she was Greek. Jack agrees that the resistance to Greek men marrying Australian women came not from the Greeks or from Australian girls, but from Australian parents.

Maureen did not date Greek boys, although she often danced with them at local dances and went out with them in groups. She says there was no objection on the part of girls her age to marrying Greeks, but she claims that for her mother and people of her mother's generation, it was unthinkable. On the other hand, Lily, who was a waitress at the Metro Café, believes that Mrs Stathis wanted her children to marry other Greeks. Lily remembers an occasion when one of the Stathis boys announced that he was marrying an Australian girl; his mother said, "Why don't you marry Lily; at least I know her." Lily appears to have had little reluctance to marrying a Greek, but, like Maureen, says that her mother's generation would not have considered it.

The Food Factor

Food is so obviously part of the story of the Australian Greek café that it is easy to overlook the role it played in fitting a wave of 'foreigners' into a 'white Australia'. Food is a primordial focus from the moment of birth and the hub around which social life revolves; it is an integral part of christenings, birthdays, weddings, anniversaries, Christmas, Easter, even funerals. Given the capacity of food to erode barriers between people, the very act of providing food, then, rather than the quality, price, or quantity of the food, may clarify the Greek café's role in assimilating Greek immigrants.

Greeks appear to have been good business people.[293] They were often also kind.[294] More specifically, however, Greek proprietors appear to have created a family atmosphere in their cafés, over which they presided as hosts. Joanne recalls, "Dad and uncle, the two little bald brothers they were – well that's what everyone called them – had a favourite spot at the table at the front of the shop and they'd give lollies and ice-creams to toddlers coming into the café."[295] Don Risson similarly remembers that when he delivered potatoes to Greek cafés, owners told him to help himself to a piece of fish and go and cook it, always pressing him to eat more. He says, "They would greet you at the door and they'd talk to you."[296]

Certainly, the Greek respondents involved in this project were warm, welcoming people and wonderful hosts; research invariably involved conversing around a table of food and, often, taking a bundle home. Urging the researcher to partake more fully of her generous provision, one host laughed, "Typical Greek hospitality – making you eat more when you're already full."[297] It is possible then that many customers felt that Greek proprietors were sharing their table rather than just making a living.

This homely family atmosphere was enhanced precisely because the Greeks served familiar, everyday food. Café menus did not boast delicacies and gourmet delights, and unlike the Chinese café, which emphasised difference

> *Food is a primordial focus from the moment of birth and the hub around which social life revolves; it is an integral part of christenings, birthdays, weddings, anniversaries, Christmas, Easter, even funerals.*

between Australian and Chinese food and culture, there was nothing exotic about anything on the menu. Also, there was nothing special about going to Ipswich's Greek cafés. According to Maureen, going to Londy's was an everyday ritual rather than a treat, unlike a visit to the memorable Whitehouse's Café, where sophistication and upmarket elegance made dining a special occasion.[298] Owned by Anglo-Australians, Whitehouse's was a grand café in Nicholas Street. The tables were marble-topped or had starched, white linen cloths and the waitresses wore black uniforms with starched, white aprons, collars, caps, and cuffs. There was a bakery at the rear and on Saturday afternoons the café catered for up to eight weddings. Local residents describe Ipswich's Greek cafés, however, in terms of the everyday. In their role as affable hosts offering familiar food in everyday surrounding, therefore, many Greek proprietors enhanced the perception that customers shared their table.

"From a little kid I learned – respect the authority of the people of the land where you live. I have never gone to court, except to interpret for someone else."

Most Anglo-Australian respondents say they accepted the Greeks, and Greek respondents, despite being called 'dagos', acknowledge that acceptance on the part of many Australians. If customers had a sense of the everyday breaking of bread with the Greeks, the fact that the interaction between Anglo-Australians and Greek immigrants took place around food is a significant factor in the assimilation of the Greek population into Australian culture. That the cafés were the interface between an anglophile Australia and waves of Greek immigrants, and that the encounter took place around food, gives additional insight into the role the Greek café played in the developing relationship between Greek and Anglo-Australians.

The attitude with which the Greeks approached life in a new country is part of the reason that they were able to become so well established. One woman told me that her mother left Greece with this advice from her grandmother: "You must treat Australians with respect because it's their country and you are the stranger." She also advised her to take food to her neighbours and give bones to their dogs.[299] Another woman told her daughter, "Just don't tell the Australians how to run their country." Jim Bellas remembers, "From a little kid I learned – respect the authority of the people of the land where you live. I have never gone to court, except to interpret for someone else." Even in the face of the insults handed down in the *Ferry Report*, the Greek community displayed a conciliatory attitude. Two years after the *Ferry Report*, the banner of a Greek newspaper proclaimed,

"A Greek Must Always Remain a Good Greek, Because You Cannot Make a Good Australian Out of a Bad Greek. Australia Has No Need to Doubt or Fear the Man Who Loves Two Countries; the Real Danger Lies in the Man who Loves None." [300]

CHAPTER TWELVE

The Other Side of the Coin: Return to Kythera

"What imaginations must those Greek poets have had in order to have given deathless renown to this desolate, wind-bound, treeless, unfrequented island."

Viscount Kirckwall, 1864.[301]

"If you've never heard of the Greek island of Kythera," writes James Prineas, creator of the Kythera Family Website, "don't worry – most Greeks don't know where it is either. And if they have heard of it they probably don't have anything nice to say about it."[302] Until I began a research project that eventually took me to this strangely haunting place, I'd never heard of it either, but I have since discovered a link between our two islands – Kythera and Australia – which is as remarkable as it is unrecognised. Although most Australians are unaware of this link, Kytherians call their homeland 'Kangaroo Island', and for very good reason.

Kythera's population was 15,000 in the 1920s, but political instability and the poverty of an arid landscape caused such an exodus to the 'land of opportunity' that there are now only 3,000 people living on the island. There are, however, 60,000 Kytherian-born people living in Australia – that's four times as many people as were living in Kythera in the 1920s. Prineas articulates both the link between the two islands and the state of life for most Kytherians in a recent newsletter:

> It's that time of the year again . . . the coldest, dampest, most solitary period of the Kytherian winter, when many older islanders feel like the world has deserted them. In some villages only one or two houses are inhabited, their occupants huddled close to the fire. Influenza and rheumatism is the norm rather than the exception. Many dread having to go out of the house into the permanent cloud which covers most of the island.
>
> For those of you in Australia with heat-waves and droughts to contend with, you might think a bit of cold rain would be a pleasant change. It's easy to forget the isolation many of our relatives there are experiencing. Send them a bit of sunshine by calling them occasionally. They've literally kept Kythera alive so we can visit a "populated" island in the summer months, and it's the least we can do.[303]

The population on Kythera swells to about 20,000 in summer as expatriates fly back to visit aging relatives and enjoy the festival season. Little wonder that the Kytherians know Australia as 'Big Kythera'.[304] And it was the Greek café that forged this link.

Kythera is a small island to the south of the Peloponnesus. It is about 26 kilometres long and 16 kilometres wide, 282 square kilometres in all. The island's main claim to fame is the mythological birth of Aphrodite, an event that came about when Cronus cut off his father's genitals and threw them into the sea near the coast of Kythera. The severed genitals caused the sea to foam and the foam produced the beautiful goddess. Zephyrus blew upon Aphrodite, who came ashore in a giant scallop shell near the village of Paleopolis. It was also on the island of Kythera that Helen of Troy met with Paris. In addition to this wild, mythical, and romantic past, shaded terrace cafés, picturesque harbours, springs hidden in secluded, mossy grottoes, and some of the warmest people you will ever meet are part of the island's appeal. But the desolation of Kythera's mountainous landscape overshadows the visitor's first impressions.

Kythera is a barren, rocky island that rises sharply from the sea and has few natural resources. Perhaps this is because the wind, which blows you across the tarmac and into the airport, and makes the powerlines sing on the island's higher vantage points, has blown the topsoil into the deep blue Ionian Sea. At the beginning of the 20th century, olive groves and a few fertile valleys terraced with fruit and vegetable gardens barely supplied the needs of the population. Peasant farmers raised small crops of wheat, legumes, grapes, almonds, and olives, kept a few goats, and produced home-made wine and olive oil, but most were acutely poor. Others searched for

work on the mainland, leaving women and children struggling to put food on the table. Some exported olives, honey, figs, and wine to the mainland, but there was no opportunity to accumulate wealth. To make matters worse, this hand-to-mouth existence was lived in the shadow of the continual threat of war.

But to drive the roads scratched across the surface of this empty landscape, past decaying rock walls and tangles of thorny bushes and prickly pear, through silent villages with empty streets and crumbling stone houses, is to understand that Kythera has been eroded in other ways. Mass migration to Australia and other parts of the world has devastated the island. Fields are neglected, clothing, diaries, and furniture are entombed in derelict dwellings, and decaying villages, deserted of young people or abandoned altogether, have virtually become 'ghost towns'. As Alexakis and Janiszewski explain, "The principal legacy of unbridled depopulation is a landscape inhabited mostly by elderly residents, and peppered with disintegrating villages, unkempt roads, unploughed fields, collapsed windmills, and abandoned homes, schools and churches."[305]

Greek cafés were certainly the means by which desperate people gave their children a better life, but in her unforgettable photographs of villages like Fratsia, Mitata, and Trifyllianika, Alexakis documents the devastation that represents the other side of the coin: an evening purse that rots on a wall hook, a warped family photograph that fades into dust, a petrified shoe that lies amongst the rubble, a torn letter that rests beside a postcard from Australia. This is the debris of abandoned lives.[306] Prineas, whose family comes from the island, foresees in this devastation an even more tragic consequence – the demise of the simple Kytherian lifestyle.[307]

In 1900, Aphrodite's birthplace overflowed with inhabitants; 14,000 people lived in 60 bustling villages dotted across the island. The population swelled to about 15,000 in the 20s. But as the shock waves of Athanasios Comino's first Greek fish shop in Sydney began to be felt on the other side of the world, Kytherians followed a pattern of chain migration that took most of the male population to Australia, and by the 1940s villages were emptying. It was as if someone had pulled a plug that drained Kythera of fathers, brothers, and eligible bachelors. Most emigrants intended to send money home while they worked toward the day when they could come back as wealthy men to care for their families. But few returned. Sometimes families joined them in Australia. Sometimes they returned briefly to find a bride. The Greek shopkeeping family, a singularly Australian phenomenon that contributed so much to the culture of a young nation, is a wonderful story, but Australia's Greek café has its flipside. And this is played out in the villages of Kythera, where elderly people are the main inhabitants.[308]

There is a monument in Kythera that marks the place where tears were shed for loved ones who left for the other side of the world, loved ones who mostly didn't come back. Above Potamos, the port from which boats departed for Piraeus and, eventually, Australia, a plain, rectangular block rests atop a low, circular platform trimmed with blue paint and edged with a simple scallop design formed in curved metal rods. Some locals call it the 'Crying Stone'. The inscription reads:

The Place of Tears of Joy and Grief, for those who came and went, in the year 1908.

Erected in the memory of George and Cleopatra Khlentzos.

Historian, Hugh Gilchrist, describes it as "a memorial to those who went down the hill to the ships, and those who would never return."[309]

Because of the process of chain migration, many of the men who had cafés in Ipswich came from one village in Kythera, the village of Fratsia. While Ithacans appear to have opened the earliest Greek shops in Ipswich, it was the Kytherians whose businesses endured. Harry, Charles, and Jim Londy left Fratsia in the second decade of the 20th century. They operated shops in several towns, at least three in Ipswich,[310] and Harry went on to build one of the most successful and best-remembered

café businesses in that city. The story of the Londy family typifies the way whole families left their homeland behind and the way families cooperated to establish themselves in Australia through their cafés.

Harry Leondarakis migrated to Australia at a young age under the guardianship of his uncle, Harry Andronicus, in Toowoomba. He was soon joined by his twelve-year-old brother, Charley, and his brother-in-law, Jim Leondarakis. Harry and Jim had the Paragon Café in Dalby before moving to Rockhampton. When he left school, Charley worked for a proprietor who had recently to introduce the latest milk bar products from Sydney, so he learned to make ice-cream, ice-cream sodas, malted milk shakes, sundaes, and parfaits. In about 1920, Harry and Jim bought the Sydney Café near the railway station in Ipswich and Charley joined them as a full partner. The three traded under the name 'Londy Bros.' because Pennys, Woollies, and Fosseys were successful business names at the time and 'Londys' had a similar sound. Soon afterwards, the partners adopted 'Londy' as their family name.

In the early 1920's, Londy Bros opened the Café Australia in Ipswich and the American Bar in Gympie, which was managed by their sister, Arete, and her husband. Harry then established Londy Brothers Paris Café in Ipswich with Jim's son, Mick. Charley opened Londy Brothers Blue Bird Café in Bundaberg with another brother-in-law, Mick Levonis. Jim moved the Capitol Café and the Paragon Café in Toowoomba. When Jim died, his wife, Rene, set up Londy's Café in Texas, and later moved to Townsville, where she started another Londy's Café in partnership with another relative. Mick and Calliope Levonis moved on to Londy Brothers Café Mimosa in Maryborough and their sons bought out the Capitol Café in Toowoomba. The Londy family eventually went into the Theatre business on the Redcliffe Peninsula.[311]

In the wake of the Londy family's departure for Australia, the Londy home in Fratsia is abandoned and dilapidated. Stalks of grass sprawl into the open doorway, the tiled floor disappears here and there under layers of grit the wind has blown in, the black, skeletal remains of a light fitting perch on the pine table, and the chairs, which seem to wait bravely for the inhabitants to return, are weathered and broken. In the eerie silence, as the wind blows across the desolate landscape and in through the unglazed window, one can almost hear voices bringing news of a land of promise, and as the afternoon sun slides across the furniture and onto the cloud-like faded blue wash on the crumbling walls, it is not hard to imagine the silent tears of the women as they prepare the farewell meal. Those who lived to see their grandchildren grow up in their adopted homeland still carry the land of their fathers in their hearts. Speaking of the Greek migrants who eventually carved out a new life in Australia, Conomos, also a Kytherian, observes that "even 50 or 60 years of life in Australia could not make them forget

the rock from which they were hewn."[312] Those memories eventually called some migrants back. Not surprisingly, a number of café proprietors have remigrated. Jim Pavlakis is one of them. After owning a café in Ipswich for more than 20 years, Jim returned to Kythera to spend his later years amongst the homes of his ancestors. Like so many other proprietors in Ipswich, Jim was born in Fratsia and followed members of his family to Australia.

Jim's sister, Maria, brought him to Ipswich, where her husband was a partner in the Kentrotis brothers' Regal Café. After working for some time at the Regal, Jim bought Tony's Café after the proprietor, Tony Veneris, was murdered in 1962. The shop was submerged for five days beneath floodwaters in 1974, but otherwise Jim's business flourished. He made good food, his customers liked him, and his shop was the hub of Ipswich's youth car culture. During the 1980s, Jim built a house near the city centre. It is much like any other two-story brick Queenslander except that the wide front steps and deep verandah are covered with tiles and edged with an impressive white concrete balustrade. The house encapsulates the history of Greek immigrants who have embraced Australian culture but manage to

imprint it with something of their earlier identity. For those who know about the Greek café phenomenon, however, the seven letters welded into the front gate tell the whole story. Jim called his Queensland home FRATSIA.

Unfortunately, not long after work on the house began, Jim suffered some health problems and over a period of years decided to return to Kythera. That was nearly 20 years ago. Jim became mayor of Fratsia and is still active in the community there. He is even restoring some of his family's homes, or at least trying to prevent further deterioration. The houses in Fratsia are mostly two-storey rectangular buildings with wide arches on the bottom level, a strong construction method that accounts for the fact that so many still survive. They are made of stone and plastered with concrete. There is not a verandah in sight. Jim feels a strong attachment to Ipswich and is grateful for the opportunities it brought into his life, but when I ask him why he returned to Kythera, he explains, "Well I just did not want to die in Australia, you understand." When I visited Jim, his lovely wife, Lumbrini, and their gang of feline hangers-on, I stayed with them in their home.

I follow Jim across the silent street to the house he has restored. A black iron gate swings open and I step onto the tiles of the front patio. On the concrete wall beside the front door, seven letters are written in gold and framed with marble – IPSWICH.

CHAPTER THIRTEEN

End of an Era: The Demise of the Greek Café

The façade of Londy Bros. Blue Bird Café in Bundaberg.

Greek cafes were "forced to transform into takeaways or be relegated to memory or oblivion."

Janiszewski and Alexakis

The Greek café is a cultural icon of the Australia of the 50s and 60s. During the middle decades of the 20th century, about 13 of them operated in the centre of Ipswich.

When they were so much a part of the city's social tapestry, it is hard to comprehend why few survived into the 70s. Eventually, however, they all closed their doors for the last time. The Central Milk Bar was the last to go; it was leased to non-Greeks in 2006 but at the time of writing was also closed for business. Ipswich residents offer a variety of reasons by way of explanation for the demise of the Greek café. Although some reasons are suggested more frequently than others, multiple factors caused Greek shops to close, and the combination of factors is different in the case of each café.

Fast-Food Chains

The pace of life increased radically as the 20th century progressed and the pace at which we ordered and ate our food increased along with it, hence the term 'fast-food'. The link between Australia's Greek café and American food outlets is evident in the first decade of the 20th century, but, sadly, an American-led fast-food industry contributed to the demise of the Greek café. Fast-food chains like McDonalds and Hungry Jack's began to replace family-based food catering concerns and sit down meals gave way to rushing customers and takeaway food. Some respondents suggested that the 1960s saw a shift to 'the instant society', with people no longer wanting to sit and wait for meals on a daily basis.[313]

Perhaps this has come full circle with European-style cafés now dotted throughout most Australian towns and cities, including Ipswich. These 'sophisticated' cafés offer a different product from that offered at McDonalds, and they target a different demographic, but in the 1960s, Greek cafés were catering to the kind of market McDonalds targets today. They could not compete with the prices or the speed offered by fast-food chains. As Janiszewski and Alexakis explain, many Greek cafes were "forced to transform into takeaways or be relegated to memory or oblivion."[314] This is the case with the Central Milk bar, where proprietors took out the front wall and plastered the interior and exterior of the building with garish signs in order to increase the shop's street presence and encourage motorists to pull up out front. Collins et al. describe this kind of Greek takeaway as the "modern reincarnation" of the classic Greek café.[315] If Greek takeaway outlets still manage to survive, it is partly because they are usually staffed by family members and because proprietors do not have to pay rent, since many have been in business for decades and own their premises, usually on prime pieces of real estate. Harry's Shop on Lutwyche Road is an example of this.

When Harry and Maroula left the Sydney Café in Ipswich in 1962, they bought a convenience store in Lutwyche Road, Brisbane. Nearby homes were removed to widen the road, so they converted their shop into a snack bar to attract passing traffic. Charcoal Chicken moved in nearby and McDonalds built right next door. But still Harry's Shop survived. In 2002, after forty years of trading on Lutwyche Road, Harry and Maroula finally closed their doors because they could not afford to cover the increased cost of insurance premiums. The couple then moved into the front of the shop, where they live under a menu board that still advertises corned beef sandwiches, Hawaiian burgers and Chico Rolls.

Professional Second-Generation Migrants

For most first-generation Greek migrants, a café was a means to an end, and proprietors endured the hardship involved in owning a café precisely so that their children would not have to. Collins et al. note that post-WWII Greeks, in particular, viewed small business as a way to achieve upward mobility. He claims that children of post-war Greek immigrants sought careers as doctors, lawyers, and teachers rather than shopkeepers.[316] Jupp notes that Australians of Greek parentage were entering professions as early as the 1920s.[317] Constantinos Karanges, of the Niagara Café in Newcastle, also explains that all of his children have fulfilled the dreams he once had for himself – dreams of going to university and becoming a teacher. No third generation Karanges has a café.[318]

Several of the second-generation, Greek men I interviewed studied at tertiary institutions and are now pharmacists, accountants, doctors, and the like. Peter Kallos recalls that if he ever displayed any reluctance to do his homework, he was dragged into the kitchen and shown a pile of dirty café dishes. Similarly, Peter Cominos explains that as a child he saw the hard work and long hours his father put into the café. This first-hand experience of what was involved in running a café ensured that Peter, like many other 'café kids', had no desire to follow in his father's footsteps and run the family business. Many high-profile Australians can trace their origins to a humble café. George Miller, for example, the director of hit films like, *Mad Max*, *Babe, Pig in the City*, and *Happy Feet*, is from a Kytherian café family.

His children have fulfilled the dreams he once had for himself – dreams of going to university and becoming a teacher.

Hotels, Clubs and Restaurants

Lunch was a common reason for visiting the local Greek café. As hotels and clubs began to serve counter lunches and inexpensive evening meals, they drew custom away from Greek cafés. It is difficult to establish when hotels began to serve meals to non-resident patrons, but most Ipswich hotels now offer simple, reasonably-priced counter meals. Some, like the Federal, the Prince Alfred, the Metropole and others, boast restaurant-quality meals, décor, and service. In addition to hotels, a number of clubs – the Golf Club, the RSL, Brothers Football Club, the United Services Bowls Club – and taverns serve meals in Ipswich, and many of these now have the added allure of poker machines.

It should be remembered that until relatively recently restaurants were not widespread, although, as Symons points out, "Every generation of Australians has believed it has enjoyed the country's first decent dining out."[319] Except for Chinese restaurants, however, there were few restaurants in regional 20th century Australia prior to the 70s. Ipswich had a Chinese restaurant, which offered take away meals, but when people ate out it was mostly at cafés. The number of restaurants increased dramatically from the 70s and this affected café trade. Ironically, while Greek cafés sold British-Australian food, the popularity of later restaurants is due to the 'non-Australian' food they offer: French, Italian, Mexican, Indian, Thai, Japanese, Moroccan. Just as ironically, the recently-emerged café culture has in turn had a detrimental effect on restaurants. This is discussed later in the chapter.

While they waited for the lights to go down, they entertained one another with guessing the names of the stars whose biographies were written on the Fantales wrappers

Many café stories refer to hotel patrons. Waitresses mentioned that between them, the Greek café and the pub catered for the entire community. Often men would go into the café for a meal after the pubs shut, and this would cause problems for waitresses if they had had too much to drink. The end of six o'clock closing in Australian pubs, then, saw the local hotel develop as an evening meeting place, reducing the evening trade at the Greek café.[320]

Television and Picture Theatres

Jack Stathis notes that cafés depended on the night trade – people window-shopping or walking in family groups, who would call in for an ice cream. This was lost to television. Picture theatres encountered a similar problem. A symbiotic relationship existed between cafés and picture theatres in the middle decades of the 20th century. Cafés and milk bars had big confectionery counters, where movie-goers stocked up on boxes of Fantales and Jaffas before the 'pictures'. While they waited for the lights to go down, they entertained one another with guessing the names of the stars whose biographies were written on the Fantales wrappers, and, as the movie reached a silent, edgy moment, 'the lads' were always armed with a Jaffa or two, which they would roll down the sloped wooden floor to the screams and applause of the audience. At intermission, café staff would be inundated with orders for hot chips and more confectionery, and afterwards, especially after the evening session, cafés overflowed with people chatting over an after-theatre supper of toasted sandwiches and milk coffee.[321]

Ipswich had number of picture theatres. Helen Kentos, who owned the Wintergarden Milk Bar beside the Wintergarden Picture Theatre, judges that most people went to the pictures twice a week in the 1950s. Her husband, John, prophesying the end of picture theatres with the introduction of television, sold their milk bar in 1958. John was right. With the advent of television, drive-ins, and videos, most of the theatres in Ipswich went out of business, and this had a huge impact on cafés. As multi-cinema complexes opened, they had their own in-house Candy Bars, which sold chocolate-coated ice creams and popcorn, in addition to the kinds of items the Greek cafés sold to theatre patrons.

Rural Families

Several people interviewed for this project mentioned that families from outlying rural areas came into Ipswich for a weekly 'day in town'. The days on which the Churchill cattle sales were held were especially busy, and 'country people' usually had a favourite Greek café and would spend as many as three 'sessions' in it. But the sale yards closed and making a living on a rural property became less viable. Improved cars also meant that a trip to town was no longer such a big day out, and developers built large shopping facilities in surrounding rural areas. Cafés lost business as a result of all of these factors.

Ipswich Bypass

Catering for travellers was an important part of the café trade, but as the 20th century sped past, highways began to bypass rural townships in New South Wales and Queensland and this had an impact on regional café businesses.[322] Jack Stathis notes that the Greek cafés in Ipswich depended on the through-tourist trade, and when the Ipswich bypass was constructed, Ipswich cafés lost the business from motorists travelling between Brisbane and Toowoomba.

Motorists could use Greek cafés if they detoured into city centres, but the advent of roadhouses, which supplied both food and fuel, made this unnecessary. Several Ipswich proprietors mentioned the problem this posed for their businesses. Those who were teenagers in the 1970s reported that service stations like the Blue Star and the Caltex on the highway at Blacksoil were their 'great, good gathering places'.[323] Jack believes that Ipswich hotels suffered a similar fate as a result of the bypass.

It is worth noting that as cars evolved and highways improved, travel became speedier and more comfortable. Cars are now equipped with air-conditioning and other 'creature comforts' so they sweep along wide, smooth bitumen roads, passing more towns in a single driving period than an EJ Holden would have done in the 1960s. Thus, motorists tend to travel far longer distances before they need to stop for a drink or a meal.

Escalating Car Culture

Fewer people had cars or used cars routinely during the decades when Greek cafés flourished. In the 30s and 40s, according to Conomos and those involved in this project, people relied on buses and, at least in Ipswich, bus stops were often located outside cafés, the last bus usually waiting until the café closed at 11pm. Also, families going for an evening stroll called in for ice creams, and people would walk to shops and picture theatres, which was conducive to them calling in for an icy-cold fresh fruit drink, ice cream soda, or malted milk. This kind of continual 'passing traffic' was the basis of the café trade, but as more and more people bought cars, this decreased.[324]

In addition, when people had no cars, they tended to be in town for longer periods and needed a 'home away from home'. Many customers had a café they frequented on a regular basis, and not only did they have morning tea, lunch, and afternoon tea at 'their' café, but they might also leave shopping, suitcases and other items there.[325] As car travel became the norm, however, people walked past cafés much less often, which reduced trade, and going into town was not an all-day event.

Cars also promoted the use of service stations, rather than cafés, as gathering places. A notable exception to the detrimental effect on Greek cafés of the escalating car culture is the youth car culture, as highlighted in Bob Hudson's hit song of 1975, which features the Parthenon Milk Bar in Newcastle. Juke boxes and pinball machines installed in cafés and milk bars were an integral part of this culture and these were installed in places like the Wintergarden Milk Bar. The inner streets of Ipswich were alive with bodgies and widgies in the 50s and 60s, and even in the 70s and 80s, young people whose relationships focussed around their cars, concentrated their activities in the centre of the city on certain nights of the week. In between 'laps', they usually gathered outside one of the few cafés still trading at that time, and proprietors report that this had only a positive impact on their businesses.

Youth and Recreation

Maria Kentrotis of the Central Milk Bar notes that people, young people in particular, now have far more options in the way of entertainment than to 'hang out' together at the local café. Technological innovations like computers, video games, DVDs, and mobile phones mean that fewer young people gather just to eat and talk. If they do, they are more likely to go to a restaurant. Video game parlours are also popular. Multiplex cinemas are another common form of leisure for contemporary youth and older people alike, as is a trip to the shopping mall, where the food court is the most frequented eating place. 'Shopping', other than grocery shopping, is now no longer a job, but a leisure activity.

Economic Downturn and Economic Rationalism

The closure of Ipswich's woollen mills, relocation and employment changes in the coal and railway industries during the 1970s, and the economic downturn of the late 1980s had a negative impact on small business in the Ipswich CBD. Maria Kentrotis notes the effect on her business of the loss of jobs in these staple industries.[326]

Prepackaged Goods and Supermarkets

Perhaps the most significant changes in the way Australians shop have been the enormous number of pre-packaged goods available in recent decades and the introduction of supermarkets. Fresh fruit drinks, home-made ice cream, and loose lollies were popular items in Greek cafés. Greek proprietors introduced chocolate bars and boxed confectionery early in the 20th century, Peters Ice Cream replaced home-made ice cream in cafés during the Second World War, and bottled soft drinks can be seen in photographs of cafés taken in the 60s and 70s, but many other items were made fresh on the premises: sundaes, malted milks, ice cream sodas, and so on. Gradually, pre-packaged soft drinks, ice creams, chocolates, lollies, fruit juice, and flavoured milk replaced shop-made products and, as these began to line the shelves in supermarkets and convenience stores, fewer people purchased them from Greek cafés. In addition to confectionery and drinks, supermarkets supply fish, which Peter Londy notes was a big 'seller' in Greek shops.

The Declining Influence of Catholicism

Greek cafés were so deeply enmeshed with Australian culture, that even the declining influence of Catholicism had an effect on Greek cafés. The Catholic practice of not eating meat on Fridays meant big business for cafés that specialised in fish, as many of them did. Stan Garland explains that in Maryborough in the second decade of the 20th century, he cooked hundreds of pieces of fish on Fridays.[327] As the century wore on, Catholics maintained this practice and the repercussions were felt in the cash registers at Greek shops. This was certainly true of the two big fish shops in Ipswich; Peter Londy cooked so much fish that, while he is a keen fisherman, he cannot face eating fish today, and Harry Tanos from the Sydney Café echoes those sentiments. Together, these two men cooked over a thousand pieces of fish on Fridays during the 1950s.

Unsophisticated Establishments

Greek cafés were ordinary, everyday places.[328] Sydney journalist, Sally McInerney, notes that, while relatively rare, restaurants were reserved for celebrations prior to the 70s and people otherwise ate at cafés. This is consistent with the reports of Ipswich residents, who refer to special occasions at the upmarket Whitehouse's Café in Nicholas Street by way of contrast to the Greek cafés. Whitehouse's, a café owned by an Anglo-Australian family, catered for weddings and had starched, white tablecloths, gleaming silverware, and upstairs dining. The food was more expensive than that sold in Greek cafés and the waitresses wore uniforms with white aprons and caps. One Ipswich resident said she never went to Whitehouse's Café because it was "too posh." Although

Ipswich's Greek cafés evoke wonderful memories today, at the time there was little special about them – they were just part of people's everyday experience.

McInerney attributes the demise of Greek cafés partly to this 'everyday' factor:

> [N]ot being sophisticated in social or architectural terms, they have never had staunch defenders, so that they undergo constant metamorphosis with different owners who feel that the place needs modernizing, otherwise the customers will disappear.[329]

Renovation occurred in many cafés during the 20s and 30s, when mechanical innovations like the soda fountain and milk bar arrived from America. Many descendents of Ipswich café owners reported that their family café had undergone renovation at some time, and both of the famous Greek cafés still in operation in Australia – the Paragon in Katoomba and the Niagara in Gundagai – were updated in the 1930s in the Art Deco style.[330] While these two survive, countless others were refurbished after the war. Many cafés were, in fact, classic examples of 'modern' architecture, but as the decades passed, and design styles changed, little value was placed on their architectural features. Old buildings that survived long enough to be heritage-listed were usually elaborate or unique at the time they were built, but even this was not enough to save most buildings. Whitehouse's Café did not survive the makeover that desecrated Nicholas Street in the 1980s. Like most of the Greek cafés in Ipswich it too was demolished.

The Coffee Club

The story of Australia's Greek café is astounding and heart-warming, and to know that it has all but come to an end brings sadness and not a little regret that younger generations will never experience this aspect of Australian cultural history. You can imagine, then, my delight upon discovering that the ongoing narrative of the Greek Café phenomenon in Australia has a resurrection ending in the popular chain, The Coffee Club, which is the brainchild of three Greek-Australians. Even more exciting are the parallels between this successful enterprise and the cafés of earlier generations of Greek-Australians.

Unlike early Greek café owners, The Coffee Club directors are passionate about great coffee; they source the best beans and employ highly trained baristas to grind and 'espress' them, so that every cup of Coffee Club coffee is perfect. Coffee was not a priority for proprietors in Greek cafés, although it was one of their top sellers. But in many other aspects, The Coffee Club success story is redolent of the spread of Greek cafés throughout Australia. First, it began with a spur of the moment idea, much like Athanasios (Arthur) Comino's inspiration for a fish shop in Sydney in 1878. After Emmanuel Drivas and Emmanuel Kokoris had been enjoying dinner in Brisbane one night, they decided it was time for coffee. When they couldn't find anywhere open late at night, they realised that thousands of people must be in the same predicament. Here was an untapped market.

An emphasis on giving customers whatever they want whenever they want it reflects the successful foundation of the Greek café.

With a display of imagination, hard work, determination, and good business sense typical of earlier generations of Greek café owners, they opened the first shop in the Eagle Street Pier complex in 1989, under the management of John Lazarou. And, like Comino's fish shop, it was an instant success. In much the same way that the ripple effect of chain migration spread a network of family-related cafés throughout NSW and up into Queensland, The Coffee Club then expanded. Shops now operate all over Australia: From Darwin to Adelaide, Cairns to Sydney, Melbourne to Perth and many places in between, people pop into The Coffee Club for everything from a quick coffee to a leisurely dinner.[331]

Like Greek cafés, which ranged from elegant, upmarket establishments to more basic shops, The Coffee Club exists in a range of forms. Kiosks, Clubs, and Café Bar Restaurants feature different menus and are appropriate to different and unique locations. An emphasis on giving customers whatever they want whenever they want it also reflects the successful foundation of the Greek café, and menus reveal that, while the Australian palette has changed in 50 years, The Coffee Clubs offers a wide range of well-known foods at reasonable prices, as did the Greek café

Finally, Greek cafés were popular meeting places; they were part of the social fabric of large cities and rural towns. The Coffee Club echoes this aspect of its ancestry too. The business' mission statement is to provide a welcoming, relaxed meeting place that offers good food, great service, and excellent coffee, and the answer to the question, 'Where will I meet you?'[332] This phrase is repeated throughout *The Coffee Club Franchise Information* booklet and features in various advertising media. Like the Greek cafés of earlier decades, the brochure encourages customers to take time out from the busy workday, catch up with friends, and indulge in a little people-watching. "No wonder so many people are asking the question 'where will I meet you?' and answering The Coffee Club."[333]

The Rise of a Contemporary Café Culture

While this project tracks the evolution of the Greek café from its origins in the oyster saloon of the late 19th century to its demise in the 1970s, a brief discussion of the recently-emerged café culture, of which The Coffee Club is part, is appropriate as a means of comparison with Greek cafés, particularly since Greek cafés were, as journalist Lenore Nicklin observes, "Our Original Café Culture."[334]

From the mid-80s, Australians began to embrace a sophisticated, European-style coffee culture. Panini with sun-dried tomato and camembert replaced toasted ham, cheese and tomato sandwiches in cafés that sprang up like mushrooms the inner-city streets. Arty chalkboards usurped the role of laminated table menus in trendy suburban cafés, where the list of coffee styles seemed to grow daily. Even in country towns, chrome chairs and black umbrellas sprawled onto dusty footpaths as Australians dreamed of the Parisian sidewalk café. What made this widespread café culture so remarkable was the lack of similar haunts and hangouts in the preceding decades. There had, of course, been cafeterias in department stores, snack bars in strip shopping centres, and coffee lounges in 'shopping towns', but the new coffee culture was an explosion of European style sophistication that resonated with Australians so that there still seems to be no end to the number of cafés a chic street can support. Even McDonalds leapt onto the bandwagon with its McCafé.

More recently, 'café bars' have evolved, blurring the distinction between the café and the pub, a boundary that was once clearly defined; Londy's Café and the North Star Hotel, adjacent to each other in Brisbane Street, Ipswich, are a good example of this distinction. The décor in the 'café bar' is contemporary, perhaps a music video plays on a flat screen television, fragments of rocket and char-grilled vegetable litter empty plates, baristas wear the mandatory café black, tables may spill out into a shaded courtyard or onto the footpath, and a bar running along one side of the room dispenses chardonnays as well as lattés. The café bar extends the café's market base by being open longer hours without offering a full restaurant menu.

Journalist, Luke Slattery, discusses the recent café culture in terms of a "phenomenon" that "exploded" in inner-city streets and extended to country areas. This echoes the descriptions of Janiszewski and Alexakis and Conomos, in their analyses of Greek cafés. On the other hand, Slattery explains that the contemporary café is an emblem of European-style sophistication, a taste for which was acquired by Australians travelling in Europe.[335] The Greek café was never an attempt to import a foreign culture and most were not renowned for their sophistication. Publisher of *Melbourne Café Guide*, Michael Sabey, defines cafés in terms of the provision of outstanding coffee, value for money food, and hours that extend from breakfast until late. This foundation, however, with the possible exception of outstanding coffee, was laid down over a century ago by Greek immigrants. Based on research carried out in 1989, Sabey claims that in reshaping the restaurant market, cafés are a force to be reckoned with: "Cafés have fundamentally changed the whole eating patterns of discerning foodies."[336] Again, this echoes the spread of Greek cafés in Australia.

Journalist and food critic, Cherry Ripe, however, observes that cafés have been blamed for driving restaurants out of business and "diluting the nation's gastronomic standards." Others accuse cafés of taking over whole streets, invading bookshops, pushing up the price of inner-city real estate, and driving out

Even in country towns, chrome chairs and black umbrellas sprawled onto dusty footpaths as Australians dreamed of the Parisian sidewalk café.

other kinds of businesses.³³⁷ According to Slattery, a whole way of life now adheres to the new coffee culture and cafés are "breeding like cockroaches along the fashionable streets of our cities."³³⁸ Greek cafés similarly had a significant impact on the way Australians lived. Although doubtless their competitors also suffered because the Greeks opened for very long hours seven days a week, on the whole, the Greek café was a welcome addition to Australian society and had a positive effect on Australian culture.

CHAPTER FOURTEEN

Café Heritage: Tracking the Signs

History never looks like history when you are living through it. It always looks confusing and messy, and it always feels uncomfortable.

– John W. Gardner[339]

The story of Australia's Greek café is largely unrecognised in the wider community. Although older Australians remember their local milk bars and cafés with fondness, they may not understand the broader significance of the Greek shopkeeping phenomenon, and many people from subsequent generations know nothing of the Greek café.

The purpose of this chapter is to outline some of the methodologies involved in this research and to offer tools that readers may use to track Greek cafés in their area.

One research method, and a good place to start, is reading the work of historians who have turned their attention to Greek migration, Greek shopkeeping, Australian food history, and Australia's shopping heritage. Historian, Leonard Janiszewski, and documentary photographer, Effy Alexakis, have undertaken some of the most significant work to date – they explore the Greek café's role in Australian culture and in immigrants' lives, although they focus primarily on cafés in rural New South Wales. Denis Conomos makes a wonderful contribution to Queensland history in his documentation of a huge number of Greek cafés in that state, although his research ends at 1945. In both cases, specific cafés are noted, although the work on cafés is part of a broader interest in the lives of Greek immigrants and Greek communities in Australia.

Most other historians, however, make only passing reference to Greek cafés: Michael Symons allocates two lines to the topic in his history of eating in Australia, failing to note the disproportionate number of Greek oyster saloons and cafés; Hugh Gilchrist, in a 1,300-page three-volume history of Greeks in Australia, allocates a brief chapter to the shopkeeping phenomenon, but few pages refer to cafés in Queensland; Craig Turnbull and Chris Valiotis' study is a further celebration of New South Wales cafés.[340] Joy McCann and Jock Collins et al. also mention Greek cafés, but their references are minor portions of a broader interest in shopping and ethnic small business.

Aphrodite and the Mixed Grill is the first body of research to focus on Greek cafés in a single town in order to understand the impact Greek shopkeepers had on the local community, and little information was available from the sources just mentioned. Ipswich was among the first towns in Queensland to have a Greek café and subsequently had many Greek cafés, and several proprietors remained in business there for long periods of time. Although Conomos and Janiszewski contributed key pieces of information about Greeks in Ipswich, few historians mention Ipswich cafés. Even local Ipswich historian, Robyn Buchanan, in a recent account of Ipswich in the 20th century, fails to mention the city's abundance of Greek cafés and milk bars.

Official records are useful resources. The Fire Department Block Plans detail property locations and, in most cases, proprietors' names and businesses, but plans of Ipswich are available only for 1918. Similarly, Ipswich City Council Land-Use Maps are only available for 1979. But Block Plans and Land-Use Maps cannot provide a complete list of Greek cafés, even for those years, because immigrants anglicised their names and the documents do not indicate ethnicity – Mavrokefalos, for example, changed his name to Black, Andreatidis became Andrews, Megaloconomos became Conomos, Leondarakis became Londy, and so on. Building Applications, Electoral Rolls, Post Office Directories, and newspaper clippings offer other useful snippets of information, but the picture is incomplete and often contradictory.[341] Some shops opened, changed hands, changed name, or closed down within short periods of time and if premises

> *Ipswich was among the first towns in Queensland to have a Greek café and subsequently had many Greek cafés, and several proprietors remained in business there for long periods of time.*

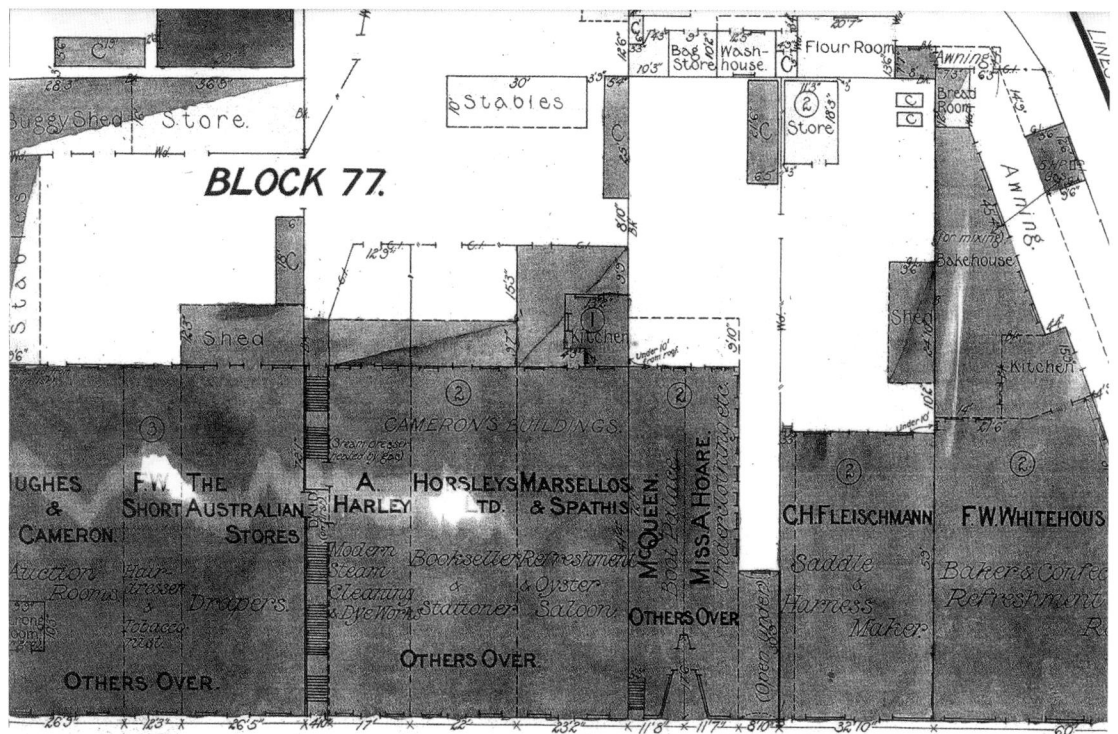

Nicholas Street, Ipswich, showing Marsellos and Spathis' second Oyster Saloon near Whitehouse's Café.

were leased, rather than bought, proprietors' names may not have been recorded. The Greek practice of reusing names according to family patterns compounds the problem of tracing family history and café ownership and employment.[342] A complete and accurate account of the city's Greek cafés and their proprietors is an elusive goal.

Histories and official sources, while they indicate that the situation in Ipswich was consistent with claims that Greek cafés dotted rural New South Wales and Queensland by 1910, are therefore inadequate for identifying the extent to which Greek cafés claimed the Ipswich streetscape, much less understanding what they meant to the people who worked and ate in them.[343] By 1910, Ipswich already had several Greek cafés. In the 1950s there were ten. Unfortunately, while Victorian and Federation buildings are often now preserved, fewer art deco buildings survive. The 'golden age' of Greek cafés passed and most of the buildings they occupied in Ipswich were demolished. Now that the Central Milk Bar has closed down, Australia's original café culture is all but erased from the Ipswich streetscape. It now exists primarily in photographs, artefacts, and, especially, memories. Oral history, then, in conjunction with academic and official sources, is the best means of constructing a history of Ipswich's Greek café venues and proprietors.

The real strength of oral history, however, is not its ability to track the growing number of cafés in Ipswich from the early 20th century, but its potential to describe what it was like to be a Greek or to work for Greeks in 20th century Ipswich. Because it offers access to the meanings of everyday practices and the stories of ordinary people, oral history is the primary means by which Greek cafés may be understood as a cultural phenomenon. A project of this nature has not previously been undertaken in Ipswich and, because the current generation of 70 to 80-year-olds is the main source of information about the role of Greek cafés in that city, the need to record this history is pressing.

The Ipswich Art Gallery's oral history morning tea – *Milkshakes and Wedding Breakfasts: Cafés and Milkbars of Ipswich* (April 2004) – was an excellent vehicle for learning about Ipswich's cafés and milk bars, but the women involved with Ipswich's Greek cafés are mostly older women for whom English is a second language, and they were reluctant to speak publicly. They were more comfortable with the idea of being interviewed in their own homes. Written notes, audio tapes, and video recordings of private interviews, as well as telephone conversations therefore proved the best way to document their stories. The conditions under which these took place were an important factor.

A video interview with Maria, for example, was almost unusable because she was working at the time amidst traffic noise in the open-fronted Brisbane Street café. Subsequent video and audio interviews were recorded in homes where it was relatively quiet and the women seemed more relaxed. This was not always possible, since people who have owned their homes for several decades often live on streets that are now major roads and noise is deafening. Situations where there were multiple interviewees also caused difficulties. Audio tapes made at such gatherings produced a cacophony of sound, although the benefit of having several respondents is that they prompt each others' memories. Language was sometimes a problem, as many older Greek-Australian women have limited English, and this is why many of their stories are paraphrased rather than quoted here. Sometimes a translator was necessary.[344]

The Popular Café in Mullumbimby exhibits Art Deco features, but these, while retained, are apparently not valued. The cubicles are good examples of the period but a blackboard menu all but covers the original name.

The original subjects for this project included a Greek woman who worked in several cafés over nearly 50 years, a non-Greek woman who worked at Londy's Café in the 40s and 50s, a café proprietor's daughter who 'grew up' at the Regal Café in the 70s, and a produce merchant who delivered to Greek cafés. The research process followed a 'snowballing' effect, however, as respondents and local historians who have lived all their lives in Ipswich and are valuable sources of local information, provided access to other potential subjects.[345] Most people were interviewed several times to clarify information or better understand their experience as women, children, and/or Greeks. In addition, generous offers of photographs, documents, and artefacts associated with milk bars, which were then copied or photographed, were a serendipitous and particularly satisfying aspect of the project's oral history component.[346]

Stories related during the course of this project enable contemporary and future Australians to access the past in an intimate way and gain insights that would otherwise rarely be written down. Maureen's account of the time she worked as a waitress at Londy's Café, for example, illuminates a particular slice of Australian life – what it was like to be a local woman working for Greek proprietors in the 40s and 50s – and Maria's story of a 50-year journey from Kythera to the Central Milk Bar in Ipswich is a personal account of how it felt to be called a 'dago' every day by everyday Australians who 'didn't mean anything by it.'

As oral historian Barry York explains, they invite an emotional as well as intellectual response in the reader.[347]

For those interested in researching the history of Greek cafés in other locations, field work is a surprisingly rewarding means of tracking down some of these great Aussie icons. Armed with snippets of information from sources such as those outlined above, the researcher is able to track the signs of the Greek café through rural towns and regional cities in the eastern states of Australia. While hundreds of Greek cafés have disappeared from Australian streetscapes, observant travellers will find in country towns evidence of the Greek cafés that once dotted the rural Australian landscape.

Apart from the exquisite Paragon Café, several Greek cafés in Katoomba, for example, are still standing, and some even operate as cafés, although with non-Greek owners. Art Deco façades, signs, and interior features are still evident in many of them, most notably the Niagara Café in Main Street. Janiszewski and Alexakis also note the Art Deco architecture and/or décor in the Busy Bee in Gunnedah, the Yenda Café in Yenda, the Paragon Café in Harden, the Astoria Café in Newcastle, the Olympia Café in Murrurundi, the Monterey Café in Coonamble, and Lismore's Crethar's Café, only some of which still operate as cafés.[348]

Elements of Art Deco style or lettering in buildings that might originally have been cafés can indicate the site of a Greek café, as

Left: The Niagara Café in Katoomba has changed hands several times since it was owned by Greeks, but its classic Art Deco façade remains intact.

Right: The Savoy in Katoomba was once a Greek café. The new owners have retained its classic features, including the doors and the front of the curved milk bar with its chrome, milky green and white bands.

might typical café names formed in masonry facades, painted on shop awnings, or hanging over footpaths, especially if they are Greek names. The Cameo Café in Tenterfield, the Oasis Café in Charleville, and the Laconia Café in Chinchilla, for example, may have been operated at some time by Greek proprietors.

While names like Laconia, Ellisos, or Olympus almost certainly indicate Greek proprietors, not all cafés with typical Greek café names – Niagara, Paragon, Australia, Busy Bee, Blue Bird, Golden Gate, and Majestic – were necessarily operated by Greeks. There is no evidence to suggest that Greeks ever ran the Majestic Café in Bell Street, Ipswich, for instance. Although the café operated at least as early as 1918, when many Greeks traded in Ipswich, residents can only recall non-Greek Australian proprietors at the Majestic.

In other instances, Greek names on the facades of other old buildings – like the Corones Building in Cunnamulla and the Comino Building in Charleville – indicate a Greek presence in early business communities. While these buildings are not café buildings, many Greek businessmen became established through café businesses. Theo Comino, for example, opened what was probably Charleville's first Greek café in about 1908, although all evidence of this is now gone, and while Charleville's historic Hotel Corones is a popular tourist destination, Harry Corones' illustrious career as a publican began in the café business.

Discussions with older local residents or the current occupants of premises that appear to have been cafes, or that bear Greek names on their façades, may confirm the presence of an old Greek café. Often, the façade remains intact although the building is significantly altered to fit its capacity as another kind of shop, as in the case of the Miles Newsagency. At other times, cafés are taken over by non-Greek Australians and undergo a name change in keeping with a contemporary Australia, as in the case of the Café Zuppa in Katoomba Street, which was once a Greek shop called the Florida Café. While new owners continue to operate the premises as cafés, they are likely to strip interiors of their classic charm in

Further investigation reveals that Greeks ran a Cameo Café in Tenterfield in the late 1930s, and that the Laconia in Chinchilla belonged to the Greek parents of George Miller, director of Australian hit films.[349]

Above: Café Majestic can still be seen, written in low relief in the space above the awning of the Miles Newsagency. The tiled front and curved display windows are classic café features.

Laconia Cafe, Chinchilla.[350]

Left: A chat with the owners of Samios Trading Post in Mitchell reveals that their building, a red brick structure with Samios Bros. written in low relief above the awning, was a magnificent three-room café when it was built in 1928.

When the Central Milk Bar in Ipswich was converted to a takeaway outlet, its front wall was opened up to maximise its street front potential. The milk bar still has cubicles along one wall.

an effort to 'keep up with the times' and so remain viable in a competitive marketplace. Even Greeks owners were forced to transform their cafés into takeaway outlets in order to compete with fast food chains. In this case, cafés lose their 'old-fashioned' façades. The least change of all occurs when a Greek café is sold to new owners who choose to highlight the café's classic features as a means of drawing patrons, the Paragon Café being, once more, a classic example. But as regional towns struggle to survive, and as small businesses crumble in the face of multi-national chains that take over the cultural landscape and homogenise towns, businesses that were once Greek cafés close down and their future hangs in the balance.

Historical research, official documents, and newspaper articles are useful sources, which, when used in conjunction with the knowledge of older residents, can build up a history of a town or city's Greek cafés. Field work and old photographs provide perhaps the most thrilling aspect of this kind of research because following a trail of clues is like solving a mystery, and when an existing facade matches that of an image from the 1920s another piece of the puzzle fits into place. Talking to older people about their lives and the way Australians lived was, for me, the most enjoyable part of the research. But since many of the people who established or worked in Greek cafés are now in their 70s and 80s, don't leave it too long to make time to talk to them.

The Inland Café in Tamworth was once a Greek Café. It still trades in coffee and meals and the physical layout of the classic café form has left its mark, but no trace of the original interior has been retained.

In Conclusion

A photograph of Maria's fairytale wedding. The photograph includes many other families from Ipswich's Greek café: Vasi and George Kentrotis, Helen and John Kentos, Peter Marendy, and George Kallinicos.

Maria indicated the five-gallon metal bucket under the refrigerated counter. "Once upon a time, I have four of those in here," she said. "Once upon a time."

It's the first Saturday of the month and I wander across the sticky bitumen to the local flea market. A woman in a patchwork dress smiles hopefully at me from behind a pyramid of crocheted Dolly Varden toilet roll covers.

A sunburnt second-hand dealer keeps a watchful eye on the blokes poking around in his trailer-load of trash and treasure. Mothers with jumbles of cots, toys, and baby clothes wrestle with grubby toddlers and other people's advice. Green-thumbed gardeners fuss over clutches of ugly, straggling plants, and share their propagating secrets with anyone who'll listen. And jam-makers, stamp-collectors, Teatree oil devotees, and a dozen other stall-holders cram beneath the sprawling fig trees at the edge of the park. I head for the second-hand bookseller – she had an old Carter Brown last month. As usual, she's managed to nab a spot in the blazing sun.

Battered kids' books, romances with gold embossed titles, a stash of non-fiction texts jammed up one end, *Out of Africa* (I've already got a copy, but . . . a dollar each or fill a bag for five dollars . . . this one's in better condition than mine), pillar-box-red Pan paperbacks from the 1950s (lucky I brought my hat) – thousands of books baking in the Queensland sun. Soon a dozen copies are piled up in my arm. My shirt sticks to my skin and, after half and hour of straining to read titles printed on spines stacked this way and that, my neck aches. I think about going. As I promise myself just one last row, four little letters reach up and grab my trailing fingers. *All Over the Shop*. Simple white font on a plain orange Penguin cover, but these days anything with the word 'shop' in it leaps from the periphery of my life like a tiger in an Indian jungle.

The blurb on the cover says that Tony Maniaty's memoir about 'a half-Greek, half-Australian kid' growing up in Brisbane in the 1950s and early 60s is witty and passionate. Now books are like boyfriends - wit is good and passion's a bonus – but, as with boyfriends, you can't judge a book by its cover. For a start, the author usually writes the effusive lines of praise written on the back. I turn to page one: "My father comes from an extraordinary line of Greeks – Plato was in fact a distant relative. So was Dionysus, which explains why Dad went into the food trade: battered savs, fish and quite passable chips." I like this book already. "He's always coming and going on the tram to the Astoria Café where he runs the kitchen – steak and chips, banana sundaes, nothing Greek at all." The story is so familiar now; it's almost feels like my story too:

On the father front, nothing has changed: Dad's still cooking away at the Astoria Cafe, where his closest friend, his fili George Vourakis also works. When they come home at night you can smell them coming; steak and chips and frying fat and sweat, all day long. You'll never guess what we have for dinner: steak. [. . . .]

We go shopping. Up to the shops, Mum and I, to shop, to do the shopping. 'Shop!' my mother calls as we walk into the shop. The shopkeeper appears. At this tender age I'm completely unaware that shops will become the central focus of my life for the next twenty years. But already Mum knows her fate, because dad is dreaming up schemes right now, as he peels yet another potato at the Astoria Cafe. 'Escape, fili – escape!' he says to Uncle George, and they dream of what their first shops will be like: a couple of dreamers still in their twenties. 'No more kitchen slaves!' says Dad, hurling another raw steak on the grill. [. . . .]

We go to the Astoria to visit Dad: this is wonderful, the fires going in the middle of the day and all the Greeks sweating like pigs and yelling, and dodging around each other and shouting and laughing. It's like a soccer game, except there's no ball. Instead they throw onions around and chop up tomatoes in four seconds flat, and have about fifteen different things going on at once and know exactly how long to keep it going and when to stop. Not like classical Greece, believe me: as Dad says, waving his hand, 'the glory that was Greece' is nowhere to be seen. (21-2)

By now I'm sweating like Tony Maniaty's Dad, so I stuff the books into a shopping bag, hand over my five dollars, and wander back across the road. Everyone knows that serendipity works tiny miracles in your life when a research project consumes you as Aphrodite and her mixed grills have consumed me for the last few years, but what are the chances of me and this book finding each other like this?

All Over the Shop is certainly witty and passionate, but it's much more than that. Like a Greek version of Hugh Lunn's *Over the Top with Jim*, it brings to life the experience of a Greek shopkeeper's son growing up in Brisbane in the 1950s and 60s. For most Australians, Greek cafés were part of daily life. We frequented them because the food was plentiful, cheap, and familiar, and because they were always open. They were the 1940, 50s, and 60s equivalent of Macca's. Some of us even got to know proprietors and their families, although, for most, they would always remain the local 'dagoes'. But Maniaty provides a unique insight into life on the other side of the counter. He juxtaposes hard work with good humour and on every page the smell of sweat and frying fat mingles with the fragrance of dreams. As penniless George Maniaty leaps from survivor to provider, he gets the shop he has dreamed of. And then another. And another. Until the dream fades. Once the proprietor of a shop that was the hub of the local community, George begins merely to fill the gaps – a loaf of bread, a packet of 'fags' – and the glorious days of the Greek café come to an end.

While sepia photographs and the reminiscences of older Australians might fill us with a sense of loss and longing, the Greek café has done its job. Cafés, milk bars, and fish shops provided economic independence and social mobility for thousands of unskilled migrants. They created a network through which marriages and jobs were organised, and they acted as conduits, channelling migrants away from Sydney to the remotest corners of the country. Today, Greek-Australians in all walks of life are part of the social fabric of Australia. As it turns out, the Greek café wasn't a 'Trojan Horse' just for American food-catering ideas; it also enabled generations of Greek immigrants to infiltrate the culture of their new land. They planted and maintained Greek traditions in Australia and, through their cafés, changed the way Australians think about themselves.

The story of the Greek café is a shared chapter in the histories of Greece and Australia, a chapter that is almost over. Very few Greek cafés operate as they did 50 years ago. Like so many café kids of his generation, Tony Maniaty, now a well-travelled journalist and award-winning writer, has left the shop behind. Even the ghost towns on islands like Kythera are reinventing themselves in the wake of a century of emigration. But the story of the Greek café has changed the face of both countries forever.

The Central Milk Bar closed down earlier this year, more than a century after John Black opened the first Greek shop just up the road. It was the last of Ipswich's Greek cafés. In later years, the glass shelves were bare, cardboard milkshake containers had relaced coloured aluminium vessels, the open shopfront admitted the din from the main street, and Bill didn't bother to get another nutmeg shaker when the last one was stolen from the counter. All that remained of the 'golden days' Maria so fondly recalls were the cubicles on the left hand side of the shop, which she added in 1983, long after all of the Ipswich cafés in the classic form had melted into history. Making a milkshake before she retired in December 2004, Maria indicated the five-gallon metal bucket under the refrigerated counter. "Once upon a time, I have four of those in here," she said. "Once upon a time."

Bibliography

Alexakis, Effy and Leonard Janiszewski. *Images of Home.* Sydney: Hale & Iremonger, 1995.

Alexakis, Effy and Leonard Janiszewski. *In Their Own Image: Greek Australians.* Alexandria, NSW: Hale & Iremonger, 1998.

Aliens of the Tweed and Brunswick. Chapter 2. page 5. http://freepages.history.rootsweb.com/~aliens/chapter_2.htm 4th April, 2007.

Babe: Pig in the City. Dir. George Miller, 1998.

Blythe, Andrew. Contemporary Studies Dissertation: *A Retailing History of the Ipswich Central Business district (CBD) from the Mid-1970s to 2003.* Ipswich, 2003.

Brasch, Dr R and L. *The Book of Beginnings: A Miscellany of the Origins of Superstitions, Customs, Phrases and Sayings.* Sydney: ABC Books, 2004.

Brown-May, Andrew. *Espresso!: Melbourne Coffee Stories.* Melbourne: Arcadia, 2001.

Buchanan, Robyn. *Ipswich in the Twentieth Century: Celebrating 100 Years as a City 1904-2004.* Ipswich: Ipswich City Council, 2004.

Buchanan, Robyn. "Old Theatre Put on the Ritz." Queensland Times: Lattice & Lace Column. 2nd May 1986.

Cain, James M. *The Postman Always Rings Twice.* London: Panther, 1960.

Collins, Jock et al. *A Shop Full of dreams: Ethnic Small Business in Australia.* Leichhardt, NSW: Pluto P., 1995.

Con the Fruiterer. Created by Mark Mitchell for the *Comedy Company*, Ten Network. 1988.

Conomos, Denis A. "Greek Eating Places in Brisbane in the Early 1900s." *Brisbane: The Ethnic Presence.* Brisbane: Brisbane History Group, 1993.

History of the Greek Community of Queensland to 1939. Brisbane: Denis A. Conomos, 1975.

The Greeks in Queensland: A History from 1859-1945. Brisbane: Copyright Publishing Company Pty Ltd, 2002.

Cozzolino, Mimmo. *Symbols of Australia.* Ringwood, Victoria: Penguin, 1980.

Dale, David. *The 100 Things We Loved: About the Twentieth Century.* Sydney: Pan Macmillan, 1999.

Detsimas, Effie. *No Speak English.* Brisbane: Self-Published, 2005.

Drysdale, Russell. *Maria,* 1950.

Drysdale, Russell. *Jo,* 1950

Dutton, Geoffrey. *The Australian Collection: Australia's Greatest Books.* North Ryde, NSW: Angus and Robertson, 1985.

Ferson, Mark and Mary Nilsson, eds. *Art Deco in Australia: Sunrise over the Pacific.* Sydney: Craftsman House, 2001.

"From Wintergarden to Ipswich City Cinema – that's entertainment!" *The Ipswich Advertiser's Golden Oldies,* September 16, 1986, page 16.

Funderburg, Anne Cooper. *Chocolate, Strawberry, and Vanilla: A History of American Ice Cream.* Bowling Green: Bowling Green State U. P., 1995.

Gilchrist, Hugh. *Australians and Greeks Volume 1: The Early Years.* Rushcutters Bay, NSW: Halstead Press, 1992.

Gilchrist, Hugh. *Australians and Greeks Volume 2: The Middle Years.* Rushcutters Bay, NSW: Halstead Press, 1997.

Gilchrist, Hugh. *Australians and Greeks Volume 3: The Later Years.* Broadway, NSW: Halstead Press, 2004.

Greek Family Life in N.S.W. 1900-1945: Laying the Foundations of 'Greekness'. http://www.cybernaut.com.au/greeksinoz/viewpoints/viewpoint1945.htm. 1st February, 2007.

Groom, Neil. *The Sunday Mail Nostalgia Book.* Bowen Hills, Brisbane: Queensland Newspapers, 1986.

Growing Up in Greek Cafés. Solomos Greek-Australian Cultural Society's Oral History Series. Respite Hall, Greek Community Centre, Edmonstone Street, Brisbane. 17.3.2004.

Gruen, Victor. *The Heart of Our Cities: the Urban Crisis: Diagnosis and Cure.* London: Thames and Hudson, 1965.

Happy Days. Created by Garry Marshall. First screened ABC January 1974 to 1984.

Happy Feet. Dir. George Miller, 2007.

Hudson, Bob. *The Newcastle Song.* 1975.

It's a Wonderful Life. Dir. Frank Capra, 1946.

Janiszewski, Leonard. Email from *Leonard.Janiszewski@humn.mq.edu.au.* Re: Greek Cafes. 3:17 pm Saturday 6th August 2005.

Janiszewski, Leonard and Effy Alexakis. "American Beauties at the Niagara: The marriage of American food catering ideas to British-Australian tastes and the birth, life and demise of the classic Australian 'Greek' Café." Paper presented at *Out There? Rural and Regional Conference.* National Trust of Australia (NSW), National Trust Centre, Sydney, 10th March 2003. http://www.kythera-family.net/index.php?nav=135-143&cid=281&did=6636&pageflip=1. 14th March 2005.

Janiszewski, Leonard and Effy Alexakis. "'That Bastard Ulysses': An Insight into an Early Greek Presence, 1810s – 1940." *Minorities: Cultural Diversity in Sydney*. Eds. Shirley Fitzgerald and Garry Wotherspoon. Sydney: State Library of NSW Press, 1995. 14-34.

Janiszewski, Leonard and Effy Alexakis. "The Greek Café: The Future of Australia's Past." Paper presented at *Greek Australians in the Twenty-first Century*, a conference at Macquarie University, 2nd – 4th April 2004.

http://www.agc.org.au/web_images/Janisewski%20and%20Alexis%20paper.pdf. 15th June 2005.

Jupp, James. *Arrivals and Departures*. Melbourne: Cheshire-Lansdowne, 1966.

Jupp, James. *The Australian People: An Encyclopedia of the Nation, Its People and Their Origins*. North Ryde, Sydney: Angus & Robertson, 1988.

Lower, Lennie. *Here's Luck*. Sydney: Angus and Robertson, 1930.

Low, John. "Zacharias Simos." *Australian Dictionary of Biography Supplement: 1580-1980*. Ed. Christopher Cunneen. Melbourne: n. pub., 2005. 362-3.

Lunn, Hugh. *On the Road to Anywhere*. Sydney: Hodder, 2003.

Mad Max. Dir. George Miller, 1979.

Mainland Greece: Athens and the Ionian Islands. Neos Guide, Michelin Travel Publications. 2002.

Maniaty, Tony. *All Over the Shop*. Ringwood, Victoria: Penguin, 1983.

Milkshakes, Sundaes and Café Culture Exhibition Education Kit. MGF NSW. *http://www.mgnsw.org.au/files/resources/Cafe%20Edu%20Kit%20Primary.pdf*. 14.12.06.

Marvellous Melbourne. "Café Culture." *http://www.museum.vic.gov.au/marvellous/postwar/café.asp*. 20th February 2007.

McCann, Joy. *A Lot in Store: Celebrating Our Shopping Heritage*. Parramatta: NSW Heritage Office, 2002.

McInerney, Sally. "A Thirst for Milkbars of the 50s." *Sydney Morning Herald*. 5th November 1983. p36.

Merriam-Webster Dictionary of Quotations. Massachusetts: Merriam-Webster Inc., 1992.

Montanari, Massimo. *The Culture of Food*. Trans. Carl Ipsen. Oxford: Blackwell, 1994.

Moyer, Judith. *A Step-by Step Guide to Oral History*. *http://www.dohistory.org/on_your_own/toolkit/oralHistory.html#WHATIS*. 3rd October 2005.

Muller, Linda. "Top Tales of Funny Types of Aussies." *Bayside Bulletin*. Books, 49. January, 2006.

Mumford, Lewis. *The Culture of Cities*, 3rd ed. New York: Harcourt, Brace, Jovanovich, 1970.

Nicklin, Lenore. "Our Original Café Society." *Sydney Bulletin*. 10 October 1995. p44-45.

Oldenburg, Ray. *The Great Good Place: cafes, coffee shops, bookstores, bars, hair salons, and other hangouts at the heart of the community*. New York: Marlowe, 1999.

Oral History Association of Australia. *http://www.ohaa.net.au/guidelines.htm*. 12th August 2005.

Prineas, James. "A Village on Kythera." *http://ourworld.compuserve.com/homepages/designerdock/KytheraIntro.html* 14.7.06.

Prineas, James. "Winter on Kythera." *james@kythera-family.net*, Email 5.2.07.

Ripe, Cherry. "Thirst for Café Culture." *The Australian*. 13th October 1998. p15.

Robertson, Beth. *Oral History Handbook*. Adelaide: Oral History Association of Australia (South Australian Branch) Inc., 1995.

Rosen, Sue. *We Never Had a Hotbed of Crime: Life in Twentieth-Century South Sydney*. Alexandria, NSW: Hale & Iremonger, 2000.

Rudofsky, Bernard. *Streets for People: a Primer for Americans*. New York: Doubleday, 1969.

Slattery, Luke. "Gone Troppo: Cafes Breeding." *The Weekend Review in The Australian*. 18/19th November 1995. p3.

Symons, Michael. *One Continuous Picnic: A History of Eating in Australia*. Adelaide: Duck Press, 1982.

The Blob. Dir. Irvin S. Yeaworth Jr., 1958.

The National Handbook of Australia's Industries. Ed. Ambrose Pratt. Melbourne: The Specialty Press, 1934.

The Sundowners. Dir. Fred Zinnermann, 1960.

Toussaint-Samat, Maguelonne. Trans. Anthea Bell. *History of Food*. Oxford: Blackwell, 2000.

Turnbull, Craig and Chris Valiotis. B*eyond the Rolling Wave: A Thematic History of Greek Settlement in NSW*. *http://www.heritage.nsw.gov.au/heritagensw/aut02/8_art.htm* 12th March 2005.

York, Barry. *Speaking of Us: Voices from Twentieth-Century Australia*. Canberra: National Library of Australia, 1999.

Interviewees

Bellas, Athena.
Bellas, Jim.
Bromley, Frank.
Burke, Lily.
Castan, Con. President of the Solomos Greek Australian Cultural Society.
Colless, Alf.
Colless, Tom.
Cominos, Peter George.
Emanuel George Cominos.
Stamatoula Cominos.
Detsimas, Effie.
Dull, Arnold.
Fellows, Myrtle.
Freeman, Narelle.
Girdis, Marina.
Green, Pearl and Jim.
Hawkins, Yvonne.
Hicks, Merrilyn.
Kallinicos, Manuel.
Kallos, Peter.
Kennedy, Dot.
Kentos, Helen.
Kentrotes, Bill.
Kentrotis, Bill.
Kentrotis, Maria.
Kentrotis, Vasiliki.
Londy, George.
Londy, Peter.
Londy, Mary.
Marendy, Helene.
Marsden, Trevor.
Pavlakis, Jim.
Penglis, Jim.
Pisasale, Charlie.
Poulos, Peter.
Prineas, Effie.
Reinke, Maureen.
Risson, Casey.
Risson, Don.
Rossiter, John.
Samios, Michael.
Samios, Yiota.
Schofstakosty, Ivan.
Sheppard, Maureen.
Simonidis, Maya.
Stathis, Jack.
Stathis, Zeta.
Stathis, Jim.
Stewart, Joanne.
Tanos, Andrew.
Tanos, Harry
Tanos, Maroula.
Thompson, Ruth.
Veneris, Doris
Veneris, Theo.
Wagner, Anne.

General discussions took place at St Mary's Hostel, Ipswich in August, 2005 and at a meeting of the Solomos Greek Australian Cultural Society at the Greek Club, West End, Brisbane in September, 2005. References to specific people are not given in the text.

Notes

1. Komninos qtd in Jock Collins et al., *A Shop Full of dreams: Ethnic Small Business in Australia* (Leichhardt, NSW: Pluto Press, 1995) Introduction.

2. Quoted in Geoffrey Dutton, *The Australian Collection: Australia's Greatest Books* (North Ryde, NSW: Angus and Robertson, 1985) 127-130.

3. Drysdale observed that, "It's a curious fact that the alien Greek cafékeeper has become a symbol of the Australian country town – whenever one goes out west there is always 'the dagoe's' to eat in… people with courage to work and save and give their children a better way of life in a new land." Quoted in Leonard Janiszewski and Effy Alexakis, "The Greek Café: The Future of Australia's Past" (A paper presented at *Greek Australians in the Twenty-first Century*, a conference at Macquarie University, 2nd - 4th April 2004. http://www.agc.org.au/web_images/Janisewski%20and%20Alexis%20paper.pdf. 15th June 2005) 11.

4. *The Newcastle Song.*

5. Mitchell created the Greek characters for the *Comedy Company*, a skit show that first appeared in Australia on the Channel Ten Network in 1988. Con and Marika had twin sons, Nick and Rick, and daughters Roula, Toula, Soula, Voula, Foula, and Agape.

6. Several historians refer to Australia's Greek café in these terms: Leonard Janiszewski and Effy Alexakis, "American Beauties at the Niagara: The marriage of American food catering ideas to British-Australian tastes and the birth, life and demise of the classic Australian 'Greek' Café" (Paper presented at *Out There? Rural and Regional Conference*. National Trust of Australia (NSW), National Trust Centre, Sydney, 10th March 2003. *http://www.kythera-family.net/index.php?nav=135-143&cid=281&did=6636&pageflip=1.*
14th March 2005) 1; Hugh Gilchrist, *Australians and Greeks Volume 1: The Early Years* (Rushcutters Bay, NSW: Halstead Press, 1992) 190; Denis Conomos, *The Greeks in Queensland: A History from 1859-1945* (Brisbane: Copyright Publishing Company Pty Ltd, 2002) 117.

7. Michael Symons, *One Continuous Picnic: A History of Eating in Australia* (Adelaide: Duck Press, 1982) 23, 113. Historian, Leonard Janiszewski, and documentary photographer, Effy Alexakis, have done some wonderful work that confirms and elaborates the abundance of Greek cafés in Australia and provides new insight into the Americanisation of Australian eating habits, but their work is primarily concerned with New South Wales cafés. In a three volume history of Greeks in Australia, to which he devotes nearly 1,300 pages, Hugh Gilchrist allocates a chapter to the shopkeeping phenomenon, with only five pages about cafés in Queensland (1: 232-238). *Beyond the Rolling Wave: A Thematic History of Greek Settlement in NSW. http://www.heritage.nsw.gov.au/heritagensw/aut02/8_art.htm 12th March 2005*, a project for the NSW Heritage Office by Craig Turnbull and Chris Valiotis, is a further example of the celebration of Greek cafés in NSW. Former solicitor and member of South-East Queensland's Greek community, Denis A. Conomos, on the other hand, documents a great many Queensland cafés in his excellent study of Greeks in Queensland, but these form part of a more general history, and one which concludes at 1945. Joy McCann, in *A Lot in Store: Celebrating Our Shopping Heritage* (Parramatta: NSW Heritage Office, 2002) and Jock Collins et al. also mention Greek cafés, but their references are minor portions of broader research into shopping and ethnic small business. Even local Ipswich historian, Robyn Buchanan, in a recent account of Ipswich in the 20th century, fails to mention that city's abundance of Greek cafés and milk bars (See Robyn Buchanan, *Ipswich in the Twentieth Century: Celebrating 100 Years as a City 1904-2004* (Ipswich: Ipswich City Council, 2004).

8. Conomos, *The Greeks in Queensland* 133.

9. Gilchrist 1: 190.

10. Conomos, *Greeks in Queensland* 118-9, 264.

11. Janiszewski and Alexakis, "American Beauties" 2, 7.

12. Also see Conomos, *Greeks in Queensland* 318.

13. Also see Conomos, *Greeks in Queensland* 551.

14. Katoomba's Paragon Café features on page 19 of *Art Deco in Australia: Sunrise over the Pacific* by editors Mark Ferson and Mary Nilsson (Sydney: Craftsman House, 2001), which is one of the few books dealing with Art Deco in Australia.

15. *Growing Up in Greek Cafés.* Solomos Greek-Australian Cultural Society's Oral History Series. Respite Hall, Greek Community Centre, Edmonstone Street, Brisbane. 17.3.2004.

16. Conomos, *Greeks in Queensland* 125-6.

17. An unidentified speaker at *Growing Up in Greek Cafés*, who quoted a video at the Qantas Museum in Longreach, in which a woman relates her experiences in Cominos' Café.

18. Peter Cominos interviewed 28th July, 2005. Emmanuel Cominos, *Growing Up in Greek Cafés*.

19. Maya Simonidis remembers the green glass.

20. The Regal Café had four tapestries on the walls, which were there when George Kentrotis bought the café – one of Venice, one of a Bridge with a man and a cart, one of mountains and a forest, and one of a bullfight, according to recollections of owners and customers.

21. Photograph of Katoomba Street at night with the Paragon Café sign on the right-hand side is courtesy of the Blue Mountains City Council archives and can be found on their images website.

22. Interviews with Tom Colless of Colless Foods and Peter Poulos of Theo Poulos Realty (13th November, 2006).

23. John Low, "Zacharias Simos," *Australian Dictionary of Biography Supplement: 1580-1980*. Ed. Christopher Cunneen (Melbourne: n. pub., 2005) 361-3.

24. *Milkshakes, Sundaes and Café Culture Exhibition Education Kit* 11-12.

25. Hugh Lunn, *On the Road to Anywhere* (Sydney: Hodder, 2003) 234.

26. Also see McCann.

27. See demographer and historian, James Jupp, *The Australian People: An Encyclopedia of the Nation, Its People and Their Origins* (North Ryde, Sydney: Angus & Robertson, 1988) 507. The title for the chapter is borrowed from a book by Jock Collins at al. *A Shop Full of Dreams Ethnic Small Business in Australia.*

28. Jupp, *The Australian People* 95.
Leonard Janiszewski and Effy Alexakis, "'That Bastard Ulysses': An Insight into an Early Greek Presence, 1810s – 1940." *Minorities: Cultural Diversity in Sydney*. Eds. Shirley Fitzgerald and Garry Wotherspoon (Sydney: State Library of NSW Press, 1995) 16-17.

29. See Conomos, *Greeks in Queensland* vi.

30. See Conomos, *Greeks in Queensland* vi, 23-4, 30-46.

31. Jupp, *People* 508-510; Janiszewski and Alexakis, "Bastard" 19.

32. See Conomos, *Greeks in Queensland* 17- 22, 188-9 for detail about the political situation that precipitated the crisis. Also see Alexakis and Janiszewski, *In Their Own Image* 120-1.

33. *Greeks in Queensland* 199-200.
34. Jupp, *People* 95; Conomos, *Greeks in Queensland* vi-vii.
35. See Conomos, pages 60-77, for accounts of voyages to Australia; Theo's story is on page 75.
36. See Jupp, *The Australian People* 508-510.
37. See Lenore Nicklin, "Our Original Café Society" *Sydney Bulletin* (10 October 1995) 44.
38. Conomos, *Greeks in Queensland* 79-80, 84-5, 92, 104-5, 122, 137; Janiszewski and Alexakis, "American Beauties" 7. It should be noted that employers and their families worked the same long, hard hours, even after their cafés began to prosper.
39. For detailed accounts of life in Kytherian villages, see Effy Alexakis and Leonard Janiszewski, *Images of Home* (Sydney: Hale & Iremonger) 1995.
40. See Conomos, *Greeks in Queensland* vii; Jupp, *People* 510 and Collins et al. 44-5, 63, 65, 82-3. Others confirm this phenomenon: "In the early years of [the 20th century], it was estimated that 85 per cent of first generation Greeks owned or worked in cafés, milk bars, fish and chips shops and other small businesses" (Wilton and Bosworth qtd. in Collins et al. 64); Conomos also notes that 140 of the 176 Greeks in Brisbane in 1916 worked in the café industry (*Greeks in Queensland* 117); while Alexakis and Janiszewski set out to contradict the stereotype of the Greek shopkeeper, they too acknowledge the pronounced Greek presence in the food catering trades. Effy Alexakis and Leonard Janiszewski, *In Their Own Image: Greek Australians* (Alexandria, NSW: Hale & Iremonger, 1998) 8, 9 and 14.
41. See Conomos, *Greeks in Queensland* 79-80. Also see Nicklin 45; Collins et al 44; Gilchrist, 1: 195; *Greek Family Life in N.S.W. 1900-1945: Laying the Foundations of 'Greekness'* http://www.cybernaut.com.au/greeksinoz/viewpoints/viewpoint1945.htm. (Feb 1st 2007); Turnbull and Valiotis 2.
42. *Milkshakes, Sundaes and Café Culture* 6.
43. Conomos, *Greeks in Queensland* 80.
44. *Mainland Greece: Athens and the Ionian Islands.* (Neos Guide, Michelin Travel Publications, 2002) 253. *Greek Family Life in N.S.W.* The kind of impact that one shop could have was to become a feature of the Greek shopkeeping phenomenon. Constantinos Karanges, for example, claims that 113 members of the Karanges family can trace their history to the Niagara Café, which opened in Newcastle in 1898. Many went on from there to establish their own cafés and milk bars throughout Australia (Nicklin 44).
45. Oysters had been popular in London for centuries. They were cheap and they were associated with poverty. In *Pickwick Papers* of 1837, Charles Dickens wrote that there was an oyster stall to every half-dozen houses (See Symons 23).
46. Gilchrist, 1: 192
47. Collins, et al explain that running a fish shop required relatively little initial capital, involved skills that were easy to acquire, and poor English was not an insurmountable problem (45). Peter Cominos, whose father ran Cominos' café in Cairns, agrees that the move to set up oyster saloons was not unexpected in a nation of fisherman. Also see Alexakis and Janiszewski, *In Their Own Image* 106.
48. This information is available in the displays at the Corones Hotel, in Conomos, *Greeks in Queensland* 295-6, 473, 480-1, and in a souvenir booklet produced by Harry Corones and available at the hotel in the Public Bar.
49. *Greeks in Queensland* 104, 111, 112, 117; Janiszewski and Alexakis, *American Beauties at the Niagara* 1.
50. Paul Comino ran his Childers café for 56 years and Harry Andronicus traded in Toowoomba for over 40 years (Conomos, *Greeks in Queensland*, 104-112). Conomos' records show that Greek cafés traded in at least 21 Queensland towns by the end of the first decade of the 20th century, and more than half of them were owned by Kytherians. He records cafés in the following towns and these were not necessarily the first in those towns: Murwillumbah, 1906, Mareeba, 1901, Ipswich, 1901, Toowoomba, 1901-2, Bundaberg, 1903, Childers, 1905, Townsville, 1903-4, Charters Towers, 1908, Mackay, 1905, Cairns, 1907, Gympie, 1904, Warwick, 1906, Charleville, 1908, Roma,1909-10, Goondiwindi, 1908, Laidley, 1908, Pittsworth, 1908, Clifton, 1908, Maryborough, 1909, Ayr, 1909, Chinchilla, 1909, Gatton, 1910, Allora, 1910, Oakey, 1910, Kingaroy, 1910. (83, 104, 106-111).
51. Local Katoomba residents remember the AB (All-British), Aroney's, the Savoy Café (beside the Savoy Theatre), the Niagara, Astor, Victory, Florida, and Waratah cafés, as well as the Plaza Café at Echo Point. In Tamworth, the White Rose Café, Dreamland, the Ritz Café, the Golden Bell, the Tamworth Café, and the Royal Café still find a place in the hearts of older residents.
52. Gilchrist 1: 233; Conomos, *Greeks in Queensland* 78, 94, 97.
53. Conomos, *History* 81, 88, 98-9, 103, 117.
54. Photograph copyright Thomas Mathewson, kindly loaned by Sandy Barrie.
55. Conomos, *Greeks in Queensland* 112
56. Gilchrist 1: 114, Conomos, *Greeks in Queensland* 112, official records cited by Leonard Janiszewski in an email dated 6th August 2005, 3:17pm.
57. Conomos *Greeks in Queensland* 104. This shop should not be confused with another Australia Café on the opposite side of Brisbane Street, which the Londy family sold to the Marendy family, who operated it from about 1935–1950.
58. Conomos, *Greeks in Queensland* 140.
59. See Conomos, *To 1939* 10 and *History* 104, 140. Since the 1918 Block Plans indicate that Marcellos and Spathis owned two oyster saloons, one in Brisbane Street and one in Nicholas Street, it is likely that Black sold both establishments to them.
60. Denis Conomos establishes this in interviews conducted by 1980-84.
61. See Block 10 IPS. P1/171 and Block 77&77A IPS. P1/171.
62. Denis Conomos establishes this in interviews conducted by 1980-84.
63. Interview with Jim Penglis, 7th January, 2006.
64. "Ipswich Opportunities: Early Businesses Laid a Solid Commercial Foundation." *Queensland Times*, March 3rd, 2006, History Section, page 8. This pre-dates the first Kytherian oyster saloon in Sydney by two years. This may indicate that Chubb was not a Greek immigrant, or, alternatively,. p65. See Symons 23.
66. This was possibly the Stratigos who later bought the City Café from Peter Spathis.
67. See Block Plan IPS. P1/169. This shop would be situated at approximately 139 Brisbane Street.
68. Gilchrist, 1: 208; Conomos, *Greeks in Queensland* viii, 134, 112, 106.
69. "The Ipswich Advertiser's Golden Oldies," 16th September 1986, page 17. Also, Robyn Buchanan includes a photograph of Marble Bar on page 56 of *Ipswich in the 20th Century*. The shop is located next door to Thomas' Hairdressing Saloon and has two female waitresses posing in the doorway.
70. Mrs Klopsch had Refreshment Rooms about six doors uphill from Marcellos & Spathis in Brisbane Street; the Khaki Tea Rooms and pastry cook , E. H. Wilson, were just across the street; the Café Majestic, later known as Marsh's café was several doors around the corner from Brisbane Street in Bell Street; W. J. Berry's Refreshment Rooms were several doors around the corner from Brisbane Street in Nicholas Street with I. Ham's

Refreshment Rooms opposite; Bearkley's Café was near Ham's Refreshment Rooms, several doors closer to the railway line on a site remembered as the Capitol Café of the 1940s; Whitehouse's Café was near the railway line in Nicholas Street. According to ex-Ipswich café proprietor, Jim Pavlakis, Whitehouse's Café was also, at one time, owned by a Greek family, Londys, but this is unconfirmed.

71. Denis Conomos establishes this in interviews conducted by 1980-84.
72. Denis Conomos establishes this in interviews conducted by 1980-84.
73. Interview with Mick Londy, conducted by Conomos 1980-84; Conomos, *History* 420. The Greeks employed a relatively small number of café names; there were Niagara, Majestic, Paragon, and Australia Cafés in many towns. There were possibly three Australia Cafés in the Ipswich CBD between 1900 and 1920.
74. Photograph of Nicholas Street – Copyright F. A. Whitehead.
75. Conomos, *History* 111, 120, Jim Penglis 7th January, 2006, Gilchrist,
    1: 234, Manuel Kallinicos 8th December, 2005
76. Arriving at a definitive number of cafés is complicated by the fact that shops passed from hand to hand. Londy's, for example, was sold to the Coplin brothers and then passed to the Samios family, so this shop was the site of three separate family businesses. Does each new owner constitute another business, or are only the premises to be counted?
77. Denis Conomos and Jack Stathis confirm this.
78. Mick Londy remembers that the family briefly owned another shop, also called the Australia Café, in Nicholas Street. This later became the Sydney Fruit Market, and, probably later still, the Sydney Café.
79. Peter and Mary Londy, interviewed 3rd February, 2006.
80. Janiszewski and Alexakis, *American Beauties at the Niagara 6*.
81. Narelle, interviewed 9th August 2005.
82. Don Risson.
83. Jim Penglis 7th January, 2006.
84. Robyn Buchanan, "Old Theatre Put on the Ritz."
85. Interview 8th December, 2005.
86. Interviewed 12th February, 2006.
87. Family history by Ruth Thompson, April 2006.
88. This information is courtesy of a family history by Ruth Thompson, April 2006.
89. Telephone conversation with Ruth Penglis, 7th Jan 2006.
90. Quoted in Symons 254.
91. This definition derives from Janiszewski and Alexakis, "The Future of Australia's Past."
92. Nicklin 44.
93. Luke Slattery, "Gone Troppo: Cafes Breeding." *The Weekend Review in The Australian* (18/19th November 1995) 3.
94. Andrew Brown-May, *Espresso!: Melbourne Coffee Stories* (Melbourne: Arcadia, 2001) 2.
95. Brown-May 32-9, 42, 48, 89. Also see David Dale, *The 100 Things We Loved About the Twentieth Century* (Sydney: Pan Macmillan, 1999) 24-6.
96. 'Espresso' is an Italian word meaning 'pressed out' (Brown-May 30-1).
97. Peter Bancroft was an Australian whose Jewish father was born in England. See Andrew Brown-May xiii, 8, 32, 33, 35, 42, 51.
98. Photograph courtesy of Marvellous Melbourne, "Café Culture." http://www.museum.vic.gov.au/marvellous/postwar/café.asp.
99. Brown-May 46, x, xiii.
100. Photograph courtesy of Marvellous Melbourne. "Café Culture." http://www.museum.vic.gov.au/marvellous/postwar/café.asp.
101. The Legend's customers "were primarily linked to a pursuit of style." The refurbished café opened at 280 Bourke Street in 1956. Having utilised the talents of sculptor, Clement Meadmore, to complete the makeover, it had a mosaic tile exterior and an Italian-style stone floor and drop lights. The Legend closed in 1970, when the building was demolished. See *Marvellous Melbourne*. "Café Culture." http://www.museum.vic.gov.au/marvellous/postwar/café.asp. (20th February 2007).
102. Brown-May 51-2, 73-74.
103. Brown-May 39.
104. Participants in *Growing Up in Greek Cafés* note that Melbourne was ahead of its time in relation to serving ethnic food in shops because shops sold Greek food in the 1950s. Con Castan makes the point that these shops should be thought of as 'restaurants for Greeks', upon which Australians had stumbled, rather than as 'Greek restaurants'. Perhaps they have been omitted from most historians' work because they do not conform to the definition of a Greek café as it is explored here, but would form part of a useful study of ethnic restaurants.
105. Brown-May, page 11. Marcus Clarke qtd in Brown-May 12.
106. Quoted in Symons 136.
107. Brown-May 39.
108. Also see Symons 229.
109. Brown-May 66.
110. Prior to the invention of the espresso machine, coffee was made by various methods. In it simplest form, a drink is produced in much the same way as tea is made, by pouring hot water over ground coffee beans and straining the resultant liquid. Percolation is popular in the US. The art of filtering coffee is a popular European method introduced during the 30s, when the plunger or French Press was also invented (see Brown-May 89).
111. Even today, in cafés and restaurants in Greece, where coffee seems expensive when compared with other items on the menu, the price of a cup, in most cases, buys the patron the right to sit and chat for a considerable period of time without further interruption.
112. Greek immigrants quoted in James Jupp, *Arrivals and Departures* (Melbourne: Cheshire-Lansdowne, 1966) 105 & 125. Picnics also feature prominently both in historical accounts and respondents' recollections: Conomos, *Greeks in Queensland* 171, 173, 260; Maureen recalls picnics with employers; Peter Kallos, Peter Londy, and Jack Stathis relate stories of picnics at Kholo and meeting with Toowoomba Greeks at Murphy's Creek or Helidon.
113. See Alexakis and Janiszewski, *In Their Own Image* 218 and Conomos, *Greeks in Queensland* 27, 157-8.
114. Brown-May x – 5. On coffee, also see Massimo Montanari, *The Culture of Food.* Trans. Carl Ipsen (Oxford: Blackwell, 1994)121-8.
115. Brown-May xiii.
116. Slattery 3 and Con Castan, President of the Solomos Greek Australian Cultural Society in Brisbane. The Kafeneion, like the sixteenth century European and British coffee house, is a men-only establishment.
117. Ray Oldenburg, *The Great Good Place: cafes, coffee shops, bookstores, bars, hair salons, and other hangouts at the heart of the community* (New York: Marlowe, 1999) 2. Also see Lewis Mumford, *The Culture of Cities,* 3rd ed. (New York: Harcourt, Brace, Jovanovich, 1970 – first published in 1938) and Victor Gruen, *The Heart of Our Cities: the Urban Crisis: Diagnosis and Cure* (London: Thames and Hudson, 1965) and Lyn Lofland, *A World of Strangers: Order and Action in Urban Public Space* (New York: Basic, 1973) and Bernard Rudofsky, *Streets for People: A Primer for Americans*
(New York: Doubleday, 1969).

118. Conomos, "Eating" 88.
119. Janiszewski and Alexakis, "American Beauties" 5-6.
120. Sally McInerney, "A Thirst for Milkbars of the 50s" *Sydney Morning Herald* (5th November 1983) 36.
121. For example, see Janiszewski and Alexakis, "Bastard" 24-5 and Conomos, *Greeks in Queensland* 157. One exception is Gilchrist, who observes that Meimarakis' Brisbane café "became a favourite rendezvous as a kafeneion for local Greeks" (1: 236). Cafés are distinct from Greek coffee houses; the kafeneion was often situated above a café (see Conomos, *Greeks in Queensland* 420).
122. See Janiszewski and Alexakis, "American Beauties" 2. Also see Symons 60-61.
123. Constantinos Karanges, quoted in Nicklin 44.
124. Janiszewski and Alexakis "American Beauties" 2-3 and "Bastard" 22.
125. Soda water fountains are evident in America from the early 19th century. Flavoured soda water enhanced the industry's popularity from the late 1830s, with hundreds of flavours available by the end of the century: almond, cognac, orange sherbet, mint julep, quince, orris root, and the like. Ice cream sodas came onto the scene some time in the second half of the 19th century. See Chapter 4 of Anne Cooper Funderburg, *Chocolate, Strawberry, and Vanilla: A History of American Ice Cream* (Bowling Green: Bowling Green State U. P., 1995) on the invention of sodas and ice cream sodas in America (85-110).
126. Symons 129; Janiszewski and Alexakis, "American Beauties" 3.
127. Janiszewski and Alexakis "Bastard" 22.
128. Janiszewski and Alexakis, "American Beauties" 4; *Milkshakes, Sundaes and Café Culture Exhibition Education Kit* 7; McCann, *A Lot in Store* 12.
129. Funderburg 106-7.
130. See Funderburg.
131. Janiszewski and Alexakis, "American Beauties" 4; "Bastard" 22; Conomos, *Greeks in Queensland* 118-119.
132. Conomos, *Greeks in Queensland* 118-119.
133. *Milkshakes, Sundaes and Café Culture* 10.
134. Nicklin 44.
135. Julie Nichles, among others present for *Growing Up in Greek Cafés*.
136. Conomos records a similar story, *Greeks in Queensland* 546.
137. *The National Handbook of Australia's Industries*. Ed. Ambrose Pratt (Melbourne: The Specialty Press, 1934) 202-3, 566.
138. Symons 130 and Janiszewski and Alexakis, "Bastard" 23. Long before Americans 'discovered' ice cream, frozen desserts were favoured by the upper classes in Europe, but Americans developed the unique taste and texture of ice cream as it is known today. They also consumed so much of the sweet, cold confection that ice cream soon became as American as apple pie and Coco-Cola (Funderburg 3-28). In America, the harvesting of ice, its handling during shipment, storage in icehouses, and its home use in ice chests – known as refrigerators – developed over the course of the 19th century. As mechanical refrigeration became more efficient, industries converted their natural ice plants to circulating brine and then to ammonia refrigeration (Funderburg 29-49).
Also see Maguelonne Toussaint-Samat, Trans. Anthea Bell. *History of Food* (Oxford: Blackwell, 2000), who notes that the Chinese are credited with a device that could make sorbet and ice cream, using the principle that salt lowers the freezing point of water to below zero, and that Marco Polo brought this device to Italy. The first refrigerator to make ice, as opposed to storing natural ice, was exhibited at the Great Exhibition of London in 1859, although it was the 1920s before the technique of freezing was completely mastered (749-54).
139. Janiszewski and Alexakis, "The 'Greek Café': The Future of Australia's Past" 3.
140. *The National Handbook of Australia's Industries*, Ed. Ambrose Pratt (Melbourne: The Specialty Press, 1934) 566.
141. Dr R and L Brasch, *The Book of Beginnings: A Miscellany of the Origins of Superstitions, Customs, Phrases and Sayings* (Sydney: ABC Books, 2004). 961-2. Also see Funderburg, who offers more detail on the invention of the sundae during the 1880s in America, 100-107.
142. Jack at St Mary's Hostel, interviewed August 2005.
143. *Milkshakes, Sundaes and Café Culture* 10-11.
144. Symons 140-1.
145. For information about Dalby's cafés see Conomos *Greeks in Queensland* (500) and *Growing Up in Greek Cafés*.
146. *Growing up in Greek Cafés*.
147. Casey Risson, interviewed January, 2007.
148. Julie Nichles, *Growing Up in Greek Cafés*.
149. Quoted in Symons 61.
150. Symons 61, 127, 178. Kelvinators were the first electric model in the US and these were imported to Australia in 1926.
151. Interviewed 6th January, 2007.
152. See Wikipedia.
153. Janiszewski and Alexakis "Bastard" 21; Brown-May 52. Melbourne is generally considered 'ahead of its time' in regard to ethnic food because of the concentration of post-war migrants who opened shops there. These shops should perhaps be thought of in terms of 'restaurants for Greeks' rather than 'Greek restaurants' or 'Greek cafés' as these are defined here.
154. See Janiszewski and Alexakis, "American Beauties" 8. Gilchrist also affirms that from the beginning the Greek café proprietor did not serve traditional dishes: "[The Greek proprietor] gave his Australian customers what they wanted and expected: fish and chips, oysters on shell, grilled steak and eggs, plain boiled vegetables, bread and butter, tea or coffee, fruit salad, and [....], unlike some Australian shop-keepers, he provided such fare at almost any hour into well into the night" (1: 192).
155. *Growing Up in Greek Cafés*. Speakers also claim that Melbourne was different in this regard, in that they had Greek restaurants in the 1950s because a far greater proportion of the post-war immigrants went to Melbourne and influenced the food introduced there. Con Castan notes, however, that these ought to be considered "restaurants for Greeks" that Australians had stumbled into, rather than "Greek restaurants." I am sure some readers will disagree with Con's statement, remembering that they encountered the pleasures of Chinese food in places like Chinatown in Fortitude Valley and Dixon Street in Sydney from at least the early 1950s.
156. Symons 255.
157. Symons 137. Symons records the gastronomic delights offered by European chefs in bohemian restaurants in Sydney and Melbourne at the beginning of the 19th century, but he claims that the austerities of the First World War "killed off restaurant society" (110-124).
158. Casey Risson, interviewed January 2007. It should be noted that the word 'mad' is used in this sense to indicate that the concept of the Mixed Grill is 'fabulous' not 'insane'.
159. Andrew Arnaoutopoulos, *Growing Up in Greek Cafés*.
160. The exclusion of wives from Australian men and their fishing yarns is the basis of advertising campaigns like the Castlemaine Perkins' Fourex Gold and Carlton Mid-Strength of the early 21st century.

161. Interviewed 31st January, 2006.
162. Interviewed July 2005.
163. Interviewed 5th August 2004.
164. As told to Denis Conomos in interviews conducted between 1980 and 1984.
165. Interviewed 16th April 2004.
166. Interviewed 9th march, 2007.
167. See Brown-May 25 for the story about Hope Gibson.
168. Joanne of Kentrotis' Regal Café.
169. Interview conducted 2nd October 2005.
170. Interviewed 12th February, 2006.
171. *Growing Up in Greek Cafés,* question time.
172. Interviewed at Council Chambers 14th, May, 2006.
173. The first meeting of Eleni Levounis and Vince Hellen, quoted in Conomos, *Greeks in Queensland* 222.
174. James Jupp, *The Australian People* 95.
Janiszewski, and Alexakis, "That Bastard Ulysses" 16-17.
175. Recorded in Leonard Janiszewski's database, email dated 6th August 2005, 3:17 pm.
176. Gilchrist 1: 191. A census in 1871 shows only 19 females born in Greece and living in Victoria at that time compared with 127 males (Jupp, *People* 508). Gilchrist claims that in 1901, only 63 of Australia's 878 Greeks were women, and a decade later, they still accounted for only 105 of a Greek-born population of 1,798 (1: 190-1). Only fourteen of 262 Greeks living in Queensland at that time were women (Gilchrist 1: 236). Even during the inter-war period, women numbered only approximately 25% of the total number of Greek immigrants (Jupp, *People* 510).
177. Gilchrist 1: 191.
178. Conomos, *Greeks in Queensland* 216.
179. Peter Cominos said this of his father, and Conomos notes this too, *Greeks in Australia* 90, 87.
180. Conomos, *Greeks in Queensland* 170.
181. Jupp, *People* 518.
182. Many older female respondents came from Greece in their 20s and married older men. While their English is not as good as many male respondents of the same age, it should be noted that their husbands, the original male immigrants and café proprietors, have been dead for twenty or thirty years and the male respondents are 'café children' – Australian-born Greek Australians. The difficulty in understanding older female respondents was a significant issue in this research and accounts for the fact that many of their stories are paraphrased rather than quoted directly.
183. Conomos, *Greeks in Queensland* 216-7, 224. Helen Kentos, Peter Londy, and Jack Stathis all recalled instances of photographs that were deliberately misleading.
184. *Mainland Greece* 252.
185. "Them days, no boys to marry. The girls were glad to find someone who would marry them" (James speaking of his marriage to Despina in 1939 qtd. in Alexakis and Janiszewski, In Their Own Image 128). This is a "forgotten aspect" of the Greek Australian migration experience (111, 115). Jack Stathis also notes that women could not get husbands.
186. Jack Stathis and Peter Londy, interview 22nd October 2005. Conomos adds that no dowry was necessary if women were prepared to come from Greece to Australia, *Greeks in Queensland* 210.
187. Interviewed 15th December, 2005.
188. Conomos, *Greeks in Queensland* 139, 269. Some residences, like those of the of the Londy and Stathis families, still stand in Limestone Streets (Stathis opposite St Stephens), Helen and John Kentos' house in Warwick Road is now a funeral parlor, and the wives of George and Jim Kentrotis of the Regal Café still live in the inner-city homes they occupied when they were first married.
189. Interviewed 2nd October 2005.
190. Conomos, *Greeks in Queensland* 506.
191. Conomos, *Greeks in Queensland* 479-82
192. Conomos, *Greeks in Queensland* 269.
193. Interviewed 5th August 2005. Similarly, Conomos relates the story of Stella Garland, who met George Marcellos of Ipswich in her capacity as orders/accounts clerk in her brother's café in Maryborough (*Greeks in Queensland* 227-8).
194. Interviewed 16th April 2004.
195. See Conomos, *Greeks in Queensland* 84-5, Janiszewski and Alexakis, "American Beauties" 7.
196. Phone conversation 11.2.2007.
197. For feminist analyses of women in ethnic small business see Collins et al. Chapter 9, "And I'd Like to Thank My Wife…" (191-205).
198. See Collins et al. on the use of child labour in ethnic family businesses, Chapter 9 (191-205).
199. Beulah Castan in *Growing Up in Greek Cafés.*
200. Conomos, *Greeks in Queensland* 139.
201. *Greek Family Life in N.S.W.* 35.
202. *Growing Up in Greek Cafés.* Cominos' Café in Cairns was a departmental café with separate accounting done for each section.
203. Interview 8.12.05
204. Interview 22.10.05.
205. *Growing Up in Greek Cafés.*
206. Interviewed 8th December 2005.
207. The term 'greaser' arose from the fact that the Greeks ran fish shops. Peter Veneris remembers that when his family bought the Blue Bird café in Lockhart, his name at school changed from dago to greasy dago (Janiszewski and Alexakis 7).
208. Interview 22nd October 2005.
209. Interviewed 12.2.06.
210. Interviewed 2nd December 2005.
211. Merriam-Webster 184.
212. Conomos, *Greeks in Queensland* 99.
213. For further analysis see Conomos, *Greeks in Queensland* Chapters 5, 6, 7 & 27, especially pages 132-3 & 290.
214. Video interview 5th August 2004.
215. Given that the Greeks I met during the research process tended to provide more than ample food on most occasions, this is a culturally-based assessment. It is likely that there was enough food to feed an army after the proprietors took the situation in hand.
216. Interviewed 16th April, 2004. Collins et al also note this problem: a Greek who spent his childhood in a Richmond café recalls that drunks staggered from the pub and ate bread and butter soaked in Worcestershire sauce to sober them up before main course (introduction). Jack Stathis also remembers it being an issue.
217. Jack, a resident at Saint Mary's Hostel.
218. Interviewed 16th April 2004.
219. Story related by Nick's son, Jim Penglis and confirmed by Harry Tanos and several other members of the community.
220. Interviewed 8th December, 2005.
221. Sue Rosen 172. Also see pages 171-6.

222. The ex-SP bookie claims that many SPs became registered bookies when the TAB was established. He claims, however, that SP booking is still big business; with cars and mobile phones, it is virtually impossible to catch a bookie in the act.
223. *Growing Up in Greek Cafés*.
224. Interviewed 2.2.2006.
225. Rosen 100.
226. Jean Jurd and Terry Glebe quoted in Rosen 100.
227. Manuel Kallinicos interviewed 8th December 2005.
228. John Curtin, 19th August, 1942 qtd. in Adam-Smith, Patsy. *Australian Women at War*. Melbourne: Nelson, 1984, 335-6.
229. Symons 165.
230. Symons 166.
231. Interviewed 2nd October 2005.
232. Conomos, *Greeks in Queensland* 544.
233. Jennifer Isaacs, *Pioneer Women of the Bush and Outback* (Sydney: Lansdowne, 1995) 72.
Patsy Adam-Smith, *Australian Women at War* (Melbourne: Nelson, 1984).
234. Neil Groom, *The Sunday Mail Nostalgia Book* (Bowen Hills, Brisbane: Queensland Newspapers, 1986) 124.
235. Buchanan, *Ipswich in the 20th Century* 94, 95.
236. "From Wintergarden to Ipswich City Cinema – that's entertainment!" *The Ipswich Advertiser's Golden Oldies*, September 16, 1986, page 16.
237. Sydney 'children' have similar memories (see Rosen, 93-4).
238. Buchanan, *Ipswich in the 20th Century* 97, 104.
239. Rosen 96.
240. Rosen 98.
241. *Growing up in Greek Cafés*.
242. Conomos, *Greeks in Queensland* 544-5.
243. *Growing Up in Greek Cafés*.
244. Buchanan, *Ipswich in the 20th Century* 98.
245. Conomos, *Greeks in Queensland*d 541.
246. Growing up in Greek Cafés.
247. Conomos, *Greeks in Queensland* 541.
248. Conomos, *Greeks in Queensland* 542, 545.
249. Conomos, *Greeks in Queensland* 546.
250. Conomos, *Greeks in Queensland* 545.
251. Conomos, *Greeks in Queensland* 544, 546.
252. Effie Detsimas, *No Speak English* (2005) 20.
253. Conomos, *Greeks in Queensland* 549.
254. Conomos, *Greeks in Queensland* 549.
255. Kay Saunders "Racial Conflict in World War II" *Brisbane at War*, quoted in Buchanan, *Ipswich in the 20th Century* 98.
256. Buchanan, *Ipswich in the 20th Century* 98.
257. Opening lines of *A Tale of two Cities*.
258. Janiszewski and Alexakis, *American Beauties at the Niagara* 2, 7.
259. Inscriptions underneath the photos also indicate the close relationships between Greek families – Londy's Café employed a number of Greeks other than the Londy family. Marendy and Kentrotis family members are present at Esther Londy's wedding and staff photos include people from the Kentrotis and Stathis families. Maureen claims that the Greeks usually married other Greeks and spoke Greek to each other and to their children.
260. Photograph, courtesy of Maria Kentrotis, given to her husband, Jim, who was a partner in the Regal Café.
261. Jack Stathis and Peter Londy, interviewed 2nd October 2005.
262. Conomos, *Greeks in Queensland* 360.
263. Quoted in Jupp, *People* 511, Conomos, *Greeks in Queensland* 355-6.
264. Quoted in *Greek Family Life in N.S.W.* For further information on the Ferry Report see Conomos, *Greeks in Queensland* 354-6, although these sources do not always agree.
265. Con Castan quoting Anthony in *Growing Up in Greek Cafés*.
266. *Greeks in Queensland* 538-551.
267. Conomos, *Greeks in Queensland* 358-9.
268. Discussion with the Londy and Stathis families, 2nd October 2005.
269. *Greek Family Life in N.S.W.* 4.
270. Quoted in *Greek Family Life in N.S.W.* 4; Alexakis and Janiszewski, *In Their Own Image* 17; Janiszewski and Alexakis, 'That Bastard Ulysses' 21, 15.
271. *People* 95, 511.
272. Also see *Growing Up in Greek Cafés* and Janiszewski and Alexakis, 'That Bastard Ulysses' 28.
273. Janiszewski and Alexakis, 'That Bastard Ulysses' 28-9; Conomos, *Greeks in Queensland* 179. See also Conomos, *Greeks in Queensland* 174-186.
274. Quoted in *Greek Family Life in N.S.W.* 20-1
275. *Greek Family Life in N.S.W.* 7; Conomos, *Greeks in Queensland* 188-202.
276. *Greek Family Life in N.S.W.* 3; Alexakis and Janiszewski explain that riots had also occurred in these towns in 1916 (*In Their Own Image* 200).
277. In Greek families, the first-born son takes the name of the father's father, and the daughter that of the father's mother, and subsequent sons and daughter, the mother's father and mother.
278. Telephone conversation, 17th July 2005.
279. Interview 5th August 2005.
280. Quoted in Nicklin 45.
281. Interviewed 28th July 2005. Jack Stathis believes that the later arrival of Asian immigrants deflected racism away from Greeks and Italians.
281. Helen Kentos, Jack and Zeta Stathis, Peter and Mary Londy, interviewed 22nd October 2005.
283. Conomos, *Greeks in Queensland* 87
284. Quoted in Conomos, *Greeks in Queensland* 311-2.
285. Janiszewski and Alexakis, *American beauties at the Niagara* 7.
286. Conomos, *Greeks in Queensland* 136.
287. *People* 511.
288. Conomos, *Greeks in Queensland* 86, 124, 136.
289. Letter dated 14th February, 2007.
290. Julie Nichles in *Growing Up in Greek Cafés*.
291. "Funny Types of Aussies" an article by Linda Muller in the *Bayside Bulletin*, January 2006, page 49.
292. Alexakis and Janiszewski, *In Their Own Image* 122.
293. Produce merchant Don Risson admires the way the cafés worked together to help each other in business and notes that serving big meals was a "clever" business move.
294. Peter Cominos notes that his father always donated 1% of his huge cafés takings to the local Ambulance Brigade and Helen Kentos believes that she would be a millionaire if she could collect on the IOUs her husband received. Also see Elpiniki Black's recollection of Gero Black in Conomos, *Greeks in Queensland* 99.
295. Interviewed 16th April, 2004.
296. Interviewed September 2005.

297. Yiota Samios, interviewed 2nd November 2005.
298. Whitehouse's is remembered as a different type of venue from the local Greek cafés. Food was more expensive and it offered more formal upstairs dining. One Ipswich resident said she never went to Whitehouse's Café because it was "too posh." Some earlier Greek cafés, and some in other towns, such as the Paragon in Katoomba, were certainly upmarket establishments, but Greek cafés were generally part of people's everyday experience.
299. Solomos Club, 21st September 2005.
300. Nikolas Marinakis qtd in Gilchrist 2: 344.
301. Quoted in Prineas, "A Village on Kythera" Introduction.
302. "A Village on Kythera."
303. James Prineas, "Winter on Kythera."
304. *Mainland Greece: Athens and the Ionian Islands* 253. Similar patterns of emigration are evident in Ithaca and other parts of Greece.
305. *In Their Own Image* 115.
306. See *In Their Own Image*.
307. Prineas, "A Village on Kythera." It should be noted that the simple Kytherian lifestyle of which Prineas speaks is not dead yet; Jim Pavlakis has vats of home-made wine and olive oil maturing in his cellar. But, as Prineas pints out, when someone dies, there is no one to replace them.
308. Conomos, *Greeks in Queensland* 30; Prineas, "A Village on Kythera."
309. Janiszewski and Alexakis, *Images of Home* 9.
310. 2: 237.
311. Family history written by George Londy, the son of Charles Londy/Leondarakis, April 2007.
312. *Greeks in Queensland* 58.
313. Jack Stathis.
314. *American Beauties at the Niagara* 5.
315. Page 83.
316. Page 63.
317. *People* 511.
318. Quoted in Nicklin 45.
319. Symons discovers French-style restaurants with French chefs, good wines, and elegant dishes in Australia at the end of the eighteenth century. See pages 112-4.
320. See the Education Kit accompanying the exhibition, *Milkshakes, Sundaes and Café Culture*, page 12.
321. Conomos describes the benefit cafés derived from the growth of the movie industry. See pages 121 & 133.
322. See Janiszewski and Alexakis, *American Beauties at the Niagara* 5
323. Ray Oldenburg uses this term to describe the function of places like hairdressers, bookshops, cafés, beer gardens, etcetera.
324. Also see Conomos, *Greeks in Queensland* 134.
325. See chapter 7.
326. Andrew Blythe records the results of this – see pages 43-5.
327. Conomos, *Greeks in Queensland* 131.
328. Page 36.
329. Page 36.
330. Jack from the City Café, Bill and Maria from the Central, Peter from Londy's, Manuel from the Ritz, and Harry from the Sydney Café all mentioned their cafés being renovated.
331. *The Coffee Club Franchise Information Booklet*, page 3.
332. *The Coffee Club Franchise Information Booklet*, page 10.
333. *The Coffee Club Franchise Information Booklet*, page 2.
334. Page 44.
335. Page 18.
336. Quoted in Ripe 15.
337. Quoted in Slattery 18.
338. Page 18.
339. Merriam-Webster 195.
340. Gilchrist, Volume 1, pages 232-238. Turnbull and Valotis, *Beyond the Rolling Wave*, a project for the NSW Heritage Office.
341. For example, while Conomos notes that a John Dennis Black operated the Australia Café in Brisbane Street, Ipswich, from 1901 to about 1915 (104, 140), the Post Office Directories indicate that a John Black traded as a fishmonger in Brisbane Street from approximately 1904 to 1920, and that the Londy Brothers had the Australia Café in 1922 and 1923 (QSA Blocks 2, 10, 77 & 77A IPS). The 1918 Plans show no record of the Australia Café or John Black.
342. Other factors further limit the usefulness of academic and official sources in tracing cafés (see Conomos, *Greeks in Queensland* 89).
In Greek families, names are used repeatedly in families because the first-born son takes the name of the father's father, and the daughter that of the father's mother, and subsequent sons and daughter, the mother's father and mother. All four of the brothers in the Regal Café's Kentrotis family, for instance, named their first son Billy, and three of the 11 children in a photo of the Londy family cousins taken in 1930 are called Esther (see Conomos, Greeks in Queensland 52). The use of nicknames further confounds the problem of tracing cafés.
343. Janiszewski and Alexakis, "American Beauties" 1; Conomos, *Greeks in Queensland* 104-117.
344. The Oral History Association of Australia website is a useful guide to the nature of oral history and how to conduct interviews: *http://www.ohaa.net.au/guidelines.htm*.
So too is Judith Moyer's website, *Do History: A Step-by-Step Guide to Oral History: http://www.dohistory.org/on_your_own/toolkit/oralHistory.html#WHATIS*.
345. Ian Wilson, President of the Ipswich Historical Society, local historian John Rossiter, and long-time Whitehead Studios employee Anne Wagner each played a role in trailing the history of local cafés.
346. Joanne Stewart, Maureen Sheppard, Jack and Zeta Stathis, Helen Kentos, Peter and Mary Londy, and most of the other participants in this project kindly loaned photographs, documents, and crockery. Whitehead Studios, established locally in 1883, is a valuable, though expensive, source of early photographs of Ipswich.
347. See pages 2-5.
348. "American Beauties at the Niagara," 7.
349. The photograph of the Cameo Café, taken in 1930, is courtesy of *Greek Family Life in N.S.W. 1900-1945: Laying the Foundations of 'Greekness'* website, page 18. The site is a useful source of information about life for Greek migrants in Australia.
http://www.cybernaut.com.au/greeksinoz/viewpoints/viewpoint1945.htm, Feb 1st 2007.
350 Athens Bellas discussed the history of the Laconia Café in a telephone conversation January, 2007.

Life in Australia

Life in Australia has now been reproduced in both an original Greek version and in an English translation. The book, written in 1916, was the first book printed and published in Australia in the Greek language. It was an important first chronicle about Hellenic involvement in Australian history and culture.

The book was produced and funded by John Comino, Sydney Merchant and leader of the Greek Orthodox Community. It was written by Georgios Kentavros and the brothers Kosmas and Emmanouil Andronikos. The book was designed to convey to Hellene "patriotes" living in Greece, just how quickly they had obtained wealth and acceptance in the Australian community.

It was published to teach prospective Greek immigrants about the history, geography and the culture of Australia, and to provide them with guidelines about what to expect, and how to "behave" when they arrived in the country. It stressed that virtues such as hard work, honesty, diligence, and civic duty were highly valued in Australia, and would ensure success there. It helped to assure prospective Greek immigrants that they would quickly enjoy a "very good life in Australia".

The 368 page book details the state of the Greek Communities, and the Greek Orthodox Church in Australia, in 1916, and provides about 150 pages of micro biographies and photographs of Greek immigrants, deriving from all parts of Greece, who had achieved a considerable measure of success in Australia, by that date. Many of us will recognise our great grandparents, grandparents, fathers, mothers, and other relatives in these pages. The contents chronicle the history of many family's migration to Australia, going back over 150 years. This seminal book transports you back in time.

It is thus an important link with subsequent generations of Hellenes in Australia. It ensures that the descendants of the pioneering generation are made aware of the achievements of the first generation of immigrants, and that they have access to this very important history. Hopefully the re-publication of this book may stimulate further research by subsequent generations. How has the family of the pioneer featured in the book, fared since 1916? What are the great-grandchildren doing now?

The publication of *Life in Australia* has emerged from the very important work undertaken by the management team and

HARALAMABOS NIK. SAMIOS

In one of the most central locations in the great city of Sydney stand two establishments together. One of these, consisting of five storeys, serves as a hotel and contains about 100 rooms. The other, consisting of three floors, is a richly furnished café/restaurant.

Any who gaze on these magnificent buildings can only admire the commercial spirit of the Greek who, without any help, in a foreign land,

manages in a short time, thanks to his construction of these splendid establishments, to be a notable contributor to the progress made by this great city. And so, admiration and praise are rightly the lot of the managers and owners, who come from Kythera, Messrs. Haralambos and Ioannis Nik. Samios, together with their cousin, Mr Konstantinos I. Kasimatis.

IOANNIS ATH. LAZANAS

Hailing from Potamos, on Kythera, Mr Ioannis Ath. Lazanas, is married to the sister of the extremely wealthy Mr J. Comino. He is the owner and manager, together with his sons, of the lucrative establishment standing in one of the most central locations in the great city of Sydney.

Mr I. A. Lazanas is to be included among the successfully established Greeks of Australia.

Mr I. Ath. Lazanas with his sons.

GEORGIOS PAPANIKOLAOU

In the country town of Merriwa, in New South Wales, stands the establishment belonging to Mr G. Papanikolaou (Nicholas), from Pireaus, which he opened with his brother. Their commercial name is *Nicholas Bros*.

Messrs. the brothers Nikolaou also have an ice factory in Merriwa. They are to be regarded as belonging to the successfully established Greeks, something that they have achieved through their ability and hard work.

---

contributors to www.kythera-family.net. Regular users of kythera-family.net will know that numerous excerpts from Life in Australia are available for all to view and/or download, on the website. After sale and distribution of the book, these entries will become more extensive.

Every Hellenic family in Australia, and beyond, should own a copy of this very important book, in both Greek and English. The books are handsomely presented and would make an ideal gift for family members.

Individual versions, AU$50.
Purchase of both an English and a Greek version – 2 books for AU$80.
Additional postage and handling costs – $10, for up to 3 books.
Credit cards (Visa and Mastercard only) accepted.

Available in Australia from:

George C. Poulos
Email: transoz@bigpond.net.au
Ph: 61 2 9388 8320

Angelo Notaras
Email: info@atomindustries.com.au
Ph: 61 2 9810 0194 ext.711 (24hrs)
Fax: 61 2 9810 6691

The Island of Kythera. A Social History. (1700-1863)

by GEORGE N. LEONTSINIS

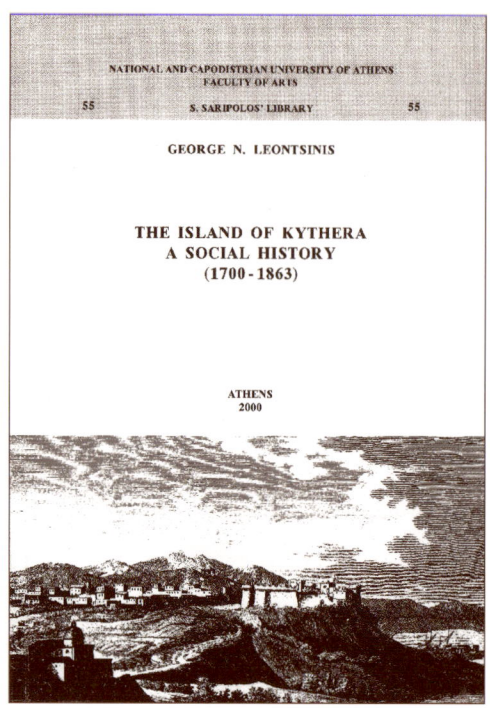

This superb history of Kythera was the thesis submitted, in August, 1981, for the degree of Doctor Of Philosophy (History) in the School of Modern Languages and European History, at the University of East Anglia, Norfolk, England. It has recently been re-printed in a revised edition. George Leontsinis' study examines the social history of the island of Kythera, from the beginning of the eighteenth century, to 1863. On 21 May 1864 the seven Ionian islands united with Greece, marking the end of the British Protectorate on Kythera.

Leontsinis' work is a penetrating analysis of the sociological infrastructure and historical processes at work in those 164 years. To understand the relatively distant Kytherian past is to understand the Kythera in which our great-grandparents, grandparents and parents grew up. It provides us powerful insights into why our immediate ancestors acted, felt and thought in the unique way that they did. These insights, in turn, allow us to better understand the Kythera of the present day, and to anticipate the Kytherian future. In Kytherian Australian circles *The Island of Kythera* is known affectionately as "..the white book on Kythera."

What was the Kytherian "aristocracy", and how did it arise? What is the origin of the mesa (inner) and exo (outer) thimo (government), and how did it arise? What impact did that have on the functioning of the island? What was the impact on Kythera of the rise of educational institutions and enhanced beaurocracy under the British? What processes radicalised the Kytherian peasantry? What precipitated the shifts in demography and patterns of migration to and from Kythera? All these questions are answered in *The Island of Kythera. A Social History*.

For Leontsinis, English is a second language. Despite this, the book is very fluidly written. *The Island of Kythera* is another book which must be on the library shelves of every "Kytherian" home in the world. George Leontsinis currently holds the position of Professor of Modern Greek History, and the Teaching of History, at the University of Athens.

He has organised several Greek and International Conferences in Kythera, including the First International Conference of Kytherian Studies

Kythera: Myth and Reality, in 2000, and Greek Benefaction and Kytherian Bequests, 2005. The proceedings of these Conferences have been published in book form and are available from George Leontsinis. Other Conferences he has organised include The Agricultural Development and the Environmental Education, (2000) National Conference on Church, Education and Culture in Kythera, (2001), Symposium on Scientific Research in Kythera, (2003) and Kytherian Migration: Historic Diaspora and Contemporary Massive Population Movement. (2004). George, and his wife Athanassia have also produced a superb DVD called Kythera: Myth and Reality. This arose out of insights gained from the proceedings of the First International Conference of Kytherian Studies.

In 2007 George published a biography, written in Greek, of prominent Australian Kytherian violinist and music teacher, Nicholas P Leontsini, copies of which can be purchased from him in Europe, and from George C. Poulos on transoz@bigpond.net.au in Australia. He has completed the Manuscript, Kythera: The Ecclesiastical Situation, in English. This will be published and made available for distribution in the near future.

Leontsinis is currently supervising a Ph.D thesis by Kytherian born Kalypso Michalakakis, on the History of the Kytherian Associations around the world, including those in Smyrna and Alexandria at the turn of the 20th century. This thesis will be completed and submitted shortly. George Leontsinis' willingness to mobilise resources in areas such as Conference organisation and Ph.D research, serve to further enhance our knowledge of Kytherian history, and help us to understand and appreciate more fully the Kytherian sense of identity.

For more information about George Leontsinis see,
http://www.kythera-family.net
GeorgeLeontsinis
The Island of Kythera. A Social History.
(1700-1863).

In Europe, order from:

George & Athanassia Leontsinis,
gleon@primedu.uoa.gr or
aleon@ppp.uoa.gr

Available in Australia from:

George C. Poulos
Email: transoz@bigpond.net.au
Ph: 61 2 9388 8320

Angelo Notaras
Email: info@atomindustries.com.au
Ph: 61 2 9810 0194 ext.711 (24hrs)
Fax: 61 2 9810 6691

The Programme for Proceedings of the "Greek Benefaction and Kytherian Bequests" Conference, held in the Kytherian Association Hall, Hora, Kythera, 21st-25th September, 2005. One of the superior features of George Leontsinis work is that all of his Conference proceedings have been subsequently published. This allows the Kytherian community, around the world, to access an encyclopeadic body of knowledge about Kythera, and its politics, religion, environment, science, and culture.

Kythera. A History of the Island and it's People.

by PETER D. VANGES

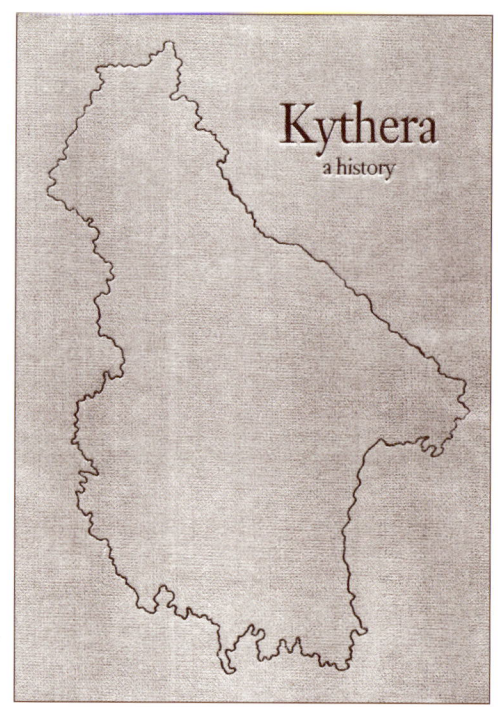

A readable, detailed and enlightening history of Kythera, from mythological times to the present day. It remains the best overview of the history of Kythera in the English language. Kytherian Australians refer to it affectionately as "..the green book on Kythera".

Peter Vanges' motivations to write the book are clearly expressed in the preface. "Firstly to write a history of Kythera in English which would help many Australian-born, American-born and other diaspora Kytherians, learn about the birthplace of their parents and grandparents. Secondly, having read this book, those who may visit the island will be able to understand it, and hence enjoy and appreciate it more. My aim is to provide some background information on Kythera and the Kytherians".

This background is divided into five chronological periods; The Early Days: 2500BC-AD1700; The Venetian Occupation: AD1200-1700; The Years of Suffering: 1799-1800; Struggling for Freedom: 1800-1940; World War II and Later Years: 1941-1990.

Part Six of the book deals with the buildings, places and traditions of Kythera; historic buildings, the Monastery of Myrtidiotissa, public works, architecture, Kytherian dress, ports and aerodrome, tourism, and the Toponymia of Kythera. Part Seven deals with the Kytherians of the Diaspora, concentrating on the Kytherian Brotherhood of Athens, Kytherians in Asia Minor, Kytherians in Africa & Egypt, Kytherians in America, Kytherians in Australia, and the history of the then Kytherian Brotherhood (now, Association) of Australia. This book must be on the library shelf of every "Kytherian" home in the world.

Book Price: A$30.00 plus A$10.00 postage, within Australia. Additional postage applies to overseas orders.

Available from:

The Kytherian Association of Australia
Rockdale Post Shop
PO Box 183 Rockdale NSW 2216
Australia

Email: info@kytherianassociation.com.au

Or contact **George C. Poulos**
Email: transoz@bigpond.net.au
Ph: 61 2 9388 8320

Angelo Notaras
Email: info@atomindustries.com.au
Ph: 61 2 9810 0194 ext.711 (24hrs)
Fax: 61 2 9810 6691

Australians and Greeks, Vol's I-III.

by HUGH GILCHRIST

It is impossible to convey the impact of the publication of Hugh Gilchrist's encyclopaedic three volume history of Greeks and Australians on Greek Australian historiography. A new high standard was set for all future research, and the study of Greek Australian history was taken far more seriously, amongst Australian intellectuals. Gilchrist has inspired subsequent historians and researchers to research, write and publish works of a similar, very high standard.

Volume I, The Early Years, published in 1992, encompasses the period from Ancient Greek history to the beginning of the First World War. For background information on the heavy involvement of Kytherians in early 20th century Australia, readers are referred in particular to *Chapter 11, The Shop-keeping phenomenon*.

Volume II, The Middle Years, encompasses the period between 1914 and 1939, the beginning of the Second World War.

Volume III, The Later Years, encompasses the period from 1939 to 30 March, 1953, when Dimitrios Lambros, the first Greek Ambassador to Australia, was appointed.

Australians and Greeks, Volumes I-III must form the centrepiece on every Greek Australian library in Australia.

"Gilchrist has created a monumental and praiseworthy work of three volumes, which will be treasured not only by historians but also by the community at large, both in Australia and Greece. One can be assured that the contents of this invaluable reference book will enlighten the reader about Australia's ties with Greece and Greece's relationship with Australia". – John Yiannakis, Curtin University of Technology.

Hugh Gilchrist has been a Philhellene all his life. From 1945 until his retirement in 1981 he served in the Department of External Affairs. From 1968-1972 he was Ambassador to Greece in Athens.

Australians and Greeks, Vol's I-III.
Book Price: $A60.00 per volume, plus A$10.00 postage.

Available in Australia from:

George C. Poulos
Email: transoz@bigpond.net.au
Ph. 61 2 9388 8320

Angelo Notaras
Email: info@atomindustries.com.au
Ph: 61 2 9810 0194 ext.711 (24hrs)
Fax: 61 2 9810 6691

Katsehamos and the Great Idea.

A true story of Greeks and Australians in the early 20th Century.

by PETER PRINEAS

"The Mass migrations that followed the early 20th century turmoil in the Balkans laid the foundations for that great Australian institution the Greek country café... Peter Prineas's spirited account of migrants building small empires of cafés and cinemas, is also tinged with the loneliness and isolation they experienced in xenophobic bush towns."
- Tony Maniaty, *Weekend Australian*

" I found the book fascinating because it contains the dreams and aspirations of all Greek immigrants of my father's generation, a world that has faded from the collective Greek consciousness as much as the Great idea. Most of all, however, I was struck by the literary quality of the book, which is far superior to almost all works of this type that I have read." – Nicholas Gage, Pulitzer prize-winning journalist and author of 'Eleni'.

" ...lyrical style and effective use of imagery, as well as the skillful juxtaposition of biographical detail with historical fact... A poignant celebration of early Greek migrants." – *Odyssey* Magazine

" ...will delight any cinema aficionado and historian." – John Adey, *Kino Cinema Quarterly*

" ...a tale of struggle, courage, stoicism, doggedness and pride which is profoundly recognisable to the children of the Greek Diaspora, echoing in the secret part of our soul." – Kiriaki Orfanos, *www.kythera-family.net*

" ...strong portraits of individuals... strong descriptions of different places." – Associate-Professor Janis Wilton, University of New England.

Book Price: A$34.95 (incl. postage within Australia):

Order from:

George C. Poulos:
transoz@bigpond.net.au
Ph: 61 2 9388 8320

or

**Plateia, 32 Calder Road,
Darlington,
NSW, Australia.**
Email: plateia@ozemail.com.au,
Phone 61 2 9319 1513

Also from **Gleebooks**,
49 Glebe Point Road, Glebe NSW
and selected bookshops.

The Greeks in Queensland.

A History from 1859-1945.

by DENIS A. CONOMOS

A detailed history of the Greeks in Queensland from the beginning of Statehood in 1859, to the end of the Second World War.

This book deals with the life in Greece, departure, voyage, arrival and experiences in Australia of the Greek migrants, who settled in Queensland prior to 1946. Source material used by Denis Conomos includes: the stories told to him by 250 pioneer migrants who arrived in Queensland prior to 1946; contemporary articles and reports that appeared in Greek-Australian newspapers; naturalisation records; a scrap album kept by the Greek Consul, Christy Freeleagus, and much other documentary evidence. The interviews with the pioneer migrants took place from 1980 to 1983. Almost all of them have since passed away. Hence, much of the material contained in the book is not available anywhere else and is therefore of immense historical importance. The migrants who told their stories came from all parts of Greater Greece – Kythera, Asia Minor, Ithaki, Athens, Castellorizo, Cyprus, Crete, Rhodes, Samos, Peloponnesos, Epirus and elsewhere. In this book, the reader meets many of the leading figures of the Greek Community in Queensland, and some in New South Wales, who helped to shape the life of the Greeks in those states. The reader also meets some colourful Greek characters who settled in Queensland in the 19th century.

Published, 2002, by *Copyright Publishing Co Pty Ltd*. A 628 page soft cover book, with over 140 b/w photographs. ISBN 1 875401 97 0

Sales for delivery within Australia. Recommended retail price: $A49.50 (incl GST and free pack & post).

Sales for delivery to countries other than Australia. RRP US$45.00 (incl. pack & post surface mail). Add US$19.00 for Overseas airmail delivery.

Available from:
info@copyright.net.au
Tel: 61 7 3229 6366   Fax: 61 7 3229 8782

Postal address:
Copyright Publishing Co Pty Ltd.,
GPO Box 2927 Brisbane
8th Floor 371 Queen Street
Queensland Australia 4001
Brisbane Queensland Australia 4001

In Sydney, Available from:
Kytherian Association of Australia
Rockdale Post Shop
PO Box 183 Rockdale NSW 2216
Australia

Email: info@kytherianassociation.com.au

or contact **George C. Poulos**,
on 61 2 9388 8320,
Email: transoz@bigpond.net.au

Panayotis Fatseas: Kytherian Faces, 1920-1938.

by JOHN STATHATOS

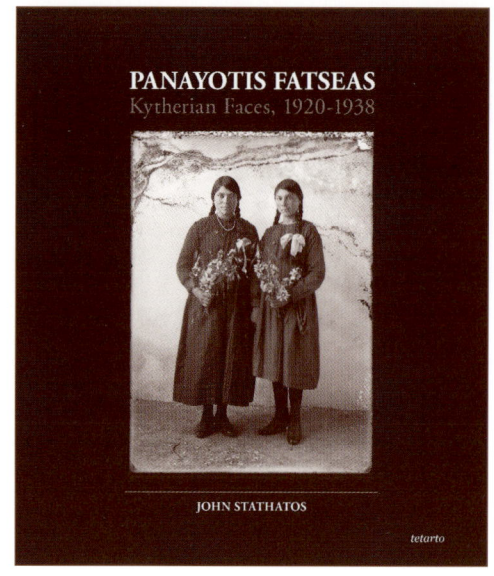

Panayotis Fatseas (1888-1938) was the first professional Kytherian photographer, through whose studio in Livadi passed many Kytherians seeking to have their portrait taken; some on their way to Australia or the USA, others to send a precious image of parents, wife or children to the emigrant many thousands of miles away. When he died, Fatseas left behind an archive consisting of several thousand glass negatives. Forgotten for decades, the archive was rescued at the very last moment by the Kythera Cultural Association, and restored thanks to the generous sponsorship of Angelo and John Notaras of Sydney.

In February 2008, a major exhibition of Fatseas' work was presented at the prestigious Benaki Museum in Athens under the title "Faces of Kythera, 1920-1938", attracting many thousands of viewers and enthusiastic critical response. The exhibition was accompanied by the publication of a high-quality monograph in Greek, which included 122 full-page duotone illustrations, and an extensive essay by the exhibition curator, photographer and photographic historian John Stathatos. Following the success of the Greek edition, "Panayotis Fatseas: Faces of Kythera, 1920-1938", an English edition is now being prepared for publication.

"The exhibition is not merely an interesting addition to the history of photography, but a revelation. The self-taught Kytherian who founded the island's first photographic studio, could be included among the five best Greek photographers, of the first half of the 20th century".

Margarita Pournara, Kathimerini newspaper.

"The Kytherians photographed by Fatseas do not seem like impersonal figures, symbolic perhaps of some nostalgically viewed past, but preserve their individual personalities. The two or three days' wages which they paid the photographer turn out to have been a good investment, since alongside the postcard-sized prints mailed to a father or son in Australia, they were – all unwittingly – also purchasing a small fraction of immortality. Not just because their faces have travelled down the years to reach us, but above all because the photographer's alchemy proves such that, before these miraculously resurrected photographs, we pause involuntarily to study their image, and wonder who they were, how they lived and what passed before their eyes."

John Stathatos

Hard-bound, 160 pp., 29.5 x 25cms, printed in duotone. Available in Australia at a cost of A$70 per volume, plus A$10 postage, from **George C. Poulos**: transoz@bigpond.net.au
Ph: 61 2 9388 8320
or, **Angelo Notaras**:
info@atomindustries.com.au
Ph: 61 2 9810 0194 ext.711 (24hrs)

Society of Kytherian Studies.

The Society of Kytherian Studies is a non profit society based in Athens. It was established in 1982 (Athens Court ruling 1386/82) and registered in the *Associations Record of Athens* (no. 11151/27.7.82).

The Aims of the Society include:

a) Research in any subject related to Kythera and Antikythera

b) The dissemination of the findings of this research.

c) The preservation of monuments, art, history and literature

d) Providing moral support to individuals or organisations whose work corresponds with the purposes and aims of the Association.

Members

i) Regular members: Scientists and scholars with an origin in Kythera and Antikythera and who reside in the area of the former Jurisdiction of the Capital, as well as scientists whose expertise and fields of interest can facilitate the Association to accomplish its aims.

ii) Honourary members: Individuals who have provided decisive help in the Association's efforts.

iii) Corresponding members: Kytherian scientists living outside the region of the former area of the Jurisdiction of the Capital.

Activities the Society include:

1. Scientific publications and other scholarly work

**Professor Nikos Petrochilos.
President**

2. Support of archaeological research on Kythera & Antikythera

3. Support of the historical archive of Kythera

4. Preservation and restoration of monuments

5. Conferences, organsisation and facilitation

6. Other activities (museum visits, lectures, excursions, guided tours)

The most important aspect of the Society's work centres around its publications on Kythera and Antikythera. The Association's publishing activity began in 1987 and has so far covered a wide range of topics. 17 significant books and pamphlets have been published to date. A complete list of these publications can be found at – *http://www.kythera-family.net/SocietyofKytherianStudies*. The Association's books promote the local culture of Kythera and aim to publicise sources of local history along with other subjects related to literature, folklore, scientific research, ecology, traditions, and the island's local dialect. All the Society's books have been published in Greek. They include the superb, *Kytherian Surnames*, an encyclopaedic volume, which details the history of the origin of all Kytherian surnames on the island.

A representative sample of some of the other published books include:

Kytherian Dictionary. Dimitris L. Komis (editor), 1996, 504 pages.

Registry Archive of Kythera. Parish of Panagia Ilariotissa, Potamos (1731-1856). Emmanuel Drakakis (editor), 2003, 1161 pages.

History of Kythera. Volumes A & B. Panagiotis Tsitsilias. 1993, 1994, 358 & 344 pages. (Researched 1920's & 1930's. Compiled 1965)

Tsirigotika. Panos Fyllis. 1999. 356 pages.

Population Census of Kythera, 18th Century. Maria G. Patramani, Antonia K. Marmareli, Emm. G. Drakakis (editors). 1997. Volumes A, B, & C. 484, 588, & 132 pages.

Kythera. On the bird route. Theodoros P. Kominos. 1995. 128 pages. (Ornithology Study).

Memories of a Doctor. From the village, the hospital, his life. Haralambos Evangelos Kritharis.1996. 384 pages.

Central distribution:

The Association of Kytherian Studies
5 Themistokleous Str., 8th floor,
Athens 106 77
Tel: 210 3844915, 3838190
Fax: 210 38844915, 3820293

To place orders for books or to contact the President, **Nikos Petrochilos**:
Email: nipet@hol.gr
or
Secretary, **Alexandra Lourantou**:
Email: kipa-ekm@trifilio.gr

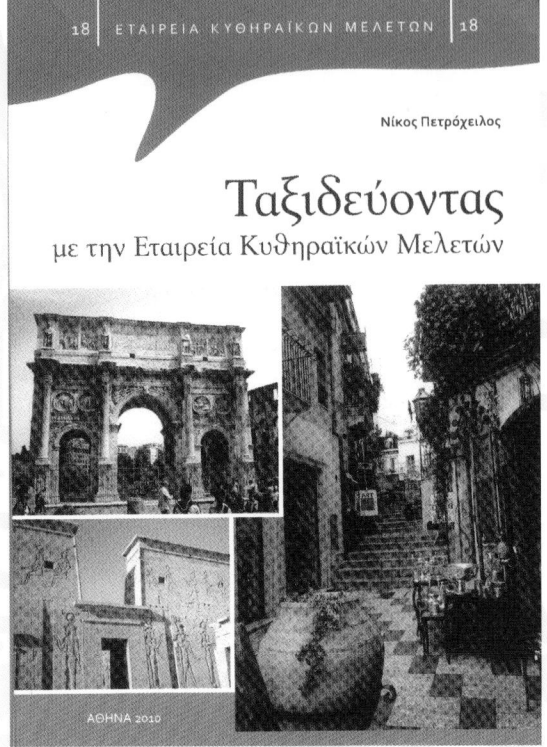

To view/download a pricelist of the books available from the Society go to:
http://www.kythera-family.net/index.php?nav=135-137&cid=275&did=17872&pageflip=1

Over the years, the *Society* has organized a series of tours, excursions and lectures to areas where Hellenic culture thrived in the past, including, Venice, Egypt, Turkey, Southern Italy and Sicily. The latest book published by the *Society*, details some of the tours that have been undertaken. Written (in Greek) by Nikos Petrochilos, it is entitled, *Travelling with the Society of Kytherian Studies in places were Greeks Lived.*

George his passion.

George his passion is the story of a loveable eccentric who was responsible for collecting funds to establish what are now considered to be premier aged care facilities catering for a vast range of needs for aged care services from southern Queensland to Coff's Harbour in NSW (and expanding). Through passionate determination, George was instrumental in turning the dream of **Feros Care Ltd.**, into a reality.

Ruby M Feros is of Kytherian heritage. She has a passion for the island from which her father came. Ruby has a great love for Greek people and their culture. Ruby was determined to see the story of her father published. She is donating the proceeds of this book to **Feros Care Ltd** to help those requiring aged care and further the work her father began. In her book she tells the story of how her father came to Australia from the Greek island of Kythera as a stowaway.

To order *George his passion* contact:

Ruby M Feros
Mobile: 0427 484 002
Email: rmferos@bigpond.co

George C Poulos
transoz@bigpond.net.au
Ph: 61 2 9388 8320

Britain's Greek Islands. Kythera and the Ionian Islands 1809 to 1864.

by PETER PRINEAS

Britain's Greek Islands tells the story of five decades in the early nineteenth century when the British ruled Kythera and the Ionian Islands. It is a very readable history, painstakingly assembled from hundreds of hand-written letters and documents, most previously unpublished. It is a meticulously researched and fascinating personal account of the Seven Islands which were "British" before becoming Greek'.

It conveys the texture and detail of life, society and politics in the island of Cerigo (Kythera) and the Ionian Islands (then known as Corfu, Paxo, Santa Maura, Ithaca, Cephalonia and Zante) and illuminates important but largely forgotten events.

Based on extensive research in the archives, and illustrated with maps, photographs and historic prints, 'Britain's Greek Islands' reveals the sometimes turbulent relations that existed in the Protectorate named the 'United States of the Ionian Islands'.

The narrative is placed within the wider history of Europe and the Near East, from the Napoleonic Wars, through the Greek War of Independence, the Crimean War, and conflicts over the 'Eastern Question' that resonate to this day.

A paperback, 415 pages, with bibliography., notes & index. ISBN 9780980672213

Book Price: A$38.50 plus A$10.00 postage, within Australia. Additional postage applies to overseas orders.

Available from:

George C. Poulos
Email: transoz@bigpond.net.au
Ph: 61 2 9388 8320

Angelo Notaras
Email: info@atomindustries.com.au
Ph: 61 2 9810 0194 ext.711 (24hrs)
Fax: 61 2 9810 6691

Also available from the author:

Peter Prineas
Plateia Press
32 Calder Road
Darlington NSW 2008 AUSTRALIA.
Email: pprineas@ozemail.com.au
Telephone: 61 2 9319 1513
Mobile: 0429 322 857